PUBLICATIONS OF THE ISRAEL ACADEMY
OF SCIENCES AND HUMANITIES

SECTION OF HUMANITIES

STUDIES IN HONOR OF SHAUL SHAKED

STUDIES IN THE HUMANITIES

STUDIES IN HONOR OF SHAUL SHAKED

Edited by

YOHANAN FRIEDMANN

AND

ETAN KOHLBERG

JERUSALEM 2019

THE ISRAEL ACADEMY OF SCIENCES AND HUMANITIES

Copy editing: Gila Brand and Deborah Greniman
Preparation for press: Deborah Greniman
Production: Yehuda Greenbaum

ISBN 978–965–208–232–9

Typesetting by Irit Nahum
Printed in Israel at Ayalon Printing, Jerusalem

CONTENTS

Foreword

The present volume is based on lectures delivered at a symposium organized by the Israel Academy of Sciences and Humanities on the occasion of the eightieth birthday of Professor Shaul Shaked, who became a Member of the Academy in 1986. The editors are grateful to the participants for their innovative contributions to the event and to the ensuing book.

Special thanks are due to Gila Brand for her first round of editing, to Deborah Greniman, Senior Editor of English-Language Publications at the Academy, for her painstaking, dedicated and professional editorial work, to Irit Nahum for her expert typesetting and to Yehuda Greenbaum of the Academy's Publications Department for overseeing the book's production.

Yohanan Friedmann
Etan Kohlberg
Jerusalem, December 2018

The Scholarly Oeuvre of Shaul Shaked, 1

Shaul Shaked and the Study of Zoroastrianism

Michael Shenkar

Notwithstanding the unusually broad scope of Shaul Shaked's research interests, the *Schwerpunkt* of his scholarly efforts since his doctoral dissertation has been his dedication to the study of Zoroastrianism. His studies of Middle Persian Zoroastrian literature, exegesis, Zoroastrian mythology, cosmogony, eschatology and ethics, and, above all, his analysis of the authors' ways of thinking and the problems that bothered them, revolutionized the scholarly understanding of Sasanian Zoroastrianism and put it on a completely new ground. This is by no means an appreciative student's respectful exaggeration, but an accurate description of the influence that Shaked has had on the field.

Given the limited scope of this introductory essay, I shall focus on just a few of the major directions of research established by Shaked that have had a decisive and formative impact on the study of Sasanian Zoroastrianism. In his 1994 book *Dualism in Transformation*, Shaked demonstrated that the definitions of Zoroastrian orthodoxy and what is to be excluded from it were probably formulated only in the post-Sasanian period.[1] This position, though it was passionately criticized by his teacher Mary Boyce, is now widely accepted, notwithstanding the state-supported attempts by the Zoroastrian clergy, apparent already in the third-century inscriptions of the Sasanian high-priest Kartīr, to define what is the 'correct' *Mazdayasnian Tradition* and what is to be considered 'heresy' and legally excluded from the approved religious practices.

Shaked insisted on the rich diversity of religious life in the Sasanian empire and was reluctant to treat the Sasanian kings as ardent champi-

1 Shaked, *Dualism in Transformation* [no. 6], p. 98. The bracketed numbers in the notes refer to the list of the Principal Publications of Shaul Shaked, in this volume.

ons of orthodox Zoroastrianism; as he observed, the Sasanian king's 'involvement in the affairs of the Zoroastrian church is not much deeper than in those of the other religious communities of the kingdom.'[2] This assessment paved the way to the numerous studies that have appeared in the past two decades exploring the place of Jewish, Christian and other religious communities in the Sasanian empire, not as tolerated or persecuted religious minorities, but as important and integral components of the empire's social fabric.

The conclusions Shaked reached about so-called 'Zurvanism' are now almost universally accepted. Most earlier scholars had argued for the existence in the Sasanian period of a separate Zurvanite 'sect' or 'movement,' or even a 'Zurvanite Church' centered on the worship of the god of time, Zurvān. Shaked, however, showed that the Zurvanite myth, in which Zurvān played a major role in the act of Creation, was only one of the numerous accepted variants of Zoroastrian cosmogony in the Sasanian period,[3] and that '[t]here is no reason to suppose that Zurvanism was an organized body of religion, comprising, besides mythology, also theology, ritual, or a church structure.'[4]

The main focus of Shaked's attention has been the elucidation and interpretation of Zoroastrianism in the Sasanian period and the transmission of Zoroastrian notions and ideas into Islam.[5] However, he has not shied away from expressing his opinion on some of the fundamental and exhaustively debated problems of Zoroastrian studies and of the broader study of Indo-Iranian religions. His approach to the Avesta, and to the *Gathas* in particular, is a masterly attempt to find a middle course between the two 'extreme' positions – that of Mary Boyce, who, in what Shaked called '... almost an act of faith that carries the reader with it,'[6] was deeply convinced that Old Avestan texts could soundly be interpreted on the basis of the much later Zoroastrian tradition, and that represented by Jean Kellens and Éric Pirart, among others, which was characterized by 'excessive reliance on the linguistic data of the Rigveda.'[7] Elsewhere, Shaked described these two approaches as 'on the one hand, regarding the Gathas as provincial Vedic texts, and, on the other,

2 *Ibid.*, p. 112.
3 *Ibid.*, pp. 20–21.
4 *Ibid.*, p. 54.
5 See his selected papers on these subjects, in Shaked, *From Zoroastrian Iran to Islam* [no. 9].
6 Shaked, 'Review of Mary Boyce' [no. 121], p. 375.
7 Shaked, 'Zoroastrian Origins' [no. 161], p. 189.

reading the whole of later Zoroastrianism into them.'[8] Not coincidentally, Shaked's treatment of this thorny subject corresponds to the Zoroastrian concept of *paymān* – 'the right measure' – to whose elucidation he himself has made a decisive contribution.[9] Shaked successfully demonstrated that between Boyce's insistence on the conservatism, continuity and orthodoxy of the Zoroastrian tradition, on the one hand, and the narrow ritualistic interpretations of the Avestan hymns, on the other, lies a vibrant, constantly changing, manifold world, full of mystical, esoteric and spiritual meanings and open to many possibilities, influences and interpretations. Approached with 'the right measure' of criticism and belief, based on breadth of knowledge and absolute command of the primary sources, the Avesta can be shown to contain the basics of what is today called 'Zoroastrianism.' According to Shaked, Zoroastrianism was never stagnant, but 'a living and changing tradition, while never betraying its essence.'[10]

This careful method characterizes Shaked's treatment of the entire corpus of the Zoroastrian written sources. As is well known, the ancient Iranians transmitted their religious literature orally for hundreds of years before starting to commit texts to writing at the end of the Sasanian period, and the Zoroastrian literature that has come down to us underwent processes of editing and compilation in the Abbasid period. Studying the history of the Zoroastrian religion in the pre-Islamic period from these multi-layered texts thus presents a serious scholarly challenge. Here, too, Shaked provides us with important methodological observations:

> Iranian literature suffered in the course of its history terrible devastation and loss, and appears to us like a table-cloth full of holes. At the same time, however, it shows a high degree of consistency and harmony. … [T]here seems to be a hard core which is recognizable as Iranian in all of the different manifestations of this literature. Each one of the chronological phases has to be studied on its own, each genre formulation has some flavour which distinguishes it from the others, and yet there is an internal affinity among them.[11]

8 Shaked, *Dualism in Transformation* [no. 6], p. 27, note 1.
9 Shaked, 'Paymān' [no. 81].
10 Shaked, 'Zoroastrian Origins' [no. 161], p. 378.
11 Shaked, 'The Iranian Canon' [no. 172], p. 23.

Shaked's balanced and exemplary discussion of the question of 'Zoroaster's Time,' which has tormented scholars for over two centuries, is yet another example of his *paymān*. His dating of Zoroaster's life to the ninth or eighth century BCE is well placed between the extreme points that have been suggested and has the merit of not contradicting any of the few established facts about the prophet of Zoroastrianism.[12]

Shaked's studies always concentrate on a specific and well-defined notion or problem in the Middle Persian literature, but his thorough knowledge of every aspect of this complex and heterogeneous corpus allows him to see the 'big picture' in the small detail and to gain insight into the very essence of Zoroastrianism as a religious system. For example, in his important discussion of whether it is possible to categorize Zoroastrianism as either 'dualism' or 'monotheism,' Shaked shows that such narrow definitions fail to fully grasp all the possibilities and aspects of Zoroastrian cosmogony and eschatology.[13]

In addition to his editions of Middle Persian texts and his expositions of the notions contained in them, Shaked has made important contributions to Middle Persian epigraphy with his publication and deciphering of inscriptions on seals, amulets and vessels. For example, his readings and publications of Jewish-Sasanian seals are essential for scholars interested in the material culture of Sasanian Jewry.[14] He has also introduced entirely new sources into scholarly use. His publication, with the late Joseph Naveh, of the documents from the archive of the Achaemenid satrap of Bactria, written in Aramaic, sheds a completely new light on the history and culture of the eastern provinces of the Achaemenid empire as well as providing us with the earliest attestation of the employment of the Zoroastrian calendar.[15] The importance of this material to settling the long-debated question of whether or not the Achaemenids were Zoroastrians cannot be overstated. After years of repetitive and inconclusive discussions based on the same exhausted evidence, this stalemate, if not completely shattered, has at least been significantly shaken.

In recent years Shaked has been directing the Middle Persian Dictio-

12 Shaked, 'Zoroastrian Origins' [no. 161], pp. 188–189.

13 Shaked, *Dualism in Transformation* [no. 6], pp. 5–27.

14 Shaked, 'Jewish and Christian Seals' [no. 55]; 'Epigraphica Judaeo-Iranica' [no. 62]; 'Jewish Sasanian Sigillography' [no. 118].

15 Naveh and Shaked, *Aramaic Documents* [no. 17]; Shaked, 'The Zoroastrian Calendar' [no. 197].

nary Project, which yields an invaluable tool for studies and students of Zoroastrianism. The project's Text Preparation Utility, now available online (to authenticated users), already contains many Middle Persian texts, greatly facilitating investigation of and searches within the extant corpus of the Zoroastrian literature.[16]

Knowledge of Semitic languages and deep acquaintance with Judaism allows Shaked easily to traverse the gap between Iranian and Semitic studies, which remains unbridgeable for many specialists in each field. This puts him in a unique position to comment upon the contacts between Judaism and Zoroastrianism and to evaluate possible influences and transmission of ideas between these two ancient religious traditions. Apparent similarities between some elements of Zoroastrianism and Second Temple Judaism had been noted early on, but the late dating of the Zoroastrian literature where these ideas are expressed gave rise to ill-founded speculations and presented a serious obstacle to any attempt to understand in which religious tradition the elements in question had originated. In his 1984 article 'Iranian Influence on Judaism: First Century B.C.E. to Second Century C.E.,' Shaked advanced the thesis that such elements should be examined in their respective contexts to determine whether they form a 'structure and coherence' within one religious tradition, 'while the overriding structure is lacking' in the other.[17] Using this method, he concluded, for example, that certain eschatological motifs found in both Judaism and Zoroastrianism originate in Iran and were borrowed in Jewish religion. In Iran, he argued, they were 'an organic development of a system' and 'formed part of a larger conception,' while in Judaism the same elements were present only 'in a more or less haphazard manner.'[18] Again, only deep and thorough knowledge of both traditions allowed him to reach such results. It comes as no surprise that despite a growing stream of studies on this subject in recent years, Shaked's article has not been superseded and remains an

16 See the Middle Persian Dictionary Project website: http://mpdp.mpdict.com/.

17 Shaked, 'Iranian Influences in Judaism' [no. 68], pp. 322–323. As he formulates the same approach in a later work: 'If these themes are more at home in Zoroastrianism than in Judaism, as seems to be the case, it is natural to assume that the parallel development reflects the impact of Zoroastrianism on Judaism.' See Shaked, 'Zoroastrianism and Judaism' [no. 148], pp. 203–206.

18 Shaked, 'Iranian Influences in Judaism' [no. 68], p. 323. See also Shaked, 'Zoroastrianism and Judaism' [no. 148], pp. 206–208, where he writes: 'the lack of a clearly defined structure within Jewish eschatology stands in contrast to the fact that Iranian eschatology can be viewed as a structural unity.'

essential, authoritative point of reference for any enquiry into the question of possible influences of Iranian religion on Judaism.

Certain priests in Sasanian Iran possessed the title *Ohrmazd mowbed* (Priest of Ohrmazd), attributing to them an extraordinary ability to see into the non-material, non-sensual world of *mēnōg* (*mēnōg-wēnišnīh*), which is unperceivable by the ordinary senses of the common people. Thus, many Zoroastrian spiritual entities that are invisible in *gētīg* (the tangible, visible world in which we live) or are believed to be manifested in *gētīg* by non-figural entities, such as natural elements, only reveal their true anthropomorphic form and appearance in *mēnōg*.[19] Shaul Shaked's abilities to discern the 'true appearance' of complex and vaguely expressed notions in the Middle Persian texts, and to perceive, via the senses and the knowledge that only he possesses, a remarkably full and vivid picture in the 'table-cloth full of holes' of the Zoroastrian literature, have made him the *Ohrmazd mowbed* of Zoroastrian studies.

19 Shaked elucidated the notions of *mēnōg* and *gētīg* and their importance in the Zoroastrian worldview and mythology in his 1971 article 'The Notions Mēnōg and Gētīg' [no. 42].

The Scholarly Oeuvre of Shaul Shaked, 2

Shaul Shaked and the Study of Judeo-Persian

Ofir Haim

Shaul Shaked's pioneering scholarship has undoubtedly revolutionized the study of the Judeo-Persian language, particularly its oldest layer, known as Early Judeo-Persian. His work laid the foundations for the study of Early Judeo-Persian texts and consequently of Jewish history in the Iranian world in the first centuries of Islam. Over the years, Shaked has published extensively on the Early Judeo-Persian language and culture and encouraged young scholars to do the same, sharing with them his expertise and advice as well as providing them with his own preliminary work on various texts.

Shaked defines Early Judeo-Persian as New Persian written in Hebrew script and datable to the pre-Mongol period, up to the early thirteenth century, and he stresses its distinctive characteristics in comparison to contemporary New Persian and later Judeo-Persian. Rather than being a 'single or unified language,' Early Judeo-Persian should be regarded as 'several varieties of New Persian used presumably in as many different localities in the Persian-speaking world.'[1] This lack of linguistic uniformity is attributable to the absence of a central authority providing models of literary writing and a uniform orthography and grammar. Different literary forms of Early Judeo-Persian thus to an extent reflect the local vernaculars of the authors.[2] After the arrival of the Mongols, which had devastating consequences for the Jewish communities of

1 Shaked, 'Classification of Linguistic Features' [no. 174], p. 450. The bracketed numbers in the notes refer to the list of the Principal Publications of Shaul Shaked, in this volume.

2 *Ibid.*

Iran, Early Judeo-Persian gave way to Classical Judeo-Persian, which differs only slightly from Standard Literary Persian.[3]

Up to the late 1960s, very few Early Judeo-Persian texts were known. Worthy of mention in this regard are a letter from the area of Khotan (Dandan-Uiliq),[4] a legal document from Ahwāz,[5] a fragmentary introduction to a Karaite book of precepts[6] and a commentary on the Book of Ezekiel.[7] Thanks to Shaked's scholarly efforts, the corpus of known Early Judeo-Persian texts increased in volume and variety, and it now amounts to some 1,000 pages. His acquaintance with the Cairo Geniza from an early stage of his career,[8] exemplified by his elaborate catalog of published Geniza documents,[9] enabled him to identify many other Early Judeo-Persian texts preserved in libraries in Europe and the United States. Later on, with the dissolution of the Soviet Union, Shaked brought to light more Early Judeo-Persian exegetical works in the Second Firkowicz Collection preserved in the National Library of Russia.[10]

The scholarly community's access to hitherto unknown texts in Early Judeo-Persian has been further facilitated by Shaked's studies, in which he illustrates these texts' importance for studying the evolution of the New Persian language. His thorough command of both Semitic and Iranian languages allowed him to edit and translate an array of difficult Early Judeo-Persian texts of different genres, such as legal documents,[11]

3 Shaked, 'Early Judaeo-Persian Texts' [no. 155], p. 198.
4 For further information, see Shaked, 'Judaeo-Persian Letter' [no. 160] and the references there.
5 For a short history of publications and improved readings and translations, see Shaked, 'Judaeo-Persian Notes' [no. 41], pp. 180–182.
6 *Ibid.*, pp. 178–180.
7 On this manuscript, see Shaked, 'Early Judaeo-Persian Texts' [no. 155], p. 195, and the references there.
8 The 'Cairo Geniza' is the designation of the hoard of manuscripts found in the Ben Ezra synagogue in Fusṭāṭ.
9 Shaked, *A Tentative Bibliography* [no. 1].
10 The Early Judeo-Persian manuscripts from the Second Firkowicz Collection probably originate in the Dār Simḥa Karaite synagogue of Cairo. For further details on these manuscripts, see Shaked, 'List of Judaeo-Persian Bible Translations' [no. 137], pp. 15–16; idem, 'Early Judaeo-Persian Texts' [no. 155], pp. 200–202.
11 Shaked, 'An Early Karaite Document' [no. 44].

letters,[12] and Bible commentaries and translations,[13] as well as literary texts.[14] Shaked also paved the way for others in the field of Early Judeo-Persian by examining the peculiarities of the language and its dialectology,[15] and by providing surveys of the linguistic features of Early Judeo-Persian exegetical texts preserved in the National Library of Russia.[16]

Shaked has also made important contributions to the field of Early Judeo-Persian epigraphy, particularly with his study of the Jewish tombstones from the mountainous region of Ghūr in central Afghanistan, which revealed the existence of the Jewish community of Fīrūzkūh (eleventh–thirteenth centuries).[17] He published several hitherto unknown tombstones and offered improved readings and translations of already-published ones, while providing erudite discussions of the names and titles engraved on them.[18] Together with Ruth Jacoby, he also published an elongated bronze rod with an inscription in Judeo-Persian datable to the pre-Mongol period, reportedly found in central Afghanistan.[19] As noted by Shaked, this rare Jewish object, possibly a Torah pointer, 'is perhaps the only inscribed metal object from Afghanistan from an early Islamic date.'[20]

Shaked's studies of Early Judeo-Persian texts have important implications for the history of pre-Mongol Iranian Jewry. Their linguistic diversity, as shown in his research, demonstrates the wide geographical

12 Shaked, 'Persian-Arabic Bilingualism' [no. 185].
13 Shaked, 'Appendix' [no. 56]; 'Two Judaeo-Iranian Contributions' [no. 63]; 'New Early Judeo-Persian Finds' [no. 173], pp. 228–245; 'A Fragment of the Book of Jeremiah' [no. 211].
14 Shaked, 'Aspects of the Early Heritage' [no. 70], pp. 35–37; 'Do Not Buy Anything from an Aramaean' [no. 95]; 'An Early Geniza Fragment' [no. 89].
15 Shaked, 'An Unusual Verbal Form' [no. 79]; 'Notes on the Preposition *bē*' [no. 93]; 'Classification of Linguistic Features' [no. 174], pp. 449–453.
16 Shaked, 'Early Judaeo-Persian Texts' [no. 155], pp. 204–217; 'Classification of Linguistic Features' [no. 174], pp. 454–458.
17 For a history of publications on the tombstones, see Shaked, 'New Data on the Jews of Afghanistan' [no. 130], p. 8.
18 Shaked, 'Epigraphica Judaeo-Iranica' [no. 62], pp. 71–82; 'New Data on the Jews of Afghanistan' [no. 130], pp. 8–13; 'New Early Judeo-Persian Finds' [no. 173], pp. 225–228.
19 Shaked and Jacoby, 'An Early Torah Pointer' [no. 163]; 'New Early Judeo-Persian Finds' [no. 173], pp. 222–225.
20 Shaked, 'New Early Judeo-Persian Finds' [no. 173], p. 223.

distribution of Jews in the Iranian orbit at the time, from Khuzistan to Bukhara, along with their rich intellectual world. Shaked showed that Judeo-Persian literature had its beginning not in the fourteenth century, as had been believed, but rather much earlier; the Cairo Geniza documents and finds from other synagogues include a wide array of literary and religious materials written in Early Judeo-Persian, some of them dating back to the tenth century.[21] Particularly important in this regard are the Early Judeo-Persian Karaite writings attesting to the Karaite presence in Iran in the tenth–eleventh centuries, which offer a glimpse into Karaite literary activity outside the scholarly circle of the famous 'Mourners of Zion' Karaite community in Jerusalem.[22]

In addition to his impressive body of work in the field of Early Judeo-Persian, Shaked, together with Amnon Netzer, has organized the Irano-Judaica conferences and edited a series of Irano-Judaica volumes.[23] The conferences gather scholars interested in the contacts of Jews with the Iranian world throughout the ages and serve as a unique platform for the study of the Judeo-Persian language and culture, from the early Islamic period to the twentieth century.

One of Shaked's significant contributions to the field of Early Judeo-Persian in recent years concerns what has been dubbed the 'Afghan Geniza,' a trove of manuscripts dating from the early eleventh to the early thirteenth centuries discovered in central Afghanistan. Shaked was the first to uncover the existence of the many literary texts written in Early Judeo-Persian in this trove, as well as the archive of a Jewish family that lived in the city of Bāmiyān in the first half of the eleventh century. His early surveys of a large portion of these texts conveyed their significance for many areas of study, and principally for the history of the Jewish communities of eastern Iran.[24] So far, he has published two specimens from this trove,[25] demonstrating its importance and uniqueness – surely a taste of things to come.

21 Shaked, 'Aspects of the Early Heritage' [no. 70], pp. 23–31.

22 See, e.g., Shaked, 'Two Judaeo-Iranian Contributions' [no. 63], pp. 304–322; 'Aspects of the Early Heritage' [no. 70], pp. 27–29; 'Early Judaeo-Persian Texts' [no. 155], pp. 202–204.

23 Shaked (ed.), *Irano-Judaica* [I] [no. 20]; Shaked and Netzer (eds.), *Irano-Judaica*, II–VI [nos. 22, 24-26, 29].

24 Shaked, 'Early Persian Documents' [no. 195]; 'Jews in Khorasan' [no. 202].

25 Shaked, 'Yima' [no. 207]; 'A Fragment of the Book of Jeremiah' [no. 211].

The Scholarly Oeuvre of Shaul Shaked, 3

Shaul Shaked on Jewish Magic

Yuval Harari

> Among the new [magical] texts there is a vast amount of information that was entirely unknown before or only vaguely understood. The picture changes rapidly and dramatically, and in some respects the changes are fundamental. (Shaul Shaked)[1]

At the age of eighty-five, Shaul Shaked is a young and driven scholar. Looking at the list of his publications during the last fifty-five years, what evokes amazement is not only his impressive productivity but also the steady pace of his publishing, year after year, including the forthcoming volume *Aramaic Bowl Spells: Jewish Babylonian Aramaic Bowls* (vol. II).[2] Magic, however, was not always a prominent concern for Shaked. Although he began publishing his scholarly work in 1964, it took twenty more years for his interest in Jewish magic to be reflected in print. Even though this involvement expanded in the following decades and became especially close to his heart, the list of publications attests that magic and magical texts were a side interest for Shaked, who focused mainly on Zoroastrian, Iranian and Judeo-Iranian issues. And yet, lo and behold, he became the leading expert on ancient Jewish magic.

Research into Jewish magic had indeed begun before Shaked directed his attention to it, but the impetus of his trailblazing research profoundly transformed the field. He greatly expanded the textual basis for the study of ancient Jewish magic, rested its research on solid philological and methodological foundations and pointed to its intra-cultural and intercultural ties, opening up for his students and his students' students

1 Shaked, 'Popular Religion in Sasanian Babylonia' [no. 128], p. 103. The bracketed numbers in the notes refer to the list of the Principal Publications of Shaul Shaked, in this volume.

2 Shaked, Ford and Bhayro, *Aramaic Bowl Spells*, II [no. 19].

a broad area of inquiry. What was seemingly a minor and relatively late interest in his intellectual life proved critical to the study of a segment of Jewish culture to which hardly anyone had paid any attention until his time. Shaked brought into the study of Jewish magic his broad knowledge, his superb linguistic tools, his marvelous ability to decode particularly difficult inscriptions and manuscripts, and his painstaking and uncompromising attention to detail. He has dealt with adjurations, demons, maladies, holy names and personal names with the same absolute seriousness that biblical and talmudic scholars devote to the canonic Jewish corpora of antiquity. In doing so, he laid the foundations for the revolution of recent decades in all that concerns the understanding of magic and its place in Jewish life in late antiquity and the early Middle Ages.

The Beginning: Folk Religion and Syncretism

The first inkling of what would become his creative research endeavor was Shaked's special interest in the cultures of 'Oriental Jews' (a term whose problematic nature he addressed in the article that opens the first volume of *Pe'amim: Studies in Oriental Jewry*)[3] and their relations with surrounding cultures. In a brief 1983 article, Shaked dealt for the first time with Jewish magic texts, spelling out the substance of his view on these materials and on the suitable approach to their study.[4] The article's opening lines point to trends in his concern with magic texts that would accompany his work in subsequent decades: intercultural ties between Jews and their neighbors in the area of folk religion, transitions and intra-cultural changes of Jewish traditions in the realm of magic, and, above all, the textual expression of these phenomena. He wrote:

> The areas of negotiation between Jews and their Muslim neighbors on matters of faith and religious practice in the late Middle Ages and the early modern period were not many. … One of the few areas of creativity that was relatively open to contacts and influences was that of sorcery and magic. … The study of this material may point to several matters of interest for the relationships between Jews and their Muslim environment in the community's folk circles as well as for the relationship between the ancient tradition and the changes

3 Shaked, 'The Heritage of Oriental Jewry' [no. 59].
4 Shaked, 'On Jewish Literature of Magic in Muslim Countries' [no. 65].

> affecting it. Our concern here is not with the magic act per se, which is a separate issue, but with expressions and formulations related to witchcraft and found in writing, that is, with the literature of magic and with the adjuration formulae in the amulets.[5]

Make no mistake. Though a linguist to his core, Shaked never confined himself to the bounds of the texts he studied; he always aspired to reach beyond them and was the first to point out cultural developments exposed in magic texts, as well as their Jewish and non-Jewish contexts. His work, however, was invariably founded, above all, on the written text, and his main interest focused on the texts themselves and their mutual relationships. On the one hand, therefore, Shaked was never really interested in theoretical definitions of the cultural domain conveyed in the magic texts he studied or in its borders vis-à-vis other cultural domains in the Jewish communities that had created these texts. 'Any one working within the field of magic in Judaism in late antiquity and the early Middle Ages,' he wrote, 'knows the difficulties besetting any attempt to define it. Despite these difficulties … there are not very many cases of hesitation when one tries to identify magic texts.'[6] Whenever he identified a text as *magic* – 'without imputing any pejorative sense to this term,' as he clarified[7] – and found it of interest, he first listened to it carefully, and then gave it his full scholarly attention. On the other hand, and from that same stance, almost no article by Shaked in the field of Jewish magic fails to explore specific texts and expose readers to a new finding, which is indeed the basis for the entire study.

Even in his first attempt, which heralds not only the trends and the method but also the breadth of his textual horizons, Shaked followed a similar path. He gathered together texts from realms separated by time and place – fragments from the Cairo Geniza, texts from Aramaic incantation bowls, passages from a book of magic recipes found in a Jewish-Persian community, and an adjuration from a modern-period metal healing bowl – to point to the cultural syncretism reflected in magic writings by Jews in Islamic lands. Shaked returned to the phenomenon of syncretism among Jews in Muslim regions in two later articles devoted to the cultural implications of textual expressions of a 'magical' kind in 'folk religion,' 'personal religious expressions,' or 'simply …

5 *Ibid.*, p. 15.
6 Shaked, 'Peace Be upon You, Exalted Angels' [no. 120], p. 197.
7 Shaked, 'Spells and Incantations' [no. 176], p. 233.

whatever is not included in the accepted form of worship,' as he termed it.[8] His fascination with religious syncretism captivated Shaked almost wherever he turned and would also accompany him to another branch, the central one, of his research on magic: the Babylonian anti-demonic incantation bowls.

Aramaic Incantations of Late Antiquity

By the time he wrote his first article on magic, Shaked was already deeply involved in two large projects, not unrelated to one another: the study of ancient amulets and incantation bowls, and the study of medieval magic fragments from the Cairo Geniza. The first of these projects took shape in the early 1980s, in his work with Joseph Naveh on *Amulets and Magic Bowls*. 'It has been our wish,' the authors wrote, 'to make available to scholars material for the study of popular religious life of Jews and pagans in the crucial period which corresponds to that of the Talmud.'[9] This was the first time scholars had gathered together Jewish magic texts from historically and geographically diverse (yet related) sources, extending from late antiquity to the Middle Ages and from Babylonia to Fustat (today's Cairo), subjected them to thorough philological study, and pointed to the existence of a well entrenched feature in the Jewish people since late antiquity – a 'permanent phenomenon,' as Shaked defined it elsewhere in an even broader historical context[10] – one that, until then, research had ignored almost entirely.

The exposure of these *insider* sources (i.e., sources from the magic culture per se), which continued even more intensely in the second volume by Naveh and Shaked, *Magic Spells and Formulae*,[11] fundamentally changed the study of Jewish magic. Until then, scholars had relied mainly on basically hostile rabbinic (or Karaite), *outsider* evidence to describe magic and its place in Jewish society. The work of Shaked and Naveh raised to the surface objective and textual expressions of this cultural phenomenon and enabled scholars to observe it and re-evaluate it without mediators.

8 Shaked, 'Between Judaism and Islam' [no. 116] (quotations on pp. 4, 9); 'Medieval Jewish Magic' [no. 138].
9 Naveh and Shaked, *Amulets and Magic Bowls* [no. 3], pp. 9–10.
10 Shaked, 'Between Judaism and Islam' [no. 116], p. 17–18.
11 Naveh and Shaked, *Magic Spells and Formulae* [no. 5].

The main force of the research in the pathbreaking volumes by Shaked and Naveh was devoted to the more ancient sources – amulets and incantation bowls. The scope and quality of these studies – the new readings of previously misunderstood texts and the readings of new texts published for the first time – made Shaked the world's foremost expert on the study of Jewish magic texts from late antiquity. This expertise would lead him to the enormous endeavor of publishing the incantation bowls from the Schøyen collection, which developed slowly and is presently in full swing. At that time, however, Shaked was actually busy with the second project that he was developing, focusing on the Cairo Geniza.

Magical Texts from the Cairo Geniza

Shaked was thoroughly familiar with the Cairo Geniza and its study from the very beginning of his scholarly training.[12] He laid the systematic foundation for the study of Geniza magic texts (including demonology, divination, astro-magic, alchemy, and so forth) in the summers of 1983 and 1984, which he spent in the library of the University of Cambridge. Adding the results of further searches in other libraries, he prepared a detailed list of some 1,700 fragments, among them amulets and passages from manuals of magic and other occult practices to which hardly anyone had hitherto paid attention. The presence of these fragments in Shaked's scientific work increased gradually in the following years, as evident both in the volumes he published with Naveh and, mainly, in his joint research with Peter Schäfer, which, during the 1990s, yielded the three volumes of *Magische Texte aus der Kairoer Geniza*.[13] In these volumes, Shaked and Schäfer published close to one hundred Geniza fragments: amulets, fragments from recipe books and parts of magic works. The sheer quantity of the texts, together with the dozens of Geniza fragments that Shaked published with Naveh, has made it untenable to go on dismissing Jewish magic as the cultural trivialities of ignorant masses. In Shaked's words, such an attitude, 'more than of magic, is indicative of the scholars' prejudices, of their unwillingness to recognize that this is a permanent phenomenon of religious

12 See Shaked, *A Tentative Bibliography* [no. 1].
13 Schäfer and Shaked, *Magische Texte aus der Kairoer Geniza*, I [no. 8], II [no. 10], III [no. 11].

life … fulfilling a significant day-to-day role hardly less important than that of the official ritual and prayer.'[14]

Furthermore, some of the works discussed by Shaked and Schäfer, such as The Use of the Eighteen Blessings, The Seven [Blessings] of Elijah (both of which suggest systematic magic use of the *Amida* blessings for the weekdays and the Sabbath), and The Use of Psalms, as well as the literary genre prevalent in them – "adjuratory prayer" – undermine, by their actual public presentation, the thin division between "magic" and "religion" that many scholars had worked so hard to build and sustain. Without pointing his textual enterprise in this direction, but constantly aware of its social, cultural and historical implications, Shaked (together with the scholars who at times joined him on this voyage) brought about a pivotal change regarding Jewish magic, by leading for over thirty years in the effort to publish magic writings. As part of this effort, Shaked also devoted articles to unusual texts from the Geniza, such as fragments from books on divination and magic that are particularly ancient or written in a unique dialect;[15] to linguistic ties between magic texts in the Geniza and Babylonian incantation bowls;[16] and to differences among the figures involved in the magic acts that these texts present[17] (and even to an ancient Afghan Jewish-Aramaic amulet written in a genre and a language familiar from the Cairo Geniza[18]). Although Shaked has not written the 'missing chapter' in Shlomo Dov Goitein's study of Mediterranean Jewish society (no one has done that yet), he has certainly made the most decisive contribution to the exposure of Geniza fragments that Goitein chose to ignore. He thereby laid the foundation for the description of magic as a vital component of Jewish culture in the Mediterranean Muslim world during the Middle Ages.

Aramaic Bowl Spells in Context

Although Jews in the Muslim realm and their folk religion were close to Shaked's heart, his main interest in Jewish magic and most of the en-

14 Shaked, 'Between Judaism and Islam' [no. 116], p. 17.

15 Shaked, 'An Early Magic Fragment' [no. 88]; 'A Palestinian Jewish Aramaic Hemerologion' [no. 107].

16 Bohak, 'From Qumran to Cairo' (with an appendix by Shaul Shaked) [no. 192].

17 Shaked, '*Dramatis Personae* in the Jewish Magic Texts' [no. 169].

18 Shaked, 'A Jewish Aramaic Amulet from Afghanistan' [no. 175].

ergy he invested in its research have focused, from the start and to this very day, on Babylonian incantation bowls. It is here that three areas of interest that have nurtured and accompanied his work throughout his years of research come together: the culture of the Sasanian Empire, Jewish magic and intercultural syncretism. In contrast to his work on the magic texts from the Geniza, Shaked found here a solid scholarly basis for his research in the works of James A. Montgomery, Cyrus H. Gordon and others, who laid the foundations for the study of the Aramaic, Syriac and Mandaic incantation bowls from Babylonia.

No dialect has been excluded in Shaked's study of these bowls, as attested by his articles dealing with Iranian elements in bowls written in Mandaic and with Manichaean bowls written in Syriac.[19] He also contributed to the study of ancient magic texts in Mandaic and Pahlavi that are not in the bowls genre.[20] Yet, when turning to the Mesopotamian-Sasanian area, where Jewish, Manichaean, Mandaic, Zoroastrian, Christian and pagan folk-religious elements came together in a spellbinding syncretism – the *mages sémitisés*, as he put it,[21] which he has recurrently addressed throughout his scholarly pursuit[22] – Shaked focused above all on the Jewish-Aramaic incantation bowls. He persistently broadened and developed this field of research and became its leading figure with regard both to the decipherment and publication of new bowl spells and to the intra-cultural and intercultural impact of this vast textual corpus.

The interest in magic bowls has accompanied Shaked since the very start of his cooperation with Joseph Naveh. It grew, intensified and developed hand in hand with his intensive concern with metal amulets from the Land of Israel and its surroundings; those texts, which were particularly difficult to read and, until then, had scarcely been published

19 Shaked, 'Popular Religion in Sasanian Babylonia' [no. 128]; 'Manichaean Incantation Bowls in Syriac' [no. 139].

20 Greenfield and Naveh (with notes by Shaked), 'A Mandaic Lead Amulet with Four Incantations' [no. 73]; Shaked, 'Notes on the Pahlavi Amulet' [no. 112]; 'Magic in Zoroastrianism' [no. 198].

21 Shaked, 'Popular Religion in Sasanian Babylonia' [no. 128], p. 114.

22 Shaked, 'Bagdana, King of the Demons' [no. 71]; Greenfield and Naveh (with notes by Shaked), 'A Mandaic Lead Amulet with Four Incantations' [no. 73]; Shaked, 'Popular Religion in Sasanian Babylonia' [no. 128]; 'Jews, Christians and Pagans' [no. 131]; 'Jews, Christians and Pagans' [no. 143]; 'Incantation Bowls and Amulet Tablets' [no. 165]; 'A Jewish Aramaic Amulet from Afghanistan' [no. 175].

(mostly incorrectly), were also a central tier in the two volumes published with Naveh.[23] As is true of many studies of this kind, their study began, as they noted, almost by chance, out of a limited inventory of bowls available to them at the time. The rumor spread, however, and additional texts were brought to their attention.

What had begun as a humble initiative, then, 'a desire … to do a modest work on a number of Aramaic magic bowls which at that time (almost ten years ago) were in Jerusalem in the hands of dealers and the collection of the Institute of Archaeology of the Hebrew University,'[24] grew to become the basis for a new field of research: ancient Jewish magic. Its borders were determined by three types of sources that he and Naveh assembled and published: Babylonian incantation bowls (28); amulets from the Land of Israel and its surroundings (32, most of them Jewish); and Geniza magic fragments (29). In their view, these sources shed light on one another and, together, allow us to trace the folk-religious phenomenon common to Babylonian Jews and the eastern Mediterranean in late antiquity and the early Middle Ages. In the introductions to their books, Shaked and Naveh began to trace the profile of this phenomenon. They discussed the religious and liturgical world of the magic texts, their conceptions of sickness and healing, their use of biblical verses, and their connection to the Jewish esoteric literature of antiquity—*Hekhalot* and *Merkavah* literature. Shaked has added to and continued to develop these research trends up to the present, never ceasing to locate, decipher and publish new texts. In the last twenty years, he has exposed and studied many more amulets and incantation bowls[25] and persistently prepared the ground for the systematic publication of the 650 incantation bowls in the Schøyen collection.

Work on the Schøyen collection began in the 1990s, when the collection was deposited in the University of London, and is still ongoing. 'In 2001,' Shaked writes, 'I finished the first stage of the work, with most of the bowls in the three major languages [Jewish Aramaic, Syriac and Mandaic] transcribed and provided with provisional translation.

23 Naveh and Shaked, *Amulets and Magic Bowls* [no. 3]; eidem, *Magic Spells and Formulae* [no. 5].

24 Naveh and Shaked, *Amulets and Magic Bowls* [no. 3], p. 9.

25 Kotanksky, Naveh and Shaked, 'A Greek-Aramaic Silver Amulet' [no. 106]; Shaked, 'Notes on Some Jewish Aramaic Inscriptions from Georgia' [no. 171]; Shaked and Elitzur-Leiman, 'An Aramaic Amulet for Winning a Case' [no. 209], and the references in note 29 below.

The sheer size and complexity of the undertaking was quite daunting.'[26] The collaboration he initiated in order to complete this enterprise, this time with James Nathan Ford and Siam Bhayro, led several years ago to the publication of the first volume of the Schøyen collection bowls in the series *Aramaic Bowl Spells: Jewish Babylonian Aramaic Bowls*.[27] The work gathers dozens of incantations from two genres of bowls: (1) Ḥanina ben Dosa bowls, narrating the magic historiola about the encounter between a lilith and R. Ḥanina, who contended with her using verses from Psalms, as part of the textual-ritual mechanism for expelling demons. (2) Divorce and ban bowls, which mostly include the historiola about the mythological bill of divorce given by R. Joshua b. Peraḥia to a lilith or about the ban he imposed on her, for the same purpose. Another volume in the series, including dozens of additional bowls, is now in press,[28] and further volumes are expected in the future.

Shaked has consistently accompanied this textual research with thematic articles that shed light on the world of the bowls' writers and their clients and on the linguistic and conceptual foundations that tied them to their neighbors. Each of these articles marked a breakthrough in its field and advanced our understanding of the character and location of magic and demonology in the Jewish culture of late antiquity. Shaked dealt at length with the praxis of writing the bowls, the transmission of knowledge between writers, the typology of the incantations, the writer–client relationships and the *dramatis personae* in the magic act, as reflected in the language of the bowls. He greatly expanded our knowledge of Jewish mythological and concrete demonology, its connections with the Iranian demonic world, and its meaning in the individual's daily life as a mechanism for explaining and removing injuries and diseases, which were the context for the development of the magic genre of incantation bowls. He examined the historical-social evidence that emerges from the bowls on such topics as family size, the lack of evidence for polygamy, the high social status of some of the clients (bearing such titles as *rabbi* or *mar*), and the recourse of Zoroastrian clients to Jewish writers. He pointed to biblical elements in the language of the bowls, such as the use of biblical verses, biblical figures and biblical events, to the role of R. Ḥanina b. Dosa and R. Joshua b. Peraḥia as mythological exorcists in the adjurations, and to the possible mention

26 Shaked, Ford and Bhayro, *Aramaic Bowl Spells*, I [no. 18], p. xiv.
27 Eidem, *Aramaic Bowl Spells*, I [no. 18].
28 Shaked, Ford and Bhayro, *Aramaic Bowl Spells*, II [no. 19].

of talmudic Babylonian rabbis – Rav Ashi (owner of one of the bowls) and Rav Aḥa bar Rav Huna (a neighbor of another bowl owner) – in them. He dealt extensively with magic divorce formulae in the bowls, including some that mention dates, and noted additional rabbinic characteristics, such as unknown midrashim that occur in the incantations. He noted the bowls' linguistic and conceptual links with *Hekhalot* and *Merkavah* works and pointed to the use of liturgical components in the incantations, including two passages from Mishna *Zevaḥim* (which are the earliest Mishna manuscripts known to us). Finally, he drew connections between the linguistic expressions of Babylonian Jewish magic and the contemporaneous and later magic texts from the Land of Israel and the Cairo Geniza.[29]

Conclusion

In his varied studies of magic bowls, Shaked has woven a tight network of intra-cultural ties between them and other manifestations of Jewish culture in late antiquity. This network joined another web of ties he had worked on, as he sought to connect Jewish expressions of magic culture in Sasanian Mesopotamia to those of the neighboring religions. By following these two paths in the course of his entire research enterprise, together with the broad and rigorous philological work that underlies them, Shaked laid the foundations for the study of ancient Jewish magic and built its first tier. It is his work that, for over thirty years, has driven the discovery and publication of new Jewish texts, due to which 'the picture changes rapidly and dramatically, and in some respects the changes are fundamental.'[30] We have every reason to believe that his work will continue to foster this fortunate development, enriching our knowledge about ancient Jewish magic with the same drive that has characterized Shaul Shaked's endeavor from its outset.

29 Shaked, 'Bagdana, King of the Demons' [no. 71]; 'Peace Be upon You, Exalted Angels' [no. 120]; 'The Poetics of Spells' [no. 133]; 'Incantation Bowls and Amulet Tablets' [no. 165]; 'Form and Purpose in Aramaic Spells' [no. 166]; '*Dramatis Personae* in the Jewish Magic Texts' [no. 169]; 'Time Designations and Other Recurrent Themes' [no. 181]; 'Transmission and Transformation of Magical Formulae' [no. 186]; Bohak, 'From Qumran to Cairo' (with an appendix by Shaul Shaked) [no. 192]; 'Rabbis in Incantation Bowls' [no. 200].

30 Shaked, 'Popular Religion in Sasanian Babylonia' [no. 128], p. 103.

From Iran to Qumran and Beyond
On the Evil Thought of God

Moshe Idel

Dualism: Some Recent Shifts in Scholarship

Since the discovery of two previously unknown ancient libraries – the Nag Hammadi library, discovered in Egypt in 1945, and the Qumran library, discovered in caves overlooking the Dead Sea in 1946 – scholarship on important aspects of Western religions has changed direction. The Nag Hammadi library, containing Gnostic documents, mainly in Coptic, many of them bearing hitherto unknown texts, demonstrated that the Gnostic movement was much less dualistic than scholars had believed,[1] and much closer to Judaism than suggested by the dominant line of research until then, which had attributed a decisive influence solely to what has been called Iranian dualism, as expressed in classical Zoroastrianism.[2] The Qumran library contained a plethora of Hebrew and Aramaic treatises, largely unknown, which showed that some Jews entertained ideas closer to dualism than had been suspected by scholars of Judaism in late antiquity. In both cases, subsequent research produced not only important contributions to the study of Jewish and Christian apocrypha and pseudepigrapha, but also an entire library of scholarship that has led to a much more complex understanding of Judaism as it

* This study is a much expanded version of Idel, 'Evil Thought,' which has been reformulated on the basis of Shaul Shaked's seminal studies. It is part of a longer work, Idel, *Il male primordiale*.

1 This was the thesis of Wilhelm Bousset and Richard Reitzenstein, and, more recently, Geo Widengren. It was not rejected by H. Jonas and U. Bianchi, and it is still accepted by some modern scholars, such as Y. Stoyanov, in idem, *The Other God*. Others, like I.P. Couliano in idem, *The Tree of Gnosis*, criticized it sharply.

2 For the view that Gnosticism was much closer to Judaism, see, e.g., Couliano, *The Tree of Gnosis*, or Stroumsa, *Another Seed*; see also Idel, *Kabbalah: New Perspectives*, pp. 30–32.

was in a crucial period in the emergence of both Rabbinic Judaism and nascent Christianity.

In both Christianity and Judaism, for all their structural and conceptual differences, the dualistic elements became attenuated. However, in later centuries, dualistic elements returned to play a much more vital role in some forms of Christianity in Europe, especially after the emergence of the Bogomil and Cathar movements, and shortly thereafter they also found their way into parts of kabbalistic literature. The parallel return of these repressed elements is quite a fascinating phenomenon. The Kabbalah texts were written after the Christian dualist heresies of the Middle Ages, in the same geographical vicinity, though temporally they coincide only in part; yet they have been viewed as influenced much more by late-antique Gnostic forms of dualism and than by its medieval forms.[3] This influence was conceived as a matter of historical affinities and not just phenomenological resemblances.[4] The kinds of dualism expressed in these texts were conceived by scholars as addressing the powerful dichotomy between good and evil in both a metaphysical and an ethical sense. Discussions of questions related to the source of evil have featured prominently in critical analyses of the Kabbalah, but, apart from Isaiah Tishby's M.A. thesis on the concept of evil in sixteenth-century Lurianic Kabbalah, written in the late 1930s and later published as a monograph,[5] there has been no in-depth study of dualism and evil. Dualism has been addressed in scholarly literature over the years, but without integrating two important developments: the discovery that stark dualism was a much rarer religious phenomenon than was earlier assumed, and recent findings relating to the origins of Gnosticism.

Scholars – notably Shaul Shaked, in his incisive studies of Zoroastrian dualism,[6] Ugo Bianchi and his student Ioan Couliano, in their work on Gnosticism,[7] Guy G. Stroumsa, in his essay on Sethianism and

3 On the possibility of Cathar influences on the *Book of Bahir* and Abraham Abulafia, see Shahar, 'Catharism,' and idem, 'Écrits Cathares.' Later scholarship did not adopt these theories: See Scholem, *Origins of the Kabbalah*, p. 234, note 72; Schneider, 'The Myth of Satan'; and Idel, *Studies in Ecstatic Kabbalah*, pp. 33–44.

4 Scholem, 'Isaac ben Jacob Hakohen'; idem, *Origins of the Kabbalah*, pp. 316–320, 363–364, 389–390.

5 Tishby, *Doctrine of Evil*, passim.

6 Shaked, *Dualism in Transformation.*

7 Bianchi, *Zamân î Oúhrmazd*; idem, 'Alcuni aspetti abnormi'; idem, 'La doctrine

Manichaeanism,[8] and Petrus Francescus Maria Fontaine, in his multi-volume study *The Light and the Dark: A Cultural History of Dualism*,[9] among others[10] – have presented a broad array of dualistic approaches, but their work has not been sufficiently reflected in studies of the history of Kabbalah. Integration of what scholars have identified as dualistic elements in the Qumran texts and the new evaluations of dualism in Gnosticism can enrich the discussion of Jewish phenomena like Kabbalah, notwithstanding their later time and differing phenomenological constitutions.

Modern studies of the origins of kabbalistic dualism have tacitly retreated from a theory put forward by Adolphe Franck in 1843 on the Iranian sources and antiquity of Kabbalah.[11] Franck's proposal was based on the somewhat problematic assumption of the antiquity of certain parts of the *Zohar*, but subsequent studies have offered further evidence for contact between Zoroastrianism and Jewish themes.[12] Nevertheless, the response of modern scholarship to the possibility of direct influence of Zoroastrian dualism on Jewish mysticism, unmediated by late-antique Gnosticism, has been one of almost total silence.[13] This silence is all the more striking in light of recent scholarly discussions of Iranian influences on Judaism in other topic areas, especially early medieval rabbinic literature, such as the Babylonian Talmud.[14]

zarathoustrienne; idem, 'Le dualisme'; idem (ed.), *Le origini dello gnosticismo*; and Couliano, *The Tree of Gnosis*.

8 See Stroumsa, *Another Seed*, and idem, *Savior et Salut*, pp. 243–258.

9 Fontaine, *The Light and the Dark*.

10 See, e.g., Stoyanov, *The Other God*; Eliade, 'Prolegomenon to Religious Dualism'; idem, *The Two and the One*; and idem, *Zalmoxis*; or Frey, 'Different Patterns of Dualistic Thought.'

11 See Franck, *La Kabbale*; see also Mueller, 'On *Sefer Yetzirah*'; idem, *History of Jewish Mysticism*, p. 65; and, more recently, Stroumsa, 'A Zoroastrian Origin.'

12 See Kohut, *Ueber die juedische Angelologie*.

13 See, e.g., the studies of Peter Schaefer and Joseph Dan.

14 See Urbach, *The Sages*, I, pp. 165, 194; more generally, Bakhos and Sayegan, *The Talmud in its Iranian Context*; Elman, 'The Other in the Mirror'; idem, 'Acculturation and Elite Persian Norms'; idem, 'Scripture versus Contemporary Needs'; Widengren, 'Iran and Israel in Parthian Times'; Secunda, 'Talmudic Text and Iranian Context'; idem, 'Construction, Composition and Idealization'; and more recently idem, *The Iranian Talmud*; Neusner, *Judaism, Christianity, and Zoroastrianism*; idem, *Judaism and Zoroastrianism at the Dusk of Late Antiquity*; Schremer, *Male and Female*, pp. 15, 168–176; and Koren, *Forsaken*, pp. 81–91. See also Stoyanov, *The Other God*, pp. 50–64.

If Zoroastrian themes impacted on rabbinic halakhah, then one may presume an impact on rabbinic esotericism, too, especially given the Persian extraction of some of the key Hebrew terms in this realm, including *pardes*, *raz* and *pargod*. Thus, consideration of Iranian materials alongside the Gnostic influences seems to me an important desideratum insofar as theories of evil in the Kabbalah are concerned.[15] Some of the more recent studies on sources of Gnostic dualism also seem to have escaped the attention of scholars of kabbalistic 'dualism.' Ugo Bianchi's emphasis on the possible Orphic-Platonic sources of Gnosticism, without ignoring potential Iranian or Jewish influence,[16] and the more widespread assumption that Gnosticism was informed by Jewish apocalyptic themes,[17] have hardly modified the picture of Kabbalah that has dominated scholarship since the late 1930s, under the influence of Hans Jonas's studies.

The assumption that Jewish themes are found in Gnostic texts, which has burgeoned in the wake of scholarly analyses of the Nag-Hammadi Gnostic literature, does not rule out the possibility of Zoroastrian/Zurvanian influence on Qumran, on apocalyptic literature or on Jewish-Christian literature, and, later, on Kabbalah. The two influences could, and in my opinion did, work together. Assuming that Kabbalah drew on ancient Jewish mythologoumena that also nourished discussions found in Gnosticism, and that there might also be Gnostic influences on the Kabbalah, does not preclude acceptance of the presence of Zoroastrian themes, when they can be proven. An early Jewish matrix of Gnosticism, a later Gnostic matrix of some kabbalistic themes, and the reverberation of Zoroastrian views in the Kabbalah should not be viewed as mutually exclusive. I believe that the Kabbalah was informed by an inclusive spectrum of sources, produced by the accumulation and amalgamation of diverse elements that reached different kabbalists in various proportions, as part of the 'stream of traditions' that reached Europe from the Middle East in the Middle Ages.[18] The weaknesses of the *Religionsgeschichte* school's Iranian thesis of Gnosticism and

15 See Idel, 'Evil Thought'; idem, *Absorbing Perfections*, p. 558, note 169; and idem, *Ascensions on High*, pp. 124–125. Especially important are Subtelny, 'Tale of the Four Sages'; and Stern, *Time and Process*, pp.126–123, speaking of the 'Irano-Hellenization of the Near East.'

16 Bianchi, *Selected Essays*.

17 See, e.g., Pearson, 'Jewish Sources in Gnostic Literature'; and Stroumsa, *Another Seed*.

18 Gaster, *Ilchester Lectures*; Idel, *Ben: Sonship*, pp. 54–57 and 98–99, note 176.

dualism, in terms of some of the themes it emphasized, does not cancel out its contributions, which are quite evident, in my opinion, in explaining the case of Manichaeism, for example. While I do not propose returning to this thesis or embracing Franck's view, it seems that both approaches should be examined with a much more open mind than has been done thus far.

Zurvanism: A Subordinated Pseudo-Symmetry

Many of the dualistic forms of religion known in the history of Western civilization owe much to the classical forms of Zoroastrian dualism,[19] which presume the existence of two primordial powers: the positive spirit Ahura Mazda (on which account Zoroastrianism is also known as Mazdeism) or Ohrmazd, and the evil spirit Angra Mainyu or Ahriman. Present reality as a mixture (*gumezagih*) of the two,[20] the battle between them, and the final eschatological victory of the former over the latter, constitute the basic tenets of the religion. This type of dualism was incorporated in several other religions, most notably Manichaeism, which was quite widespread and left a strong imprint on medieval sects such as the Paulinians, Bogomils, Massalians and Euchitians, and later the Albigensians and Cathars. Other forms of Gnosticism may have borrowed from the Zoroastrian concept of dualism, too.[21]

However, there was also a less familiar and less influential form of Zoroastrianism, known as Zurvanism. It presumed the existence of a higher principle, Zurvan, the infinite time, which generated the two principles mentioned above.[22] This was a more monotheistic conception than the basically unmitigated dualism of classical Mazdeism; viewed as heterodox by Zoroastrian orthodoxy, it elevated a single principle

19 See Jonas, *The Gnostic Religion*; Stoyanov, *The Other God*; Shaked, *Dualism in Transformation*; and Oisteanu, *Religie, politica si mit*, pp. 153–164. This thesis has been disputed by scholars in the last two generations.

20 See, e.g., de Menasce, *Le troisième livre du Denkart*, Chap. 90, p. 97, Chap. 106, p. 108, Chap. 222, p. 233, Chap. 316, p. 301, and Chap. 404, p. 362.

21 Stoyanov, *The Other God*, pp. 161–174.

22 The late Prof. Shlomo Pines drew my attention to the Zurvanic material. The question of whether Zurvanism is a heresy in comparison to stricter dualistic Zoroastrianism, or just one variant of Zoroastrianism, is quite important to the history of Zoroastrianism but irrelevant to most of the following discussion. For the second position, see the seminal studies of Shaked, *Dualism in Transformation*, and Stoyanov, *The Other God*, pp. 322–323, note 127.

over the two 'classical' principles. Zurvanism regarded that single principle as the father of the two deities, which are envisioned as sons and hence as brothers, implying a preexisting shared *Urgrund.* The extent of the influence of this religious variant within broader social strata is unknown, but it was known to a variety of medieval scholars. I wish to refer to a few passages from among the array of fragments describing this heterodox vision, found solely in medieval texts written by a variety of authors – Greek, Christian and especially Arab. One of the most remarkable testimonies appears in Shahrastani's famous twelfth-century description of heresies, *Kitab al-Milal wa-al-Niḥal* (The Book of religions and sects), in the section entitled 'The Zurwaniyya':[23]

> Light brought forth persons of light, all of them spiritual, luminous and divine. But the greatest person, whose name was Zurwan, doubted something and from that doubt there came into being Ahreman the Satan. But some of them say: No, but rather [it was in the following manner]: The great Zurwan stood and prayed for 9,999 years to have a son, but did not have one. Thus there occurred [in] him a thought, and he said: 'This knowledge is perhaps worthless,' and Ahreman came into being from that one reflection, and Hormiz came into being from that knowledge, and both were in one belly. Hormiz was closer to the gate of exit, but Ahreman used a stratagem and by splitting the belly of his mother he came out before Hormiz and took possession of the world.[24] It is said that when he [Ahreman] presented himself before Zurwan, and when the latter watched him and saw the vileness, evil and corruption which was in him, he detested him, cursed him and chased him away. ... Some of the Zurwaniyya claim that there has been something vile with God from eternity, either a vile thought[25] or a vile corruption,[26] and that this is the origin of Satan.[27]

23 Namely, the Zurvanic sect. The English translation is Shaked's.

24 This episode is reminiscent of the birth of Esau and Jacob in Gen. 25:22–26, which became a topos in many kabbalistic discussions.

25 For additional references to evil thought – *pensée mauvaise* – in Arabic sources, see the footnote to the French translation of this passage in Gimaret and Monnot, *Shahrastani*, p. 639, note 25.

26 Or putridity, see below.

27 Shaked, 'Some Islamic Reports,' pp. 56–57. See also another translation in Zaehner, *Zurvan*, p. 433. For analysis, see *ibid.*, pp. 60–61, 270–271; and Shaked, *Dualism in Transformation*, pp. 17–18. For a French translation

For the sake of the following discussion, let me put into relief the themes that will preoccupy us: The evil entity emerged before the good entity, and its source is divine doubt, thought or reflection. The phrase 'evil thought' appears only in Arabic accounts of Zurvanism, which are relatively late, while other sources use terms like doubt, putridity and reflection. However, it is obvious that Shahrastani did not invent this notion, since 'evil thought' appears in original Zoroastrian texts, such as *Yasna* 30:3 and 32:5, which use the term *Aka mainyu*, as well as in a text that will be adduced below, and in another early description of Zurvanic religion as heresy. Moreover, the converse term, 'good thought,' or *vohu manah*, is found in another Zoroastrian text.[28] Thus, it seems there is no reason to doubt the authenticity of the later account as evidence of a much earlier formulation of the two types of divine thought.

The evil entity is evidently a son – unlike the more orthodox Zoroastrian view of it as an evil spirit – and he is the firstborn of Zurvan. The nature of the mother is unknown in these sources, but birth involves a female's womb. According to another view, Ohrmuz commits an incestuous act with his mother as part of the act of creation.[29] In other words, the emergence of Ahriman is the product of a misguided thought or a doubt, which engendered the evil spirit. A similar view concerning Zurvan's evil thought has been documented in other Arabic sources.[30]

To be sure, the Arabic sources are relatively late, from the twelfth century and after, and their accounts do not always match other accounts of Zurvanism. However, the expression 'evil thought' is found in 'Abd al-Jabbar's eleventh century description of Zoroastrianism,[31] which also

with important footnotes, see Gimaret and Monot, *Shahrastani*. See also the discussions of Zaehner, *Dawn & Twilight*, pp. 212–214 and 217; and Bianchi, *Selected Essays*, pp. 368–370 and 382–389. A small part of the very end of this passage appears in a Latin translation and is quoted by Franck, *La Kabbale,* p. 370, note 3, but he does not discuss the issue of Zurvan's doubt or evil thought.

28 See Shaked, *Dualism in Transformation*, p. 137.

29 See Zaehner, *Zurvan*, pp. 151–153. On Zurvan's 'wife,' see *ibid.*, pp. 63–64, 423 and 428. On ritual incest in Zoroastrianism, see Shaked, *Dualism in Transformation*, pp. 120–124; and Pines, 'A Parallel,' pp. 49–51.

30 Zaehner, *Zurvan*, pp. 421–423, 428 and 451, and after the publication of his monograph, see the material collected by Monnot, 'Pour le dossier,' *Journal Asiatique*, pp. 238 and 243–245, as well as the next footnote.

31 See Shaked, 'Some Islamic Reports,' pp. 50–51 and 73–74; and Monnot, *Penseurs musulmans*, p. 247 and note 3, where he explains that the demon was born out of evil thought. On the impact of Zoroastrianism on Ismailyya, see Corbin, *Temps cyclique*; regarding the text of Shaharastani, see pp. 24–25.

uses the terms 'doubt' and 'putridity.' It should be noted that the doubt or evil thought precedes wisdom, which is conceived as good. In any case, the reliability of the Muslim sources has not been challenged by scholars in the field. Although the above discussion implies a fourfold structure of the first divine persons – Zurvan, the unknown female and their two sons – the structure is actually triangular, or what I have called a 'subordinated pseudo-symmetry': a father and his two sons

The emergence of Ahriman from Zurvan's cognitive action, I would add, is not part of a cathartic move meant to purify Zurvan, but a manifestation of a deficiency in his character that was externalized at a certain moment, in a kind of hypostasis. Its emergence does not improve the act of creation but generates the condition for its mixture, and thus for lower nature.

Two Thoughts in Qumran

A similar triangular structure, without the presumption of fatherhood, appears in a book discovered in the Qumran caves dealing with two hypostatic spirits, one of light and one of darkness, leading several scholars to draw attention to similarities between Zurvanism and the Dead Sea Scrolls.[32] One of the passages most quoted by scholars in the so-called *Manual of Discipline* reads:

32 Michaud, 'Un mythe Zervanite,' esp. pp. 145–146; Duchesne-Guillemin, 'Le zervanisme'; Shaked, 'Qumran and Iran'; Wilderberger, 'Der Dualismus'; Winston, 'The Iranian Component'; Dupont-Sommer, *Les Ecrits esseniens*, p. 93, note 2, and pp. 94 and 96; Zaehner, *Dawn & Twilight*, pp. 50–51; Stoyanov, *The Other God*, pp. 61–62; Eliade, *History of Ideas*, p. 269 note 42; and now Elman, 'Zoroastrianism and Qumran.' On dualism in Qumran literature in general and adopting the Zurvanic explanation, see Dimant, 'Dualism at Qumran'; eadem, 'Qumran Sectarian Literature,' pp. 534–535 and 546; Kister, '4Q392 and the Concept of Light'; idem, 'On Good and Evil'; and idem, 'Body and Purification.' Dealing not with a Zurvanian theme but with a Zoroastrian theme related to evil, Shlomo Pines pointed out its impact on Qumran literature and the New Testament; see his 'Wrath and Creatures of Wrath'; and see also idem, 'Eschatology and the Concept of Time.' This impact shows that Zoroastrian concepts penetrated other areas of Jewish literature as well. A much more cautious approach to Qumranic dualism from the point of view of Zurvanic impact, based on some very keen attention to divergences in the concepts, is found in Bianchi, *Selected Essays*, pp. 370–378. See also more recently Nitzan, 'Evil and its Symbols.'

> From the God of knowledge stems all there is and all there shall be. Before they existed he established their entire design. And when they have come into being, at their appointed time, they will execute all their works according to his glorious design, without altering anything. … He created man to rule the world and placed within him[33] two spirits so that he would walk with them until the moment of his visitation: they are the spirits of truth and of deceit. From the spring of light stem the generations of truth and from the source of darkness the generations of deceit. And in the hand of the Prince of Lights is dominion over all the sons of justice. They walk on paths of light. And in the hand of the Angel of Darkness is total dominion over the sons of deceit; they walk on paths of darkness. From the Angel of Darkness stems the corruption of all the sons of justice, and all their sins, their iniquities, their guilt and their offensive deeds are under his dominion, in the compliance with the mysteries of God, until his moment. And all their afflictions and their periods of grief are caused by the dominion of his enmity; and all the spirits of his lot cause the sons of light to fall. However, the God of Israel and the angel of his truth[34] assist all the sons of light. He created the spirits of light and of darkness, and on them established every deed.[35]

The polarity here is both anthropological and cosmological: On the one hand, there are two spirits in man and two types of men; on the other, the spring of light and the source of darkness are related to two cosmic leaders, designated as the Prince of Lights and the Angel of Darkness. These polarities are also associated with the different forms of ethical behavior. However deterministic this sounds, it is clear that the sons of deceit can entrap the sons of light and cause them to go astray; not

33 There is a certain ambiguity here: It is not totally clear whether each person is given two spirits, like the two urges in rabbinic literature, or only one, creating the dichotomy between the children of light and of darkness. It seems that the latter alternative is more plausible.

34 *Mal'akh 'amito*. On this phrase, see Idel, *Golem*, p. 311; and idem, *The Angelic World*, p. 158, note 6.

35 III, 15–25, in García Martínez and Tigchelaar, *The Dead Sea Scrolls*, I, pp. 74–78; see also IV, 16–19, *ibid.*, pp. 78–79; and Licht, *The Rule Scroll*, pp. 91–92. On this passage, see Dimant, 'Qumran Sectarian Literature,' p. 533; Shaked, 'Qumran and Iran,' esp. pp. 434–435; Erder, *Karaite Mourners*, p. 147; Kister, 'On Good and Evil,' pp. 511–513; Eliade, *Zalmoxis*, p. 108; Pétrement, *A Separate God*, pp. 177–179; Levenson, *Creation and the Persistence of Evil*, pp. 41–42; or Orlov, *Dark Mirrors*, p. 13.

everything is predestined. Though the imagery is one of symmetry, the divine creator clearly sides with the spirit of truth, which is why it is more appropriate here to speak of subordinate pseudo-symmetry than of dualism. However, the present age is considered to be under the aegis of the Prince of Darkness, implying that evil comes before the final good, in a manner reminiscent of Zurvanic views.

In the above passage there is no mention of the thought of God or of 'evil thought.' Immediately afterwards, however, three terms are used in association with thought: *maḥashevet ma'ase* (thought of action), *maḥashevet qodesh* (thought of the Holy or of holiness)[36] and *maḥashevet qodeshekha* (thought of your holiness),[37] and *maḥashavto*[38] ('his' thought), referring to the thought of God. Here creation and predestination are related explicitly to divine thought. By contrast, in another Qumranic treatise we find *maḥashevet qodesho*, thought of his Holiness, juxtaposed with *maḥashevet Mastemah*, the thought of Mastemah, the angel appointed over the evil powers,[39] and *maḥashevet rish'am*, the thought of their wickedness.[40] Menahem Kister has pointed out an instance in the scrolls where the term *maḥashava* implies some form of arbitrariness.[41] Moreover, the phrase 'God of knowledge' at the beginning of the above-quoted passage alludes to the biblical expression *El hade'ot* in I Sam 2:3, and should be translated literally as 'the God of all knowledge,' since the Hebrew term is plural. Could this plural be understood here as referring to two forms of thought, and to God as existing prior to them, in the manner of the Zurvanic theological triangle?

Thus, in addition to the various 'dualisms' that scholars have already discerned in certain treatises found in the Qumran library, I see a clear polarity in the two cosmic leaders, also reflected in the two types of thought, calling to mind the Zurvanic discussions mentioned above. Again, as in the case of Zurvanism, there is nothing cathartic in the

36 IV, 4–5, in Licht, *The Rule Scroll*, pp. 95–96.
37 XI, 19, *ibid.*, p. 236.
38 XI, 11, *ibid.*, p. 231.
39 On this name for the chief of evil entities see also Jubilees 18:9; Pines, 'The Oath,' pp. 170–171; Alexander, 'Demonology of the Dead Sea Scrolls,' pp. 341–344; Segal, *Book of Jubilees*, pp. 202–210; Erder, 'The Prince Mastemah'; and idem, *Karaite Mourners*, pp. 145–148. See also Rosen-Zvi, *Demonic Desires*, pp. 55–56.
40 Yadin, *The Scroll*, p. 334 and the parallels adduced on p. 335.
41 See Kister, 'Some Lexical Features,' p. 568.

creation of the spirit of deceit insofar as the nature of God is concerned, and there is no allusion in these passages to a concept of perfection.

These ideological similarities appear to be part of a much broader Iranian impact on late antique Judaism.[42] According to some recent suggestions by scholars, views found in the Qumran cave texts could have been known to early Jewish-Christian authors[43] and even to medieval Jewish circles.[44] In any case, the assumption that Zurvanic views were known only to a few inhabitants of the caves in Qumran, and that they disappeared from Judaism with the disappearance of that group, is overly simplistic.

Traces of acquaintance with Zoroastrian thought occur in the Babylonian Talmud, a vast compilation of traditions stemming from a wide variety of rabbinic sources.[45] Here I would like to elaborate on a single concept that may reflect some kind of Zurvanic influence. In a rather difficult passage, a talmudic master refers to his younger brother as *bekhor satan*,[46] which may be rendered as 'the firstborn of Satan,' or, as proposed more recently by Israel Ta-Shma, as 'the firstborn Satan.'[47] He bases this interpretation of Satan as the firstborn of God on a comparison with the Bogomil vision of Satan as the firstborn of God. However, since the Babylonian Talmud was redacted at least two centuries before the appearance of the Bogomils in southeastern Europe, it seems that Ta-Shma's observation on the affinity between the two themes would be better served by assuming a common source

42 See Kohut, *Angelologie und Daemonologie*; and especially Shaked, 'Iranian Influence on Judaism'; and see also Frye, 'Qumran and Iran.' For a survey of scholarship exploring Iranian influence on the figure of Satan see Schaerf Kluger, *Satan in the Old Testament*, pp. 151–162, accepting the idea of Iranian influence but not dealing with Zurvanian Zoroastrianism. See also Kohut, *op. cit.*, pp. 62–72, who claims that some characteristics of Satan are derived from the concept of Agromainus. This view was accepted by Gaster, 'Satan,' p. 226. See also Greenfield and Shaked, 'Three Iranian Words'; Rosen-Zvi, *Demonic Desires*, p. 118; and Liebes, *Studies in Jewish Myth*, pp. 75–76.

43 This is, e.g., the view of Danielou, *Theologie du Judeo-Christianisme*, pp. 93–94.

44 See Wieder, *Judean Scrolls*; Erder, *Karaite Mourners of Zion*; Wacholder, *Dawn of Qumran*, pp. 141–167, 177–178; Mack, 'From Qumran to Provence'; and Ta-Shma, *Studies in Medieval Jewish Literature*, III, pp. 191–192.

45 See BT *Pesaḥim* 111a; Kohut, *Angelologie und Daemonologie*; and Schwab, *Vocabulaire de l'angélologie*, pp. 153 and 195. See also Urbach, *The Sages*, I, pp. 165 and 194.

46 BT *Yevamot* 16a.

47 See Ta-Shma, *Studies*, III, p. 194 and note 14.

for both – Zurvanism. Indeed, scholars of the Bogomil myth have proposed such an explanation for the emergence of the Bogomil trinity, consisting of God and his two sons: Satanael, the firstborn, and Jesus, the younger one.[48] Thus, the possibility remains that the Babylonian Talmud borrowed a Zurvanian view in which the firstborn is conceived as evil, or even identical with Satan.

Moreover, in a Jewish-Christian view reported by Epiphanius of Salamis, writing around 370, Jesus and Satan as described as equivalent in status:

> They state that the two classes were established by God, as I see the one is Christ and the other is the devil. And they say that that Christ received the portion of the coming age but that the devil has been entrusted with this age.[49]

While the devil is not described here as firstborn, as in some traditions, he is given dominion over the first of the two ages, meaning that his dominion precedes that of Jesus. This is reminiscent of the division of rulership between Ahriman, who reigns first, and Ohrmuz, who will reign in the future. It seems that the talmudic phrase may be better understood by resorting to pre-talmudic themes than to post-talmudic ones.

Rabbinic Traces

In rabbinic tradition, divine thought is sometimes described as impenetrable. One such discussion attributes the tragic death of Rabbi Akiva, one of the most revered figures in the rabbinic world, to divine thought.[50] A possible explanation is that divine thought may operate according to

48 See Stoyanov, *The Other God,* p. 163; Eliade, *Zalmoxis*, p. 108; idem, *The Two and the One*, p. 83; and Orlov, *Dark Mirrors*, pp. 85–120. The split between good and evil in Christianity, as personalized by Jesus and Satan, is a recurring theme in Carl G. Jung's psychoanalytic theory.

49 *Panarion* 30:16,2; English translation by Klijn and Reinink, *Patristic Evidence for Jewish-Christian Sects*, p. 183. See also Daniélou, *Theologie du Judeo-Christianisme*, p. 231; and Eliade, *Zalmoxis,* p. 108. I do not know why Carl Jung read this passage as if it were obvious that Satan was an elder son of God. See idem, *Aion*, p. 57. On p. 58, he assumes that in Jewish-Christian sources in late antiquity there were two sons of God, as mentioned earlier.

50 See e.g., BT *Menaḥot* 29b. See also Idel, *Absorbing Perfections*, p. 232. Whether there is some form of Zoroastrian influence here is a matter for separate investigation.

a different form of religious logic in which a righteous person could be relegated to an undeserved and tragic death.

In this context, let me adduce another tradition found in Jewish circles concerning an affinity between the firstborn and the chief evil power. Starting from the early Middle Ages, a few Hebrew sources assert that Adam's firstborn was not the biblical Cain but a figure described by the Hebrew consonants *'GRYMS*, which can be vocalized as Agrimas. This is the case of a late midrash that perhaps belongs with some fragments put together by several twentieth-century several scholars under the title *Midrash 'Avkkir*,[51] though its relationship to that composition is unproven.[52] Nonetheless, there seems to be a scholarly consensus that the following passage does belong to a midrash:

> Adam was an absolutely righteous person, and since he saw that death was proclaimed because of him, he practiced asceticism, fasting and separating from woman, and slept alone.[53] Lilith, whose name is Pizna, found him, and she desired his beauty ... and she [lay] beside him and gave birth to demons and liliths from him, and the name of the firstborn of Adam was Agrimas. Agrimas went and

51 See Epstein, 'Yalqut Shim'oni'; Marmorstein, *Devir*; and Buber, Introduction to *Midrash Leqaḥ Tov*, p. 40. On the affinities between this midrash and Hekhalot literature, see Scholem, *Jewish Gnosticism*, p.132; Urbach, *Sefer 'arugat habosem*, p. 174, note 22; and Beit Arié, *Pereq shira*, II, p. 81, note 103.

52 See Geula, 'Lost Aggadic Works,' who surveyed all the known data in print and manuscripts regarding this midrash. On p. 2 and note 10, and p. 97, note 635, he argues that this discussion is related not to *Midrash Avkkir*, as found in one of the earliest editions from sixteenth-century Venice, but to an anonymous, unidentifiable midrash, which he decided not to publish among the fragments of *Midrash 'Avkkir* that he assembled. See also Scholem, *Devils, Demons*, p. 134, note 60.

53 See BT *'Eruvin* 18b and *Genesis raba* 20:11. The image stems from an interpretation of Gen. 5:3, understood as the period between the death of Abel and the birth of Seth. See Ginzberg, *Legends of the Jews*, V, p. 148, notes 46 and 47. In the last footnote, discussing Eve giving birth to demons, Ginzberg refers to a polemic with a Persian source. This is a clear critique of asceticism, which provokes spilling of the seed in vain. Although the rabbinic sources mentioned here predate the passage on Agrimas, the possibility that the latter may be the source of the former should be considered, at least in principle. For a discussion of the rabbinic version of the legend as dealing with both the lower and the higher couple, see especially the text of R. Moshe of Burgos, printed by Scholem, 'R. Moshe miBurgos,' pp. 50–51. The kabbalistic text emphasizes the theme of Adam's seed.

> took for a wife 'Imrit Lilith, and she [bore] him ninety-two tens of thousands of demons and liliths.[54]

Parallel narratives in other midrashim speak implicitly, and in one case, explicitly, about Adam's seed becoming demons.[55] In a show of ambivalence, the above passage takes a positive view of asceticism and then goes on to criticize it, perhaps if it is taken too far. After relating the tremendous proliferation of demons and liliths,[56] the story goes on to say that Methuselah was given a sword engraved with the divine name that enabled him to kill demons. This is one of the earliest forms of the succubus myth. Agrimas, conceived as head or propagator of the demons, must save them from the deadly sword, and he arrives to implore Methuselah to stop decimating the demons.[57] The onus of generating the demons is put here on the feminine element, Lilith. However, in the above text, as well as in the classic rabbinic discussions of Adam's procreation of demons through intercourse with a female demon, no explanation is supplied for the origin of the demoness. This demonic vision of the feminine power is reminiscent of a Zurvanian approach that differs from the Zoroastrian approach.[58] While semen is not mentioned here, as it is in the classic rabbinic versions of this midrash, a Jewish reader of the text would easily have associated it with spilling seed in vain. If the Zurvanian nature of the passage is accepted, then we are looking at a combination of two myths of evil, as delineated by Paul Ricoeur in his *Symbolism of Evil*: the 'dominant myth' of the

54 See Marmorstein, *Devir*, p. 138. An almost identical text appears in another manuscript source from that same year, reprinted in Ginzburg, *Jewish Law and Lore*, p. 249. See also Scholem, *Kabbalah*, p. 357, and the version found in the fourteenth-century Ashkenazi treatise *The Book of Memory* (ed. Yassif), p. 113. For Lilith and Adam see the other traditions from a variety of sources, collected and discussed in Jungian jargon by Hurwitz, *Lilith, the First Eve*. Our passage is not discussed in this collection. See also the parallel pointed out by Scholem, *Jewish Gnosticism*, pp. 73–74. For a recent study that highlights the affinity between an Iranian depiction of the protoplast couple and the rabbinic view of androgyny, see Secunda, 'The Construction,' pp. 60–85. For the penitential dimension of the Adamic myth in Judaism, see Ricoeur, *Symbolism of Evil*, pp. 237–243. Cf. also Widengren, 'Primordial Man and Prostitute.'

55 See, especially, *Yalqut Shim'oni* on Genesis 5, §42.

56 Here, as in other magical texts, Lilith is not a proper name but a generic category of female demonic spirits.

57 Marmorstein, *Devir*, p. 139.

58 See Zaehner, *Zurvan,* p. 192.

so-called 'fall' of man – though the sin here is relatively transient – and the drama of creation, which presumes the existence of some seed of evil in creation itself.

The assertion that 'The name of the firstborn of the First Man [Adam] was Agrimas' recurs in several of the sources that preserved the midrashic fragment. Louis Ginzberg, one of the first scholars to publish a version of this myth, proposed to see in the name Agrimus, as he vocalized it, a variant of Angro-Mainu,[59] an earlier form of the name Ahriman. Thus, just as Ahriman, in Zurvanic texts, is the firstborn of Zurvan, or infinite time, Agrimas/Agrimus in the Hebrew sources mentioned above is the firstborn of Adam, sired with the demoness Lilith, who, according to late midrashic sources, was his first wife, who left him before he met Eve.[60] In both cases a progenitor is born to a foundational figure, and the names of the two are quite similar. It seems that the late midrash derives not from an orthodox version of dualistic Zoroastrianism but from a Zurvanian source that speaks of a divine father and two sons, the firstborn being evil. Moreover, in both Zurvanism and the midrash, Ahriman/Agrimas is the source of the demons. The occurrence of the name Agrimas allows us to exclude the possible influence of Manichaeism and later of Catharism, according to which God has two sons, the first of them evil, and of Bogomilism, in which the firstborn son was Jesus and only the second was the devil.[61] In none of these cases does the name Ahriman occur.

59 Ginzberg, *Legends of the Jews*, V, pp. 165–166, note 63. In his earlier discussion, in idem, *Jewish Law and Lore*, p. 245, he offered another explanation for Agrimus, a derivation from Greek *agrimainos*, 'wild.' He changed his mind later on without mentioning his earlier proposal. Ginzberg's later etymology was accepted by Scholem, *Origins of the Kabbalah*, p. 296, note 191; see also idem, *Devils, Demons*, p. 61; and Bidez and Cumont, *Les Mages Hellénisés*, p. 386. In Idel, *Fallen Angels*, I discuss aspects of the above-quoted passage, together with a manuscript version, in the context of the transmission of myths in Judaism relating to the fallen angels, which differ from what is found in the known apocrypha. See also Idel, *Ben*, pp. 98–99, note 176. The Mithraic/Roman form of Ahriman's name, Arimanius, is not the source of the Hebrew form. For this form, see Bianchi, *Selected Essays*, pp. 208–216.

60 Thus, there is no contradiction between the biblical narrative, where Cain is the firstborn of Eve, and the midrash, which attributes Agrimas to another mother. Although this passage relates evil to some form of procreation by relations with a she-demon, procreation itself is conceived as positive, unlike the classical Hindu view. See Doniger O'Flaherty, *Origins of Evil*, pp. 27–29.

61 See Stoyanov, *The Other God*, pp. 160–161; and Anderson, *Genesis of Perfection*, p. 173.

The theory of Zurvanic impact on the anonymous midrash is reinforced by yet another parallel. In another fragment of *Midrash 'Avkkir*, it is said, referring to the biblical verse 'Then (*'az*) Israel sang this song' (Num. 21:17), that 'the Holy One, blessed be He, clothed Himself in a garment of splendor upon which were written all the [occurrences of the word] *'az* in the Torah.'[62] In Zurvanism, *'az* represents the power of concupiscence, a negative analogue of Zurvan, and Zurvan is described as having a garment,[63] as is Ahriman, who receives this garment from Zurvan.[64] Arthur Marmorstein, too, has pointed out a possible relationship between this midrash and Iran.[65]

This midrashic material obviously made its way to Europe, as the name Agrimas is known to some Ashkenazi sources, especially those linked to the thirteenth-century Hasidei Ashkenaz,[66] some of them already mentioned by Ginzberg and Marmorstein.[67] The story is quoted almost in its entirety in the widely circulated *Commentary on the Pentateuch* by the mid-thirteenth century Ashkenazi commentator R. Efrayim b. Shimshon.[68] From these Ashkenazi sources, or from their sources or parallels, parts of the myth seem to have found their way to some sixteenth-century kabbalists. The minor Ashkenazi kabbalist R. David b. Isaac Ginsburg of Fulda included it in his voluminous treatise *Migdal David*, written in 1595.[69] More important for the history of Kabbalah is the testimony of R. Nathan Neta Shapira of Jerusalem, a mid-seventeenth century Lurianic kabbalist who enjoyed a large following in Europe, especially Italy. In a gloss to R. Ḥayim Vital's *Peri 'etz ḥayim*, he wrote:

62 This fragment was printed by S. Buber in *Hashaḥar*, 11, p. 458. For other variants of this statement see also Epstein, 'Yalqut Shim'oni,' pp. 205, 207. See also Scholem, *Jewish Gnosticism*, pp. 61–64 and 132, and the late anonymous Ashkenazi text found in MS Oxford-Bodleiana 1816, fol. 68b–69a, where *Midrash 'Avkkir* is mentioned in the context of all occurrences of the Hebrew word *'az* in the Bible.

63 Zaehner, *Zurvan*, pp. 132, 351.

64 *Ibid.*, pp. 59, 119, 121–122.

65 Marmorstein, *Devir*, p. 134, note 2.

66 Klugemann, *Commentary on the Pentateuch* attributed to R. Eleazar of Worms, pp. 95. On p. 100, *Midrash 'Avkkir* is mentioned by name.

67 Ginzberg, *Legends of the Jews*, V, pp. 165–166, note 63.

68 Klugemann, *Commentary on the Pentateuch* by R. Efrayim b. Shimshon, p. 30.

69 See Scholem, *Kitve yad beqabala*, pp. 109–110.

> In *Sefer harazim* it is written:
> When Adam separated himself from his wife for 130 years he gave birth to spirits and liliths, and these are noxious to people [*'olamot*]. And in the midrash several tens of thousands of spirits and liliths are enumerated, and they were killing people [*beriyot*], and the Holy One, blessed be He, gave permission to Methuselah the righteous, and he wrote the divine name on his sword, and he killed twenty thousands of them in one moment, until Agrimos, the firstborn of Adam, came … and according to this intention[70] he had the power to kill all, would Agrimos not have come, as noted. End of quote from R. N[athan].[71]

I have no idea what book is being referred to as *Sefer harazim* (Book of secrets), but it is certainly distinct from *Midrash 'Avkkir*, which it quotes. This means that there was a book, most probably a kabbalistic one, where the midrash had been cited, and R. Nathan Shapira had seen this later book, perhaps similar to R. Isaac of Acre's untitled text, which I shall discuss elsewhere. It seems that we have here a clear reverberation of the struggle between humans and devils found in Zoroastrian

70 *Kavanah*, i.e., some form of mystical intention that has a magical effect. This is probably a reference to a Lurianic book.

71 Vital, *Peri 'etz ḥayim*, Chap. 11: 'Qeri'at Shema' 'al hamita,' fol. 80a. A shorter version of this passage, in which the name Agrimas does not appear, was adduced by R. Ḥayim Vital from an oral tradition of R. Moses of Mintz, who quoted his teacher R. Isaac Luria Ashkenazi. See Vital, *Liqute Torah*, fol. 19a. I do not know the source of Scholem's information that this detail was found specifically in a *Book of Secrets* of R. Eleazar of Worms, but I assume that he must have seen some source; see his *Origins of the Kabbalah*, p. 296, note 191. Thus, Luria was acquainted both with the Agrimas myth and with the concept of the presence of the evil within the divine thought, as we shall see below. Lurianic Kabbalah was very fond of the midrashic/talmudic version of the legend of Adam as a progenitor of demons. See, e.g., Vital, *Sha'ar hapesuqim*, pp. 101–102 and 141. See also Magid, *From Metaphysics to Midrash*, pp. 66–71. For a discussion of the midrash about Adam that does not mention Agrimas but does mention another head of demons, Amon of No, see the late-fifteenth-century *Tseror hamor* by R. Abraham Saba, fol. 96d; and Benayahu, *Ma'amadot umoshavot*, pp. 107–108. Amon of No was already known from the demonology of a circle of kabbalists related to the *Book of Meshiv*, and Saba may have been influenced by them. For other kabbalists in Safed who cited the rabbinic version of Adam as a progenitor of demons before Luria, see Cordovero, *Pardes rimonim*, II, XXVI:8, fol. 58c, and his older contemporary R. Yehudah Ḥallewah's *Tsafnat pa'neaḥ*, MS Dublin, Trinity College, B. 5.27, fol. 51b.

sources,[72] with righteous Methuselah saving humanity with the help of God. Although the theme of Adam's wasted seed during the 130 years is not explicit, it surely underlies the proliferation of the demons. The wasted seed will play a significant role in some of the kabbalistic discussions that I shall examine below.

I refer here only to texts in which the name Agrimas/Agrimos is mentioned explicitly, and not to texts in which fragments of *Midrash 'Avkkir* are cited or copied. The latter show that the Agrimas story was available at least in principle, even if the title *'Avkkir* was not cited. Thus, some avatars of a Zurvanic myth can be traced rather convincingly in late midrash – perhaps *'Avkkir* – in some medieval Ashkenazi sources, and as late as seventeenth-century kabbalistic texts, most of them also of Ashkenazi extraction. Adam's sin is conceived as a major transgression, perhaps as important to some kabbalists as the original sin of eating from the tree of knowledge. It is hard to exaggerate the impact of this legend in a culture where the issue of seed was paramount, and the kabbalists amplified it all the more.

We may note as well that according to *Sefer pitron Torah*, a commentary on the Torah composed in Iran in the Middle Ages, the two goats sacrificed on the Day of Atonement are intended for Ohrmuz and Ahriman. This seems to indicate that there were Jews who adopted some form of subordinated symmetry or binitarianism.[73]

The Testimony of Agobard of Lyon

The midrashic treatment reflects a mythical version of what I suggest may be seen as the impact of a Zurvanic theme on pre-kabbalistic and kabbalistic forms of Judaism. However, in my opinion, an additional aspect of Zurvanic doctrine revolving around the emergence of Ahriman also left its imprint on some Jewish sources. The belief that evil is generated by divine thought runs through many kabbalistic texts, as we shall see below. However, its first known formulation in Europe appears in a text written centuries before the emergence of Kabbalah. An epistle written in the first part of the ninth century by Agobard,

72 Shaked, *Dualism in Transformation*, p. 24, note 42.

73 Urbach, *Sefer pitron Torah*, p. 64; *ibid.*, note 34; and Introduction, p. 29. For my view on the existence of binitarian tendencies in early Kabbalah, see, e.g., Idel, *Ben*, pp. 50, 201, 653, 656–657, 604–605, and the footnotes to these discussions.

Episcope of Lyon, constitutes one of the most important and relatively early testimonies of the existence of certain types of mythologoumena among Jews in Europe. While scholars in other areas have drawn attention to the short passage by Agobard,[74] little has been written about its significance for the history of Kabbalah.[75] Some of the mythologoumena mentioned by Agobard have parallels in earlier Jewish writings, especially the Hekhalot literature,[76] and other elements that he attested stem from some forms of Palestinian halakhah, as demonstrated in an incisive study by Reuven Bonfil.[77] Thus far, it does not seem that this rather anti-Jewish episcope invented weird traditions in order to attribute them to the Jews. However, among the many mythologoumena mentioned in his epistle we do find one that does not have any earlier parallel in Judaism, although several parallels are found later on, in kabbalistic literature, and in earlier non-Jewish notions.

> They also say that their deity is corporeal and is distinguished by his limbs and his corporeal features and that, like us, he hears with one body part, sees with another, and speaks or does whatever else he does with yet another; and thus the human body was fashioned in the

74 See Odeberg, *3 Enoch*, Introduction, p. 28; see also Merchavia, *The Church versus Talmudic and Midrashic Literature*, pp. 71–84; and, more recently, Langenwalter, *Agobard of Lyon*; Cohen, *Living Letters of the Law*, pp. 123–146; and Kanarfogel, *Peering through the Lattices*, pp. 27–28. Neither these scholars nor those cited in the next two footnotes have questioned the reliability of Agobard's testimony.

75 It is surprising that scholarship on the history of Jewish mysticism and esotericism, including *Shi'ur qoma*, makes no mention of Agobard's epistle, which is safely dated to the first half of the ninth century. For example, although I discussed this passage in my article, 'Evil Thought of the Deity,' published in 1980, it is overlooked by Schaefer, *Origins of Jewish Mysticism*, esp. pp. 306–315; indeed, Schaefer ignored a series of Hebrew articles directly relevant to the topics he discusses, which might problematize his proposals. See, e.g., Farber-Ginat, 'Inquiries in *Shi'ur Qomah*,' and the bibliography cited there. French and English studies on this topic fare no better: See Mopsik, *Chemins de la Cabale*, pp. 309–324; and Idel, *Ben*, pp. 91–92, note 134. On this grave omission in modern research of Jewish mysticism, see Idel, *ibid.*, pp. 71 and 123, and, p. 107, note 215.

76 See Idel, 'Evil Thought of the Deity,' p. 357.

77 See Bonfil, 'Cultural and Religious Traditions of French Jewry.' Bonfil offers some interesting reflections on the implications of Agobard's testimony for an alternative understanding of the history of Jewish mysticism. On the halakhic dimension of Agobard's epistle, see Soloveitchik, 'Agobard of Lyon.'

> image of God, except that he has inflexible, rigid fingers, inasmuch as he does not work with his hands. He sits like some terrestrial king on a throne borne by four beasts, and he is housed in some sort of great palace. *He even thinks many superfluous and vain thoughts, which, because they all come to naught, turn into demons.*[78] As we have said, they relate countless abominations concerning their god, such that they worship an image which they have fashioned and erected for themselves in the folly of their hearts, not the true, completely unalterable God, of whom they are totally ignorant.[79]

Many of the concepts noted in this passage reflect concepts found in earlier Jewish sources. Thus, the rigid fingers are mentioned in a unique version, mentioned by a Karaite author, of the speculations in the *Shi'ur qoma*,[80] though it is not corroborated in the extant texts of that work.[81] The description of God sitting on a throne in a palace and some of the comments on the divine body are reminiscent of Hekhalot literature, thus providing relatively early evidence for the spread of this type of literature far beyond the Middle East, where it originated. Moreover, immediately following this passage there are descriptions of Jewish notions concerning the letters of the Hebrew alphabet, which have been discussed recently in scholarship and are not relevant to the current discussion.[82] Only the italicized sentence has no earlier parallels in Jewish texts. Demons, or at least some of them, are described as springing from divine thoughts, which did not actualize because they are vain. I shall explore below the question of whether angels were assumed to emerge from other types of divine thought. In any case, we are not looking at extreme dualism or at an assumption of a metaphysically lower source

78 The Latin original of the sentence in italics is: *Cogitare esiam illum superflua et vana quae, quia ad effectum cuncta venire nequeant, vertantur in daemones*; see Gundlach et al., *Epistolae*, p. 189. See Idel, ' Evil Thought of the Deity,' p. 357; Oron, *Sha'ar harazim*, Introduction, pp. 25–26; and Koren, *Forsaken*, p. 91.

79 The translation is that of Cohen, *Living Letters of the Law*, p. 129, slightly modified.

80 See the Karaite description of *Shi'ur qoma* in Salmon ben Yeruhin, *Sefer Milḥamot haShem*, p. 121: 'the fingers of his hands … are linked.' This indeed appears to show a conclusive nexus between the Jews of Lyon and the ideas in *Shi'ur qoma*.

81 I hope to deal with the significance of this phenomenon elsewhere.

82 See Weiss, 'Reception of Sefer Yesirah,' pp. 41–43.

for the demons. It was divine thought, or thoughts, that produced them. The present tense used by in the original Latin implies that this was a continuous process and not just a primordial act.

I believe that the topics mentioned in the above passage reflect theological positions that may be attributed to some elite Jews. Agobard remarks that he spoke daily with Jews and that they revealed to him what he calls 'the mysteries of their errors.'[83] Isaiah Tishby, speculating that the traditions attested by Agobard perhaps stemmed from 'apostates' (*sic*!) or related only to a small number of Jews, chose to regard them as mere 'popular' traditions and hence irrelevant to later developments of the Kabbalah and its theory of evil.[84] However, had he read Agobard's epistle closely, he might have found that it presents these notions as no less than the 'mysteries' of the Jews; or he could have read Bonfil's interesting study of this very subject, relying on details found in the above passage and including a short analysis based on my article, which appears in the *Festschrift* published in Tishby's honor.[85]

To summarize: Agobard's testimony provides important evidence for the existence of a theory on the emergence of evil from divine thought, embraced by Jews in Western Europe as early as the mid-ninth century.

Evil and Divine Thought in the Kabbalah of Late Thirteenth-Century Castile

There can be little doubt that Agobard's epistle was unknown to medieval Jews. This does not mean that the ideas attributed to the Jews of Lyon did not continue to preoccupy them and Jews elsewhere. A certain interest in divine thought, specifically the 'depth of the thought' harboring the primordial *tohu*, can be discerned in the Kabbalah of Provence, though the issue of evil is not explicit there.[86] A special concern with problems of evil, far beyond what is found in earlier forms of Kabbalah, may be seen among kabbalists in Castile starting in the second half of the thirteenth century. Some deal explicitly with the concept of

83 Gundlach et al., *Epistolae*, p. 189: *cotidie ... mysteria erroris ipsorum audimus*.

84 Tishby, 'Imaginary Innovation in the Research of Kabbalah,' p. 486; and see my response, 'Old and New in the Study of Kabbalah,' pp. 495–496.

85 R. Bonfil, 'Cultural and Religious Traditions,' p. 338 and note 27.

86 See the *Commentary on the Account of Creation* by Asher Ben David, in Abrams, *Asher ben David*, p. 338.

evil thought,[87] invoking parallels to the view concerning the origin of demons described by Agobard. As we shall see a little further on, one of the principal kabbalists active in Castile, R. Moshe of Burgos, devoted an interesting passage to the nexus between divine thought and the creation of evil.

The closest parallel to the notion expressed in Agobard's epistle appears in a passage by a thirteenth-century kabbalist, presumably active in Castile, called R. Joseph Haba Mishushan Habira – that is, 'R. Joseph who comes from Hamadan,' ancient Ecbatana, the Iranian city identified by Persian Jews with Shushan, the scene of the Book of Esther. He was probably active during what I call the 'window of opportunity of Kabbalah,' between around 1275 and 1295.[88] We know hardly any significant details of his life or his origins, which might be of interest in our context, given his name, but his kabbalistic thought, as delineated in his hitherto unidentified writings found in manuscripts, has been investigated by several scholars.[89] He was a theosophical-theurgical kabbalist, meaning that he assumed the divine status of the system of ten *sefirot* and believed that human activity may have an impact on the dynamics of the sefirotic structure. In one of his writings we read:

> From where were the demons created? I already hinted to you that this stems from the thought that He thought on the calamity [*pur'anut*] of Israel, because both angels and demons were created from the thought, but [the former] were created from the pure and fine thought, and [the latter] were created from the left side.[90]

87 Oron, 'Was the Kabbalah in Castile a Continuation?' On evil in Castilian Kabbalah and Zoharic literature, see Tishby, *Wisdom of the Zohar*, II, pp. 447–474.

88 Idel, 'The Kabbalah's Window of Opportunities.'

89 On this figure, about whose life and locale we know very little, see Scholem, *Einige kabbalistische Handschriften*, pp. 19–21; Altmann, 'Concerning the Question of the Authorship of *Sefer ta'ame hamitsvot*'; idem, 'An Allegorical Midrash'; Gottlieb, *Studies in Kabbalah Literature*, pp. 248–256; Liebes, *Studies in the Zohar*, pp. 103–126; Mopsik, 'Un manuscript inconnu'; idem, *Joseph de Hamadan*; Idel, 'R. Joseph of Hamadan's Commentary on the Ten Sefirot'; and Felix, 'Theurgy, Magic, and Mysticism.' See also Liebes, *Cult of the Dawn*, p. 185.

90 Printed anonymously in *Sefer hamalkhut*, fol. 85a–b. On R. Joseph of Hamadan's authorship of this treatise see Gottlieb, *Studies in Kabbalah Literature*, pp. 251–253.

Indeed, a few lines earlier, R. Joseph had asked about the origin of angels and demons:

> From where were they created? From the pure thought [*maḥashava tehora*][91] which ascends before the Holy One, blessed be He, an angel was created, and from the thought of calamity [*maḥashevet hapur'anut*] a demon was created ... from there came demons and spirits and malign powers [*maziqin*] and *lilin*, from the attribute of the left [side].[92]

The specific nature of the thought that generates angels and demons is not clear. However, it is clearly the divine thought that has the creative power to produce these two types of supernatural beings. From the context of the above passages it is evident that the pure thought corresponds to the *sefira* of *Ḥesed* or divine mercy, while the thought of calamity corresponds to that of *Gevura*, the power related to evil. Thus, there is a substantive correspondence between the last two passages and, to an extent, the view attributed to Jews in ninth-century Lyon. Both in Agobard's testimony and in the writings of R. Joseph of Hamadan, the reference to divine thought is not necessarily part of a theogonic or cosmogonic narrative but is restricted to the creation of demons. R. Joseph's remarks indicate, at any rate, that the demons were generated by an evil power, designated as the thought of calamity, which is described as the opposite of the pure thought.[93] This vision of demons, *shedim*, as stemming from a supernal negative divine power

91 On this term and its possible sources see Scholem, *Origins of the Kabbalah*, pp. 126–127 and the accompanying footnotes; and Dauber, 'Pure Thought.'

92 *Sefer hamalkhut*, fols. 84d–85a. See also Felix, 'Theurgy, Magic, and Mysticism,' pp. 289–290. R. Joseph mentions the legend of Adam's asceticism and his siring of the demons in *Sefer hamalkhut*, fol. 85a, immediately after the above passage.

93 The use here of the phrase 'pure thought' – *maḥashava tehora* – as related to *Ḥesed* differs from its use in earlier Kabbalah in Gerona, where it stands for the supernal thought, mainly as the *sefira* of *Ḥokhma*, the locus of the ten *sefirot*. See the material, some of it transcribed from manuscripts, on the ten *sefirot* or *ḥavayot* found within the *maḥashava tehora*, in my 'The Sefirot above the Sefirot,' pp. 243–245, 266–268, and notes 132, 153, 277 and 206, where I also discussed the origin of this view in R. Abraham bar Hiya. See Scholem, *Origins of the Kabbalah*, p. 270, note 153; and Dauber, 'Pure Thought.'

is by no means consensual in Jewish literature, in which demons were described in quite traditional terms as performing most of the rabbinic precepts like any traditional Jew.[94] I wonder whether the discrepancy between the singular and plural references to demon/demons in the two quotes drawn from R. Joseph's *Toledot Adam* is significant. If the singular refers to something like an archangel and an arch-demon, the similarity to Zurvanism is even more pronounced.

Elsewhere in the same treatise, R. Joseph envisions the existence of ten groups or ranks of impurity, which were created from the ten pure *sefirot*, and describes them as the refuse (*pesolet*) of the pure ones.[95] R. Joseph does not speak of a primacy or priority of evil powers, but his reference to evil within the divine thought is important, in that it parallels Agobard's testimony as well as the Zurvanic position.

Notably, elsewhere in this treatise R. Joseph discusses the two decads of pure and impure *sefirot*, the latter being related to the ten Edomite kings, found in a passage that is unfortunately corrupted.[96] These views differ from that discussed above, adduced earlier in the book, and from another discussion by this author in his *Commentary on Genesis*, which has reached us in truncated form. There he describes the emergence of ten *sefirot* within the 'primordial *Ḥokhma*,' envisioned as the right hand, while the ten ranks of impurity are described as emerging from the left hand.[97] In short, we have here a theory of subordinated pseudo-symmetry. Indeed, the writings of R. Joseph offer a variety of explanations as to the source of evil, and any attempt to present them systematically is doomed, in my opinion, to failure. Notably, in a study dealing with Iranian influences on Judaism,

94 See Kanarfogel, *Peering through the Lattices*, pp. 224–225.

95 *Sefer hamalkhut*, fol. 102d. See also *ibid.*, fols. 98c, 102a, 103a. On God's creation of the opposites, see the views of R. Joseph discussed in Felix, 'Theurgy, Magic, and Mysticism,' pp. 83–84, and p. 86, note 145.

96 *Sefer hamalkhut*, fol. 97c; cf. also *ibid.*, fols. 97d–98a, 98c and 99a, d. These kings are described as derived from the *sefira* of *Gevura* but nevertheless as preceding the kingdom of Israel, which is related to the *sefira* of *Tiferet.* Cf. *Zohar*, I, fol. 177b, and Liebes, *Studies in the Zohar*, p. 128.

97 Mopsik, *Joseph de Hamadan*, p. 17 (Hebrew section) and pp. 82–83 (French section); *Sefer hamalkhut*, fol. 108c. For the emergence of ten impure powers from the *sefira* of *Gevura* see also his *Commentary on Ten Sefirot*, occurring anonymously in several manuscripts, e.g., MS Paris BN 835, fols. 90b–91a.

Shlomo Pines drew attention to the possible impact of Iranian sources on this kabbalist.[98]

A view similar to that of R. Joseph of Hamadan is found in an Aramaic passage that presumably pertains to the Zoharic literature, although it seems first to have been preserved by an early fourteenth-century Italian kabbalist, R. Menahem b. Benjamin Recanati. It appears in R. Menahem's *Commentary on the Pentateuch*, which is replete with authentic quotes from the *Zohar* that can be identified in printed texts and manuscripts. While this passage does not appear in the Zoharic manuscripts, it was incorporated in a late printed collection of Zoharic material entitled *Zohar ḥadash*, most probably taken from Recanati's book. This is, again, a truncated passage, dealing with the rationale of the commandment of sacrifice, and it has a rather close parallel in a Hebrew passage printed anonymously at the end of R. Moses de Leon's *Sefer hanefesh haḥakhama*. I shall deal with the Aramaic passage first:

> On the left side there is another, impure side, also called thought, and called 'evil thought,' since the rank above it is called evil, and that is the reason why it is called evil thought. This [consists of] all the bad wills, and bad ruminations, and all the bad harlotry, and all the bad things in the world, and it is the reason for all those wills by which people defile themselves. On this evil thought several impure ranks stand, and all stand in order to defile people, by means of these wills and ruminations of the evil thought, and then the person defiles himself because of them and cleaves to that side. And that is the reason why he wants to sacrifice a holocaust in order to purify himself; in sacrificing, he wants to divert his will toward the holy thought. And a cloud ascends out of these fats and some inner organs [*'imurim*] in those places, and that evil thought ascends[99] first, and all take from it and are satiated from it. Afterwards another cloud ascends that is more subtle … and when the person separates himself from the evil thought and cleaves to the pure thought,[100] so that

98 Pines, 'A Parallel,' pp. 49–51. See also Schremer, *Male and Female*, p. 175.

99 This is a play on Hebrew *'ola*, referring to the holocaust sacrifice but also a verb meaning 'to ascend.'

100 On the cleaving of thought in early Kabbalah see Idel, *Kabbalah: New Perspectives*, pp. 46–49.

> everything cleaves to the supernal enclosed thought[101] more than all, then all becomes one.[102]

What interests me first and foremost is the idea of evil thought as the source of other kinds of depravity stemming from human desire. Evil thought is reified and depicted here as standing on the left side. This understanding is based on a bold reading of the classical phrase *maḥashava ra'a* as a construct form (*semikhut*), meaning 'evil's thought' – that is, the thought over which there is an evil power, a 'rank,' a form of hypostatic entity. This lends a somewhat vague ontological status to the thought and to evil. This thought is ascribed to the left side, but I wonder whether this might be the *sefira* of *Gevura*, and whether this is how we should understand the term *ra'a*. In any case, it is this latter entity that is conceived as the source of impurity in human beings. According to this reading, the evil thought is envisioned as the source of evil in a manner reminiscent of the evil thought that generated Ahriman, the source of evil doings in the lower world.

The Zoharic passage describes the fat in the holocaust ascending and satiating the evil ranks, thus freeing human thought from the presence of the extension of the supernal evil side, and allowing the now-freed human thought to cleave to the supernal thought, bringing about a unification of the entire sefirotic realm. That is, the evil side is conceived as receiving some part of the sacrifice and being satiated by the first 'cloud' that arises from its burning. The verb *r.v.ḥ*, occurring in both the Aramaic and the Hebrew passages, reflects this satiation of the

101 The Aramaic text has *maḥashava setima'a 'ila'a*. This phrase also occurs in one of R. Moses de Leon's writings, referring to the first and third *sefirot*. See de Leon, *Sefer sheqel haqodesh*, p. 24, and idem, *Book of the Pomegranate*, p. 264. The meaning of *satum* in this instance is the existence of everything within the space of the divine power, recalling the use of this term by R. Abraham bar Ḥiya, *Hegyon hanefesh ha'atzuva*, pp. 41, 43: *hatsura hasetuma*. The use of the same phrase in the Aramaic passage in the *Zohar* and in de Leon's Hebrew book shows the terminological relationship between the two texts. However, in other places the *Zohar* uses the phrase *ḥokhma'a 'ila'a setima'a*. See Gottlieb, *Studies in Kabbalah Literature*, p. 176.

102 Recanati, *Commentary on the Pentateuch*, fol. 58c, reprinted in Margoliot, *Zohar ḥadash*, fol 46c. See Idel, 'Evil Thought of the Deity,' pp. 360–362; and Liebes, *Studies in the Zohar*, p. 188, note 182. Cf. the discussion of other Zoharic texts in Tishby, *Wisdom of the Zohar*, III, p. 892. Conversion from another religion to Judaism is portrayed in de Leon's *Book of the Pomegranate*, p. 212, in terms reminiscent of the above-quoted passage.

evil powers through their consumption of the vapors of the sacrifices. By giving a portion to the left side, or to the evil thought, it is possible to extract human thought – previously possessed by the presence of evil that is caused by the cleaving of thought to evil – from the evil thought's pernicious impact, enabling contact of human thought with the supernal thought, a move allegorized by the second cloud arising from the holocaust. Note that the emergence of the evil thought, doubt or decomposition that generated Ahriman occurred after a thousand years of sacrifices by Zurvan.

R. Menahem Recanati expresses a similar view in the introduction to his earlier *Commentary on the Commandments*:

> From the left side all the impurities and sorceries and demons emanate, as we have explained, and it is called in the Book of Zohar 'evil thought,' and from the right side it is the converse.[103]

Now let us look at the anonymous Hebrew passage, appended along with various kabbalistic secrets to the printed edition of R. Moses de Leon's book *Hanefesh haḥakhama*, but not, in my opinion, belonging to this kabbalist:[104]

> [Human] thought is the head [i.e., the beginning] of all actions, and it comes closer to the supernal thought in order to link everything together, until the thought that is called 'all.'[105]

Two types of supernal thought are mentioned here: the higher thought, also called 'enclosed thought' as in the Zoharic passage, corresponding to the first *sefira*, and the lower thought, related to the *sefira* of *yesod*, denoted here by the term *kol*, 'all.' By the ascent on high of the human,

103 Printed in R. Yehudah Ḥayat, *Minḥat Yehuda*, fol. 30a. See also in *Tiqune Zohar*, fol. 63a, where the good thought is conceived of in Aramaic as a good man – *adam tava* – while the evil thought, *maḥashava bisha*, is conceived of as a wicked man, *adam beli'al*.

104 One of the reasons I suggest that R. Moshe de Leon is not the author of this passage is the absence of the phrase *maḥashava ra'a* in his lengthy discussion of sacrifice in *Book of the Pomegranate*, pp. 262–266, whereas the word *maḥashava* appears many times.

105 Col. 15, fol. 1bc, an anonymous text found in MS New York, JTS 1883, fol. 106b, and in Y. Alemanno's *Collectanea*, extant in the autograph in MS Oxford-Bodleiana 2234, fol. 169a.

purified thought, the realm of the *sefirot*, from *Keter* to *Yesod*, is unified. Thus, two forms of sacrificial cult are discussed both in the Zoharic text and in the anonymous Hebrew one, which were both written, in my opinion, by the same author: The first is related to evil thought, which receives a bribe to release its grasp on human thought,[106] and the second converts the liberated human thought into supernal pure thought.

The sacrifice is understood to culminate in a third phase: It is meant first to free one's thinking from the dominance of the evil thought, then to facilitate cleaving to the pure thought, and finally to unify the sefirotic realm. Indeed, the assumption that sacrifice has to do with the left or impure side is articulated in an interesting way in an anonymous manuscript that reflects Castilian kabbalistic traditions: 'All the sacrifices possess something of the left side, and this is the above-mentioned refuse.'[107] Notably, according to another Zoharic discussion that asserts a nexus between the evil thought and sacrifice, the anonymous kabbalist understands the function of the ritual as being to burn the evil thought and remove it from the holiness.[108] In both cases, it is hard to discern any effort to integrate or reintegrate evil with good, as suggested elsewhere in the *Zohar*.[109]

Some Conclusions

We have surveyed some cases of what I have called subordinated pseudo-symmetry. These discussions reveal a structure that typifies the Zurvanic view, based on a triangle consisting of a supreme deity and two sons. This, it seems, was more easily acceptable in Jewish circles than the stark dualism of the more widespread Iranian sources or the Gnostic ones.

Early in his career, Scholem formulated the approach that would remain the consensus among scholars in the field for many decades:

> The concept that evil and the dark, left powers had been emanated independently by a special emanation is ancient and its root is

106 See also Tishby, *Wisdom of the Zohar*, II, p. 453, and III, pp. 892–893; and Orlov, *Dark Mirrors*, p. 144, note 34.

107 MS Paris BN 859, fol. 9c.

108 *Zohar*, II, fol. 239b, III, fol. 27a.

109 This is the main thesis of Wolfson's article on the *Zohar*, 'Light through Darkness.' See also Tishby, *Wisdom of the Zohar*, III, pp. 885, 890–895.

> certainly found in the dualistic Iranian systems, therefrom it continued into the Gnostic movement. Just as there are archangels governing the good worlds, so there are archangels appointed over the evil worlds. Understandably, a doctrine like that necessarily changed its extreme dualistic character when it entered into Jewish circles.[110]

Tishby repeated Scholem's view almost vertabim:

> The theory that evil and the dark, 'left-sided,' forces were emanated as a separate emanation is an ancient one and it certainly stems from Iranian dualistic systems, and from there it came to the Gnostic movement. ... It is clear that such a doctrine had necessarily changed its extreme dualistic nature when it penetrated into Jewish circles.[111]

Both scholars assumed that Iranian dualistic sources were only the remote origins of kabbalistic views, mediated by Gnostic appropriations of their dualism. Surprisingly, the two scholars seem to be in total agreement on this complex issue. After all, though Scholem was 'certain' of his assessment, he did not support it with any accompanying discussion or adduce any testimonies for the changes. Nevertheless, for Tishby, Scholem's proposal is 'clear.' Moreover, Kabbalah itself, as Tishby put it elsewhere, 'amounts, in fact, to a gnostic transformation of Judaism.'[112] This one-sided understanding of the historical source and nature of Kabbalah is not backed by a sustained analysis that goes beyond pointing to general parallels, many of which are scarcely convincing.

Let me stress the phenomenological problem that transpires from the two scholars' formulations: The initial source suggested for the speculations of the Kabbalah is described as having been dualistic in the extreme, leading both scholars to assume that the content of that source underwent transformations for the sake of its adoption into a monotheistic system, as Kabbalah is understood to be. This hypothetical

110 Scholem, 'Isaac ben Jacob Hakohen,' p. 31, cited verbatim by Tishby, *Doctrine of Evil*, p. 16, note 5.

111 Tishby, *Doctrine of Evil*, p. 16. This position is reiterated in his *Wisdom of the Zohar*, I, p. 237, and II, pp. 447–448. See also idem, *Paths of Faith and Heresy*, p. 26.

112 See Tishby, 'Gnostic Doctrines,' p. 146. For Scholem's strongly Gnostic interpretation of Lurianic Kabbalah, see idem, *On the Kabbalah and Its Symbolism*, pp. 109–117.

transformation is taken to explain the phenomenological discrepancies between the late-antique Gnostic sources, on the one hand, and the medieval kabbalistic visions of evil, on the other. However, given that no substantial impact of Gnosticism on Kabbalah has yet been demonstrated, this proposal remains in the realm of scholarly speculation; it may or may not be correct, but it needs some substantial evidence before it should be repeated again by a serious scholar. To the best of my knowledge, the alleged Gnostic source for the kabbalistic visions of evil has remained the single explanatory theory reigning in Scholem's school.

The monochromatic Gnostic explanation given by Scholem and accepted uncritically by Tishby for the metaphysical origin of evil in Kabbalah has never been elaborated in detail. There has been no attempt to explicate why this solution is appropriate, what philological proofs can be adduced for it, and by what historical channels these views might have been transmitted from the ancient Gnostics, and their medieval reverberations, to the early Kabbalists. It seems, rather, that Scholem made an apodictic statement that was reiterated faithfully by Tishby, though Tishby elaborated much more on topics of evil than Scholem did. He also contributed what seems to me an interesting and, for its time, original article pointing out the similarities between some aspects of the Lurianic theory of evil and Manichean theories on this subject.[113]

In lieu of Irano-Gnostic dualism, which allegedly had to be transformed in order to accommodate it to medieval Jewish monotheism, I propose the impact of Zurvanic subordinated pseudo-symmetry, which also has the advantage of having being represented in Judaism before the emergence of Kabbalah, as a more economical explanation for kabbalistic views on evil.

References

R. Abraham bar Ḥiya. *Hegyon hanefesh ha'atsuva*, ed. G. Wigoder, Jerusalem: Bialik Institute, 1971.

Abrams, Daniel (ed.). *Asher ben David: His Complete Works and*

113 Tishby, 'Gnostic Doctrines,' pp. 146–152. However, this article does not touch questions relating to the beginnings of the Kabbalah. For the possibility that Gnostic dualistic reverberations among Slavic groups could have influenced Sabbateanism in Poland, see Scholem, 'Le mouvement sabbataiste en Pologne,' p. 38, and Eliade, *Zalmoxis*, p. 92. On questions related to Lurianic theories of evil see Idel, 'The Mud and the Water.'

Studies in His Kabbalistic Thought, Los Angeles: Cherub Press, 1996 (Hebrew).

Alexander, Philip. 'Demonology of the Dead Sea Scrolls,' in P.W. Flint and J.C. Vanderkam (eds.), *The Dead Sea Scrolls: Fifty Years After*, II, Leiden: Brill, 1999.

Altmann, Alexander. 'An Allegorical Midrash on Genesis 24 According to the "Inner Kabbalah,"' in S.Y. Zimmels, Y. Rabinovitz and Y.S. Feinstein (eds.), *Sefer hayovel tifereth Yisra'el likhevod Yisra'el Brodie*, London, 5727 (1957), pp. 57–65 (Hebrew section).

—. 'Concerning the Question of the Authorship of *Sefer ta'ame hamitsvot* Attributed to R. Isaac ibn Farhi,' *Qiryat sefer*, 40 (1964–1965), pp. 256–276, 405–412 (Hebrew).

Anderson, Gary A. *The Genesis of Perfection: Adam and Eve in Jewish and Christian Imagination*, Louisville: Westminster–John Knox Press, 2001.

Bakhos, Carol, and M. Rahim Sayegan. *The Talmud in its Iranian Context*, Tübingen: Mohr-Siebeck, 2010.

Beit-Arié, Malachi. 'Pereq shira,' Ph.D. Dissertation, The Hebrew University of Jerusalem, 1967 (Hebrew).

Benayahu, Meir. *Ma'amadot umoshavot* (Studies in Memory of R. Yizhak Nissim, 6), Jerusalem: Yad Yitzhaq Nissim, 1985 (Hebrew).

Bianchi, Ugo. 'Alcuni aspetti abnormi del dualism persiano,' *Atti del convegno internazionale sul tema: La Persia nel Medioevo*, Rome: Accademia nazionale dei Lincei, 1971, pp. 149–164.

—. 'La doctrine zarathoustrienne des deux esprits,' in idem, *Selected Essays*, pp. 361–389.

—. 'Le dualisme en histoire des religions,' *Revue de l'histoire des religions*, 159 (1961), pp. 1–46.

— (ed.). *Le origini dello gnosticismo*, Leiden: Brill, 1967.

—. *Selected Essays on Gnosticism, Dualism and Mysteriosophy*, Leiden: Brill, 1978.

—. *Zamân î Oúhrmazd: Lo zoroastrismo nelle sue origini e nella sua essenza*, Turin: Società Editrice Internazionale, 1958.

Bidez, Joseph, and Franz Cumont. *Les Mages Hellénisés, Zoroastre, Ostaneàs et Hystaspe d'apres la tradition greque*, II, Paris 1938.

Bonfil, Reuven. 'The Cultural and Religious Traditions of French Jewry in the Ninth Century, as Reflected in the Writings of Agobard of Lyon,' in J. Dan and J. Hacker (eds.), *Studies in Jewish Mysticism, Philosophy and Ethical Literature Presented to Isaiah Tishby*, Jerusalem: Magnes Press, 1986), pp. 327–348 (Hebrew).

Buber, Solomon. *Hashaḥar*, 11 (1883) (Hebrew).
—. 'Introduction,' in idem (ed.), *Midrash Leqaḥ tov*, Vilna 1880.
Cohen, Jeremy. *Living Letters of the Law: Ideas of the Jew in Medieval Christianity*, Berkeley, CA–London: University of California Press, 1999.
Corbin, Henry. *Temps cyclique et gnose ismaélienne*, Paris: Berg International, 1982.
Cordovero, Moses. *Pardes rimonim*, Munkacs 1906 (reprinted Jerusalem 1962).
Couliano, Ioan P. *The Tree of Gnosis: Gnostic Mythology from Early Christianity to Modern Nihilism* (English transl. by H.S. Wiesner and the author), San Francisco: HarperCollins, 1990.
Daniélou, Jean. *Theologie du Judeo-Christianisme*, Paris: Desclee–Cerf, 1974.
Dauber, Jonathan V. '"Pure Thought" in R. Abraham bar Hiyya and Early Kabbalah,' *Journal of Jewish Studies*, 60 (2009), pp. 185–201.
De Leon, Moses. *The Book of the Pomegranate*, ed. E.R. Wolfson, Atlanta: Scholars Press, 1988.
—. *Sefer sheqel haqodesh*, ed. C. Mopsik, Los Angeles: Cherub Press, 1996.
Dimant, Devorah. 'Dualism at Qumran: New Perspectives,' in J.H. Charlesworth (ed.), *Caves of Enlightenment*, Richland Hills, TX: D. & F. Scott, 1998, pp. 55–73.
—. 'Qumran Sectarian Literature,' in Stone (ed.), *Jewish Writings of the Second Temple Period*, pp. 483–550.
Doniger O'Flaherty, Wendy. *The Origins of Evil in Hindu Mythology*, Berkeley: University of California Press, 1976.
Duchesne-Guillemin, Jacques. 'Le zervanisme et les manuscrits de la Mer Morte,' *Indo-Iranian Journal*, 1, (1957), pp. 96–99.
Dupont-Sommer, André. *Les Ecrits esseniens decouverts pres de la Mer Morte*, Paris: Payot, 1959.
Eliade, Mircea. *A History of Ideas* (English transl. by W.R. Trask), II, Chicago–London: University of Chicago Press, 1982.
—. 'Prolegomenon to Religious Dualism: Dyads and Polarities,' in idem, *The Quest: History and Meaning in Religion*, Chicago: University of Chicago Press, 1969), pp. 127–175.
—. *The Two and the One* (English transl. by J.M. Cohen), New York–Evanston: Harper and Row, 1965.
—. *Zalmoxis, The Vanishing God: Comparative Studies in the Religions*

and Folklore of Dacia and Eastern Europe (English transl. by W.R. Trask), Chicago–London: University of Chicago Press, 1972.

Elman, Yaakov. 'Acculturation and Elite Persian Norms and Modes of Thought in the Babylonian Jewish Community of Late Antiquity,' in idem, E.B. Halivni and Z.A. Steinfeld (eds.), *Neti'ot leDavid: Jubilee Volume for David Weiss Halivni*, Jerusalem: Orhot, 2004, pp. 31–56.

—. 'The Other in the Mirror: Iranians and Jews View One Another,' *Bulletin of the Asia Institute*, 19 (2001), pp. 15–25; 20 (2010), pp. 25–46.

—. 'Scripture versus Contemporary Needs: A Sasanian/Zoroastrian Example,' *Cardozo Law Review* (2005), pp. 153–169.

—. 'Zoroastrianism and Qumran,' in Lawrence H. Schiffman and Shani Tzoref (eds.), *The Dead Sea Scrolls at 60: Scholarly Contributions of New York University Faculty and Alumni*, Leiden: Brill, 2010), pp. 91–98.

Epstein, Abraham. 'Yalqut Shim'oni: … Extracts from Midrash Avkkir,' *Ha'eshkol*, 6 (1909), pp. 183–210 (Hebrew).

Erder, Yoram. *The Karaite Mourners of Zion and the Qumran Scrolls: On the History of an Alternative to Rabbinic Judaism*, Tel Aviv: Hakibbutz Hameuchad, 2004 (Hebrew).

—. 'The "Prince Mastemah" in a Karaite Work,' *Meghillot*, 1 (2003), pp. 243–246 (Hebrew).

Farber-Ginat, Assi. 'Inquiries in *Shi'ur Qomah*,' in M. Oron and A. Goldreich (eds.), *Massu'ot: Studies in Kabbalistic Literature and Jewish Philosophy in Memory of Prof. Ephraim Gottlieb*, Jerusalem: Bialik Institute, 1994, pp. 361–394 (Hebrew).

Felix, Iris. 'Theurgy, Magic, and Mysticism in the Kabbalah of R. Joseph of Shushan,' Ph.D. Dissertation, The Hebrew University of Jerusalem, 2005 (Hebrew).

Fontaine, Piet F.M. *The Light and the Dark: A Cultural History of Dualism*, Amsterdam: J.C. Gieben, 1986–2006.

Franck, Adophe. *La Kabbale ou la philosophie religieuse des Hebreux*, Paris: Hachette, 1843.

Frey, Jorg. 'Different Patterns of Dualistic Thought in the Qumran Library: Reflections on their Background and History,' in M. Bernstein, F. García Martínez and J. Kampen (eds.), *Legal Texts and Legal Issues: Proceedings of the Second Meeting of the International Organization for Qumran Studies, Cambridge 1995, Published in Honour of Joseph M. Baumgarten*, Leiden: Brill, 1997, pp. 275–335.

Frye, Richard N. 'Qumran and Iran: the State of Studies,' in Jacob Neusner (ed.), *Christianity, Judaism and Other Greco-Roman Cults: Studies for Morton Smith at Sixty*, Leiden: Brill, 1975), Part Three, pp. 167–173.

García Martínez, Florentino, and Elbert J.C. Tigchelaar (ed. and transl.). *The Dead Sea Scrolls: Study Edition*, Leiden–Boston–Grand Rapids, MI: Brill–Eerdmans, 1997.

Gaster, Moses. *Ilchester Lectures on Greeko-Slavonic Literature*, London: Trübner, Ludgate Hill, 1887.

Gaster, T.H. 'Satan,' in G.A. Buttrick (ed.), *The Interpreter's Dictionary of the Bible*, New York–Nashville: Abingdon Press, 1962, *s.v.*

Geula, Amos. 'Lost Aggadic Works Known Only from Ashkenaz: *Midrash Abkir*, *Midrash Esfa* and *Devarim zuta*,' Ph.D. Dissertation, The Hebrew University of Jerusalem, 2006 (Hebrew).

Gimaret, Daniel, and Guy Monnot (transl.). *Shahrastani: Livre des religions et des sects*, I, Louvain: Peeters, 1986.

Ginzberg, Louis. *On Jewish Law and Lore*, Tel Aviv: Dvir, 1960 (Hebrew).

—. *Legends of the Jews*, Philadelphia: JPS, 1968.

Gottlieb, Efraim. *Studies in Kabbalah Literature*, ed. J. Hacker, Tel Aviv: Tel Aviv University, 1976 (Hebrew).

Greenfield, Jonas C., and Shaul Shaked. 'Three Iranian Words in the Targum of Job from Qumran,' *Zeitschrift der Deutschen Morgenländischen Gesellschaft*, 122 (1972), pp. 37–45.

Gundlach, Wilhelm, Ernst Dümmler et al. (eds.). *Monumenta Germaniae Historica*, III: *Epistolae Merowingici et Karolini Aevi*, 1, Munich: Monumenta Germaniae Historica, 1892 (reprinted 1994).

Ḥayat, R. Yehuda. *Minḥat Yehuda*, commentary on *Sefer ma'arekhet ha'Elohut*, Mantua 1558.

Hurwitz, Siegmund. *Lilith, the First Eve* (English transl. by G. Jacobson), Einsifdeln: Daimon Verlag, 1992.

Idel, Moshe. *Absorbing Perfections: Kabbalah and Interpretation* (New Haven, CT: Yale University Press, 2002).

—. *The Angelic World: Apotheosis and Theophany*, Tel Aviv: Yedioth Books, 2008 (Hebrew).

—. *Ascensions on High: Pillars, Lines, Ladders*, Budapest–New York: CEU Press, 2005.

—. *Ben: Sonship and Jewish Mysticism*, London–New York: Continuum, 2008.
—. 'The Evil Thought of the Deity,' *Tarbiz*, 49 (1980), pp. 356–364 (Hebrew).
—. *Fallen Angels: On an Ancient Jewish Myth and Its Metamorphoses in Jewish Thought*, forthcoming (Hebrew).
—. *Golem: Jewish Magical and Mystical Traditions on the Artificial Anthropoid*, Albany: SUNY Press, 1990.
—. *Il male primordiale nella Qabbalah* (Italian transl. by F. Lelli), Milan: Adelphi, 2016.
—. 'R. Joseph of Hamadan's Commentary on the Ten Sefirot and Fragments of His Writings,' *'Ale sefer*, 6–7 (1979), pp.74–84 (Hebrew).
—. *Kabbalah: New Perspectives*, New Haven, CT: Yale University Press, 1988.
—. 'The Kabbalah's "Window of Opportunities,"' 1270–1290,' in E. Fleisher, G. Blidstein, C. Horowitz and B. Septimus (eds.), *Me'ah She'arim: Studies in Medieval Jewish Spiritual Life in Memory of Isadore Twersky*, Jerusalem: Magnes Press, 2001, pp. 171–208.
—. 'The Mud and the Water: Towards a History of a Simile in Kabbalah,' *Zutot*, 14 (2017), pp. 65–72.
—. 'Old and New in the Study of Kabbalah,' *Zion*, 54 (1989), pp. 493–508 (Hebrew).
—. 'The Sefirot above the Sefirot,' *Tarbiz*, 51 (1982), pp. 239–280 (Hebrew).
—. *Studies in Ecstatic Kabbalah*, Albany: SUNY Press, 1989.
Jonas, Hans. *The Gnostic Religion*[2], Boston: Beacon Press, 1963.
Jung, Carl G. *Aion: Researches into the Phenomenology of the Self*[2] (English transl. by R.F. C. Hull; Collected Works of C.G. Jung, 9, Part 2), Princeton: Princeton University Press, 1979.
Kanarfogel, Ephraim. *'Peering through the Lattices': Mystical, Magical, and Pietistic Dimensions in the Tosafist Period*, Detroit: Wayne State University Press, 2000.
Kister, Menahem. '4Q392 and the Concept of Light in Qumran "Dualism,"' *Meghillot*, 3, (2005), pp. 125–140 (Hebrew).
—. 'Body and Purification from Evil: Prayer Formulas and Concepts in Second Temple Literature and Their Relationship to Later Rabbinic Literature,' *Meghillot*, 8–9, (2010), pp. 243–284 (Hebrew).
—. 'On Good and Evil: The Theological Foundations of the Qumran Community,' in idem, *The Qumran Scrolls*, II, pp. 497–527 (Hebrew).

— (ed.). *The Qumran Scrolls and Their World*, Jerusalem: Yad Ben Zvi, 2009 (Hebrew).

—. 'Some Lexical Features of the Writings from Qumran,' in idem, *The Qumran Scrolls*, II, pp. 561–569 (Hebrew).

Klijn, Albertus Frederik Johannes, and G.J. Reinink. *Patristic Evidence for Jewish-Christian Sects*, Leiden: Brill, 1973.

Klugemann, Joel (ed.). *Commentary on the Pentateuch* attributed to R. Eleazar of Worms, I, Bene Beraq, 1986.

— (ed.). *Commentary on the Pentateuch* by R. Efrayim b. Shimshon, I, Jerusalem, 1993.

Kohut, Alexander. *Ueber die juedische Angelologie und Daemonologie in ihrer Abhaengigkeit vom Parsismus*, Leipzig, 1866.

Koren, Sharon Faye. *Forsaken: The Menstruant in Medieval Jewish Mysticism*, Waltham, MA: Brandeis University Press, 2011.

Langenwalter, Anna Beth. "Agobard of Lyon: An Exploration of Carolingian Jewish-Christian Relations," Ph.D. Dissertation, University of Toronto, 2009.

Levenson, Jon D. *Creation and the Persistence of Evil: The Jewish Drama of Divine Omnipotence*, San Francisco: Harper and Row, 1988.

Licht, Jacob (ed. and comm.). *The Rule Scroll: A Scroll from the Wilderness of Judaea*, Jerusalem: Bialik Institute, 1965 (Hebrew).

Liebes, Yehuda. *The Cult of the Dawn: The Attitude of the Zohar toward Idolatry*, Jerusalem: Carmel, 2011 (Hebrew).

—. *Studies in Jewish Myth and Jewish Messianism* (English transl. by B. Stein), Albany: SUNY Press, 1993.

—. *Studies in the Zohar* (English transl. by A. Schwartz, S. Nakache and P. Peli), Albany: SUNY Press, 1993.

Mack, Hananel. 'From Qumran to Provence: The Notion of a Manassite Messiah,' *Meghillot*, 3 (2005), pp. 125–142 (Hebrew).

Magid, Shaul. *From Metaphysics to Midrash: Myth, History, and the Interpretation of Scripture in Lurianic Kabbala*, Bloomington: Indiana University Press, 2008.

Margoliot, Reuven (ed.). *Zohar ḥadash*, Jerusalem: Rav Kook Institute, 1978.

Marmorstein, Abraham. *Devir*, 1 (1923) (Hebrew).

de Menasce, Jean Pierre (ed. and transl.). *Le troisième livre du Dēnkart, Traduit du pehlevi*, Paris: Klincksieck, 1973.

Merchavia, Ch. *The Church versus Talmudic and Midrashic Literature, 500–1248*, Jerusalem: Bialik Institute, 1970 (Hebrew).

Michaud, Henri. 'Un mythe Zervanite dans un des manuscriptes de Qumran,' *Vetus Testamentum*, 5 (1955), pp. 137–147.

Monnot, Guy. *Penseurs musulmans et religions iraniennes: 'Abd al-Jabbār et ses devanciers*, Paris–Cairo–Beirut: J. Vrin–Institut Dominicain des Études Orientales, 1974.

—. 'Pour le dossier arabe du mazdéisme zurvanien,' *Journal Asiatique*, 268 (1980).

Mopsik, Charles. *Chemins de la Cabale*, Paris: L'Èclat, 2004.

—. *Rabbi Joseph de Hamadan: Fragment d'un commentaire sur la Genese*, Lagrasse: Verdier, 1998.

—. 'Un manuscript inconnu du *Sefer Tashak* de R. Joseph de Hamadan suivi d'un fragment inedit,' *Kabbalah*, 2 (1997), pp. 167–205.

Mueller, Michael A. *History of Jewish Mysticism*, New York: Yesod, n.d.

—. 'On *Sefer Yetzirah*,' *Metzudah*, 2, (1943), pp. 108–109 (Hebrew).

Neusner, Jacob. *Judaism, Christianity, and Zoroastrianism in Talmudic Babylonia*, Lanham, MD: University Press of America, 1986.

—. *Judaism and Zoroastrianism at the Dusk of Late Antiquity*, Atlanta: Scholars Press, 1993.

Nitzan, Bilhah. 'Evil and Its Symbols in the Qumran Scrolls,' in Henning Graf Reventlow and Yair Hoffman (eds.), *The Problem of Evil and Its Symbols in Jewish and Christian Tradition*, London–New York: T. & T. Clark, 2004, pp. 83–96.

Odeberg, Hugo (ed.). *3 Enoch: The Hebrew Book of Enoch*, New York: Ktav, 1973.

Oisteanu, Andrei. *Religie, politica si mit: Texte despre Mircea Eliade si Ioan Petru Culianu*, Iasi: Polirom, 2007.

Orlov, Andrei. *Dark Mirrors: Azazel and Satanael in Early Jewish Demonology*, Albany: SUNY Press, 2011.

Oron, Michal (ed.). *Sha'ar harazim* by R. Todros Halevi Abulafia, Jerusalem: Bialik Institute, 1989 (Hebrew).

—. 'Was the Kabbalah in Castile a Continuation or a Revolution? A Study of the Concept of Evil in Castilian Kabbalah,' in J. Dan (ed.), *The Beginnings of Jewish Mysticism in Medieval Europe* (Jerusalem Studies in Jewish Thought, 6), Jerusalem: Jewish National and University Library, 1987, pp. 383–392 (Hebrew)

Pearson, Birger A. 'Jewish Sources in Gnostic Literature,' in Stone, *Jewish Writings of the Second Temple Period*, pp. 443–481.

Pétrement, Simone. *A Separate God: The Christian Origins of Gnosticism* (English transl. by Carol Harrison), San Francisco: HarperCollins, 1990.

Pines, Shlomo. 'The Oath of Asaph the Physician and Yoḥanan ben Zabda,' in idem, *Collected Works*, IV: *Studies in the History of Religion*, ed. Guy G. Stroumsa, Jerusalem: Magnes Press, 1996.

—. 'A Parallel between Two Iranian and Jewish Themes,' *Irano-Judaica*, 2 (1990), pp. 41–51.

—. 'Eschatology and the Concept of Time in the Slavonic Book of Enoch,' in idem, *Collected Works*, Jerusalem: Magnes Press, 1996, IV, pp. 21–36.

—. 'Wrath and Creatures of Wrath in Pahlavi, Jewish and New Testament Sources,' *Irano-Judaica*, 1 (1982), pp. 76–82.

Recanati, R. Menahem b. Benjamin. *Commentary on the Pentateuch*, Jerusalem 1961 (Hebrew).

Ricoeur, Paul. *The Symbolism of Evil*, Boston: Beacon Press, 1969.

Rosen-Zvi, Ishay. *Demonic Desires: Yetzer Hara and the Problem of Evil in Late Antiquity*, Philadelphia: University of Pennsylvania Press, 2011.

Saba, R. Abraham. *Tseror hamor*, Venice 1527 (Hebrew).

Salmon b. Yeruhin. *Sefer milḥamot haShem*, ed. I. Davidson, New York, 1934 (Hebrew).

Schaefer, Peter. *The Origins of Jewish Mysticism*, Princeton: Princeton University Press, 2009.

Schärf Kluger, Rivkah. *Satan in the Old Testament* (English transl. by H. Nagel), Evanston, IL: Northwestern University Press, 1967.

Schneider, Michael. 'The Myth of Satan in the Book of Bahir,' *Kabbalah*, 20 (2009), pp. 287–343 (Hebrew).

Scholem, Gershom. *Devils, Demons and Souls: Essays on Demonology*, ed. E. Liebes, Jerusalem: Ben Zvi Institute–Hebrew University, 2004 (Hebrew).

—. *Einige kabbalistische Handschriften im Britischen Museum*, Jerusalem, 1931.

—. 'Isaac ben Jacob Hakohen, *Ma'amar ha'atsilut hasmalit*,' *Jewish Studies*, 2 (1927), pp. 30–34 (Hebrew).

—. *Jewish Gnosticism, Merkabah Mysticism and Talmudic Tradition*, New York: JTSA, 1965.

—. *Kabbalah*, Jerusalem: Keter, 1974.

—. *Kitve yad beqabala*, Jerusalem, 1930 (Hebrew).

—. 'Le mouvement sabbataïste en Pologne,' Part 1, *Revue de l'histoire des religions*, 143/1 (1953), pp. 30–90.

—. *On the Kabbalah and Its Symbolism* (English transl. by R. Manheim), New York: Schocken Books, 1969.

—. *Origins of the Kabbalah* (English transl. by A. Arkush), ed. R.Z.J. Werblowsky, Philadelphia–Princeton: JPS–Princeton University Press, 1987.

—. 'R. Moshe miBurgos, The Student of R. Isaac,' *Tarbiz*, 5 (1934), pp. 50–51 (Hebrew).

Schremer, Adiel. *Male and Female He Created Them: Jewish Marriage in the Late Second Temple, Mishnah and Talmud Periods*, Jerusalem: Shazar Institute, 2004 (Hebrew).

Schwab, Moïse M. *Vocabulaire de l'angélologie*, reprinted Milan: Archè, 1989.

Secunda, Shai. 'The Construction, Composition and Idealization of the Female Body in Rabbinic Literature and Parallel Iranian Texts: Three Excursuses,' *Nashim*, 23 (2012), pp. 60–86.

—. *The Iranian Talmud: Reading the Bavli in Its Sasanian Context*, Philadelphia: University of Pennsylvania Press, 2013.

—. 'Talmudic text and Iranian Context: On the Development of Two Talmudic Narratives,' *AJS Review*, 33 (2009), pp. 45–69.

Sefer hamalkhut, Casablanca 1930.

Segal, Michael. *The Book of Jubilees*, Leiden–Boston: Brill, 2007.

Shahar, Shulamit. 'Catharism and the Beginning of Kabbalah in Languedoc,' *Tarbiz*, 40 (1971), pp. 483–508 (Hebrew).

—. 'Écrits Cathares et Commentaire d'Abraham Abulafia sur "Le Livre de la Creation": Images et Idées Communes,' *Cahiers de Fanjeaux*, 12 (1977), pp. 345–361.

Shaked, Shaul. *Dualism in Transformation: Varieties of Religion in Sasanian Iran*, London: SOAS, 1994.

—. 'Iranian Influence on Judaism, First Century B.C.E. to Second Century C.E.,' in William David Davies and Louis Finkelstein (eds.), *The Cambridge History of Judaism*, I, Cambridge, UK: Cambridge University Press, 1984, pp. 308–325.

—. 'Qumran and Iran: Further Considerations,' *Israel Oriental Studies*, 2 (1972), pp. 433–446.

—. 'Some Islamic Reports concerning Zoroastrianism,' *Jerusalem Studies in Arabic and Islam*, 17 (1994), pp. 43–84.

Soloveitchik, Haym. 'Agobard of Lyon, the Scroll Ahima'ats, and the Palestinian Halacha in Early Medieval Ashkenaz,' in J.R. Hacker and Y. Harel (eds.), *The Scepter Shall not Depart from Judah: Leadership, Rabbinate and Community in Jewish History – Studies Presented to Professor Simon Schwarzfuchs*, Jerusalem: Bialik Institute, 2011, pp. 207– 217 (Hebrew).

Stern, Sasha. *Time and Process in Ancient Judaism*, Oxford–Portland, OR: Littman Library, 2003.

Stone, Michael E. (ed.). *Jewish Writings of the Second Temple Period*, Assen–Philadelphia: Van Gorcum–Fortress Press, 1984.

Stoyanov, Yuri. *The Other God: Dualist Religions from Antiquity to the Cathar Heresy*, New Haven, CT: Yale University Press, 2000.

Stroumsa, Guy G. *Another Seed: Studies in Gnostic Mythology*, Leiden: Brill, 1984.

—. *Savior et Salut*, Paris: Le Cerf, 1992.

—. 'A Zoroastrian Origin to the *Sefirot*?' *Irano-Judaica*, 3 (1994), pp. 17–33.

Subtelny, Maria Eva. 'The Tale of the Four Sages Who Entered the "Pardes": A Talmudic Enigma from a Persian Perspective,' *Jewish Studies Quarterly*, 11/1–2 (2004), pp. 3–58.

Ta-Shma, Israel M. *Studies in Medieval Jewish Literature*, Jerusalem: Bialik Institute, 2004–2010 (Hebrew).

Tishby, Isaiah. *The Doctrine of Evil and the Shells in Lurianic Doctrine*, Jerusalem: Magnes Press, 1942 (Hebrew).

—. 'Gnostic Doctrines in Sixteenth-Century Jewish Mysticism,' *Journal of Jewish Studies*, 6 (1955).

—. 'Imaginary Innovation in the Research of Kabbalah,' *Zion*, 54 (1989), pp. 469–491 (Hebrew).

—. *Paths of Faith and Heresy*, Ramat Gan: Masada, 1964 (Hebrew).

—. *The Wisdom of the Zohar* (English transl. by D. Goldstein), London–Washington: Littman Library of Jewish Civilisation, 1991.

Urbach, Ephraim E. *The Sages, Their Concepts and Beliefs* (English transl. by I. Abrahams), Jerusalem: Magnes Press, 1979.

— (ed.). *Sefer 'arugat habosem* by R. Abraham b. Azriel, I, Jerusalem: Mekitze Nirdamim, 1939 (Hebrew).

— (ed.). *Sefer pitron Torah*, Jerusalem: Magnes Press, 1978 (Hebrew).

Vital, R. Ḥayim. *Liqute Torah*, Jerusalem 1972 (Hebrew).

—. *Peri 'ets ḥayim*, Dubrovna 1803.

—. *Sha'ar hapesuqim*, Tel Aviv 1962 (Hebrew).

Wacholder, Ben Zion. *The Dawn of Qumran: The Sectarian Torah and the Teacher of Righteousness*, Cincinnati: HUC Press, 1983.

Weiss, Tzahi. 'The Reception of Sefer Yesirah in Jewish Mysticism in the Early Middle Ages,' *Jewish Quarterly Review*, 103 (2013), pp. 26–46.

Wieder, Naphtali. *The Judean Scrolls and Karaism*, London: East and West Library, 1962.

Widengren, Geo. 'Iran and Israel in Parthian Times with Special Reference to the Ethiopic Book of Enoch,' *Temenos*, 2 (1966), pp. 139–177.

—. 'Primordial Man and Prostitute: A Zervanite Motif in the Sassanid Avesta,' in E.E. Urbach, R.J.Z. Werblowsky and C. Wirszubski (eds.), *Studies in Mysticism and Religion Presented to Gershom G. Scholem*, Jerusalem: Magnes, 1967, pp. 227–234.

Wilderberger, Hans. 'Der Dualismus in den Qumranschriften,' *Asiatische Studien/Études asiatiques*, 8 (1954), pp. 163–177.

Winston, David. 'The Iranian Component in the Bible, Apocrypha and Qumran: A Review of the Evidence,' *History of Religions*, 5 (1966), pp. 183–216.

Wolfson, Elliot R. 'Light through Darkness,' in idem, *Luminal Darkness: Imaginal Gleanings from Zoharic Literature*, Oxford: Oneworld, 2007, pp. 29ff.

Yadin, Yigael (ed.). *The Scroll of the War of the Sons of Light against the Sons of Darkness*, Jerusalem: Bialik Institute, 1957 (Hebrew).

Yassif, Eli (ed.). *The Book of Memory that is the Chronicles of Jerahme'el*, Tel Aviv: Tel Aviv University, 2001 (Hebrew).

Zaehner, Robert C. *The Dawn & Twilight of Zoroastrianism*, London: Weidenfeld and Nicolson, 1961.

—. *Zurvan: A Zoroastrian Dilemma*, Oxford: Clarendon Press, 1955.

Babylonian Jewish Magic in Late Antiquity
Beyond the Incantation Bowls

Gideon Bohak

Babylonian Jewish Magic and the Aramaic Incantation Bowls

Upon their first discovery, in 1853, the Babylonian incantation bowls seem to have aroused little scholarly attention.[1] A few studies were devoted to the edition and interpretation of several bowls, and there was some discussion of their chronology, their original mode of use, their relationship with rabbinic Judaism and their possible overall significance. But the scholars who studied the bowls were mostly busy establishing the correct reading and understanding of the texts inscribed upon these clay bowls, a task that proved exceptionally difficult, especially at a time when very few bowls were known, and when publications were not yet accompanied by images of the bowls themselves, so that different scholars had access to different bowls – in Paris, Cannes, London, Berlin, Philadelphia and elsewhere.[2] And yet, going through these earlier publications, one has a feeling that none of the scholars involved realized that these humble clay bowls would one day furnish a

1 I dedicate this study to Professor Shaul Shaked, mentor, friend, and path-breaking scholar, whose immense contributions to the study of Jewish magic, and especially of the Aramaic incantation bowls, made the present study possible.

2 For the most important publications, see the bowls published by Thomas Ellis in Layard, *Discoveries*, pp. 509–526; Schwab, 'Une coupe d'incantation'; idem, 'Les coupes magiques'; idem, 'Coupes à inscriptions magiques'; idem, 'Deux vases'; Hyvernat, 'Sur un vase judéo-babylonien'; Wohlstein, 'Über einige aramäische Inschriften'; Lacau, 'Une coupe d'incantation'; Myhrman, 'An Aramaic Incantation Text.' Most, but not all, of these bowls have since been re-edited in the more recent publications listed below. Here and in what follows, I essentially ignore the Syriac and Mandaic incantation bowls, since my focus in on Babylonian *Jewish* magic.

major source for the study of late-antique Mesopotamia in general, and of late-antique Babylonian Jewish culture in particular.[3]

It was only sixty years after the initial publications, and just over a full century ago, that Montgomery's exemplary edition of the Nippur incantation bowls in the University of Philadelphia's Museum provided other scholars with a sound textual basis on which to base their own analyses of unpublished bowls and of the bowl phenomenon as a whole.[4] This line of research was continued by Montgomery's disciple, Cyrus Herzl Gordon, and by Gordon's own disciples, such as Mark Geller and Edwin Yamauchi.[5] But It gained new prominence with the publication of the two volumes of Aramaic magical texts by Joseph Naveh and Shaul Shaked, in 1985 and 1993, and the subsequent publications of important corpora by Shaul Shaked, Dan Levene, Christa Müller-Kessler and many others.[6]

Today, we are on the threshold of a new era in bowl studies, with the appearance of the first volume of the Schøyen collection of incantation bowls, edited by Shaul Shaked, James Nathan Ford and Siam Bhayro.[7] Once all projected nine volumes of the Schøyen bowls are published (and especially the five volumes devoted to bowls written in Jewish Babylonian Aramaic), the corpus of published Aramaic incantation bowls will become one of the largest Jewish textual corpora from Antiquity, almost as large as the Babylonian Talmud itself. And even this will not end the stream of publications, since more bowls surface on the antiquities markets all the time, and many bowls in museums and

3 They are mentioned only briefly by Blau, in *Das altjüdische Zauberwesen*, p. 154, note 2, and idem, 'Amulet,' p. 547. Thus, even the greatest scholar of Jewish magic of the late nineteenth century was not yet aware of their importance.

4 Montgomery, *Aramaic Incantation Texts*.

5 For the most important publications, see Gordon, 'Aramaic Magical Bowls'; idem, 'Aramaic and Mandaic Magical Bowls'; idem, 'Aramaic Incantation Bowls'; idem, 'Magic Bowls in the Moriah Collection'; Rossell, *A Handbook*; Jeruzalmi, *Les coupes magiques*; Isbell, *Corpus*; Geller, 'Four Aramaic Incantation Bowls'; and idem, 'Eight Incantation Bowls.'

6 See Naveh and Shaked, *Amulets and Magic Bowls*; eidem, *Magic Spells and Formulae*; Segal, *Catalogue*; Levene, *A Corpus*; idem, *Jewish Aramaic Curse Texts*; Müller-Kessler, *Die Zauberschalentexte*; Faraj, *Coppe magiche*; and Bhayro, Ford, Levene and Saar, *Aramaic Magic Bowls*.

7 Shaked, Ford and Bhayro, *Aramaic Bowl Spells*.

private collections remain unpublished.[8] In fact, no one really knows how many unpublished bowls are out there already, and once Iraq regains its former stability, new archaeological excavations are bound to lead to the discovery of many more Aramaic incantation bowls.

The Babylonian Aramaic incantation bowls are an important source for the study of Babylonian Jewish magic and of Babylonian Jewish culture as a whole.[9] They present four major advantages over most other types of textual sources currently at our disposal for the study of ancient Jewish culture. The first is that, in the world of the bowls, there seems to be a close connection between a bowl's language and script and the ethnic or religious identity of its producers. At the very least, one may definitely assume that bowls written in Aramaic and in the square script were produced by Jews (though not necessarily for Jewish clients). The hundreds of bowls in this category that have been published thus far display many signs of the Jewish origins of their producers, and no Aramaic bowl displays clear signs of having been produced by a non-Jewish practitioner. This gives the Aramaic incantation bowls a vast advantage over such magical texts as are found, for example, in the Greek magical papyri, some of which may have been produced by Jews, but most of which probably were not, even if they display some Jewish influence. More important still, the Aramaic incantation bowls provide a much more reliable body of evidence for the study of late-antique Jewish culture than the massive body of evidence assembled by

8 For some of the most recent publications, see Gorea, 'Trois nouvelles coupes'; Moriggi, 'Aramaean Demons'; idem, 'Two New Incantation Bowls'; Abousamra, 'Une nouvelle coupe'; Abousamra and Lemaire, 'Bol magique'; Faraj, 'An Incantation Bowl'; Ford, 'A New Parallel'; Ford and Ten-Ami, 'An Incantation Bowl'; Levene and Bohak, 'A Babylonian Jewish Aramaic Incantation'; Levene and Ford, 'For Aḥata-de-'abuh Daughter of Imma'; al-Jubouri, 'An Aramaic Incantation Bowl'; idem, 'An Aramaic Incantation Text'; idem, 'A New Aramaic Incantation Bowl'; Fain, Ford and Lyavdansky, 'Aramaic Incantation Bowls'; and cf. Frankfurter, 'Scorpion/Demon.'

9 For detailed surveys of the bowls and their significance, see Yamauchi, 'Aramaic Magic Bowls'; Isbell, 'The Story'; Shaked, 'Popular Religion'; idem, 'Jews, Christians and Pagans'; idem, 'Magical Bowls and Incantation Texts'; Levene, *Curse or Blessing*; Harari, 'On the Trail,' pp. 59–67; idem, *Jewish Magic*, pp. 234–251; Morony, 'Magic and Society'; idem, 'Religion'; Bohak, *Ancient Jewish Magic*, pp. 183–193; and Müller-Kessler, 'Zauberschalen und ihre Umwelt.'

Erwin Goodenough for his monumental work on Jewish symbols, most of which probably is non-Jewish to begin with.[10]

A second advantage of the Babylonian incantation bowls is that they come from Babylonia itself and are late-antique objects, not medieval copies of late-antique texts. This means that, unlike many other bodies of ancient Jewish literature (such as most of the Apocrypha and Pseudepigrapha), their chronological and geographical coordinates are well known. In this respect, the bowls may even help us peg down some texts whose original contexts are far more obscure. Thus, to give just one example, when we find Hekhalot-related motifs, and even rather extensive passages known to us from the Hekhalot literature, in some of the Babylonian incantation bowls, we can be certain that these motifs and textual units were already in circulation in late-antique Babylonia.[11] This does not necessarily mean that they began their life there and not in Palestine, and it does not really tell us how much older they may have been, but it does provide a firm *terminus ante quem*, and one specific geographical and social context, for the early transmission of at least some textual components of the Hekhalot literature. This evidence is of great importance, since it dates to long before the references to the Hekhalot literature in the responsa of Sherira Gaon and Hai Gaon or in the *Scroll of Aḥimaaz*, and even longer before the earliest Geniza fragments of this literature, not to mention the much later manuscripts of European origin.[12]

The third reason why the bowls are such an important source is that they come in great abundance and that each bowl carries a relatively long text. Unlike tombstones, for example, which often come in great abundance but tend to be quite short, and in many cases highly formulaic and thus extremely repetitive, a typical bowl provides us with the equivalent of half a page of printed text; and while many textual

10 See Goodenough, *Jewish Symbols*.

11 For a pertinent example, see Bohak, 'Observations,' pp. 220–222; for the formula discussed there, see now Shaked, Ford and Bhayro, *Aramaic Bowl Spells*, JBA 9 (MS 2053/183), ll. 16–17. The pioneering study in this field was Shaked, 'Peace Be upon You,' and cf. idem, 'Jewish and Iranian Visions'; Shaked, Ford and Bhayro, *Aramaic Bowl Spells*, pp. 23–27; and Müller-Kessler, 'Eine ungewöhnliche Hekhalot-Zauberschale.'

12 For a useful introduction to these complex issues, see Boustan, 'Study of Heikhalot Literature.' For the earliest manuscripts of the Hekhalot literature, see Bohak, 'Dangerous Books.'

units recur in more than one bowl (often with some variation between the different parallels), the number of different textual units found in the entire corpus amounts to many hundreds. These units range in length from a line or two to ten or twelve lines of printed text, and they often contain one or two larger spells along with a plethora of smaller textual units and recurrent formulae.[13] And they have much to tell us about many aspects of Sasanian Jewish society and culture, including language, onomastics, family structures, levels of literacy, Jewish/non-Jewish cultural and social contacts, and even the knowledge and use of such texts as the Hebrew Bible, the Mishna and the Jewish liturgy. For scholars used to reconstructing ancient cultures from their scanty textual remains, this is an extremely important body of evidence, which has not yet been utilized for all that it has to offer.

Finally, a fourth major advantage of the bowls is that they clearly stem from more than one site. This is a rather sensitive issue, since most of the bowls that have come out of Iraq over the last two decades were looted from unknown locations, but those that were excavated in more peaceful times often are of a known provenance. A full study of all these different findspots, and of the possible differences between bowls found in different locations, has yet to be carried out, but enough is known about bowls from Babylon (such as those published by Ellis), Nippur (such as those published by Montgomery), Khafajah, Kish, Tell Baruda (Ctesiphon), Bidjan, Tel Omar (Seleucia), Borsippa and some sites in Western Iran to assure us of their wide geographic distribution.[14] Thus, it is clear that these bowls are not the product of some aberrant social

13 For a pioneering attempt to sort out the different *types* of textual units found in the bowls and disentangle the logic of their internal arrangement, see Shaked, 'Transmission and Transformation of Spells'; see also Shaked, Ford and Bhayro, *Aramaic Bowl Spells*, pp. 8–13.

14 See Cook, 'An Aramaic Incantation Bowl' (Khafajah); Gordon, 'Aramaic Incantation Bowls,' pp. 129–130 and pp. 276–280 (Kish); Franco, 'Five Aramaic Incantation Bowls' (Tel Baruda); Gawlikowski, 'Une coupe magique' (Bidjan, near Anah); Waterman, *Preliminary Report*, pp. 61–62 (Tel Omar); Harviainen, 'An Aramaic Incantation Bowl' (as this bowl was bought in Borsippa, and not excavated in situ, its provenance is less certain). For bowls from Western Iran, see Yamauchi, 'Aramaic Magic Bowls,' p. 512. For bowls found in other locations, see, for example, Faraj and Moriggi, 'Two Incantation Bowls,' pp. 72 and 77. And note the map provided by Müller-Kessler, 'Zauberschalen und ihre Umwelt,' which includes the Syriac and Mandaic evidence as well as the Jewish Aramaic bowls.

group or of specific local circumstances, but objects produced in great numbers, by many different producers, in many different locations, for numerous clients. As such, they represent a phenomenon that clearly is very different from that represented by the Dead Sea Scrolls, for example, or by the Gnostic library found at Nag Hammadi, each of which may have been intended for the use of one rather small group of potential readers. With the bowls, the potential readers were the demons whom the bowls were trying to thwart, but the clients on whose behalf these texts were written were both male and female, both Jews and non-Jews, living in many different towns and villages over a period of two, three or four centuries, from the fifth to the seventh or eighth centuries CE.[15]

Useful as the bowls might be, their usefulness as sources for the study of Jewish magic is diminished by several important drawbacks. On the one hand, because of the problematic ways in which they reach the markets, many bowls are without provenance and utterly devoid of any archaeological or precise geographical context. In some cases, bowls whose provenance is unknown may be ascribed to a specific location because the client for whom they were produced is known from other bowls whose provenance is known for certain, but such cases are few and far between. This is to be regretted, since the absence of provenance almost precludes any attempt to study which spells were used in which locations, and how the spells travelled from one location to the next.[16]

The lack of clear archaeological contexts for many bowls is a major handicap, but the bowls also suffer from another disadvantage, in that they are rather uni-dimensional. A vast majority of the bowls are apotropaic in nature, as they seek to bind demons and avert the dangers of witchcraft and the evil eye. In some bowls, there is implicit or explicit reference to the illnesses from which the bowls' owners suffered, and these bowls thus shed some light on the etiology of certain diseases, and the connection between magic and medicine, in late-antique Babylonia.[17]

15 The bowls' chronology is not easy to establish for certain, since very few carry specific dates or other chronological indicators, but those that do carry such indications cluster in the second half of the sixth century and in the seventh; see Shaked, Ford and Bhayro, *Aramaic Bowl Spells*, p. 1, note 2.

16 For a modest effort in this direction, see Hunter, 'Manipulating Incantation Texts.'

17 See, for example, Levene, *Curse or Blessing*, pp. 28–29; Ford, 'A New

But only some two dozen of the published bowls are aggressive in nature, and even these tend to be intended more to send the witchcraft back upon its perpetrators, with only six bowls containing aggressive spells that are not presented as counter-spells.[18] Only four published bowls are intended for erotic magic, and only one seeks to enhance its client's economic and social position by attracting people to his business.[19] Thus, a reading of the bowls might give us the impression that the Jews of Sasanian Babylonia were mostly busy with 'white' magic and showed little interest in recourse to 'black' magic. Some students of Jewish culture might be satisfied with such a conclusion, since this is the type of Jewish magical activity that is easiest for them to swallow.[20] But students of magic should be extremely skeptical of such a scenario, since in other magical traditions, and in the Jewish magic of later periods and even of late-antique Palestine, magical practices for aggressive, erotic, medicinal and divinatory purposes tend to be at least as popular, and often more so, than magic aimed for protection against demons and witchcraft.[21] That the bowls preserve mostly one type of magic must be because this type was committed to writing, and on writing surfaces that happen to be quite durable; that they were buried in the ground also helped preserve them for posterity. Other types of magical activity apparently involved different practices, including the manipulation of various objects, the uttering of oral spells, the writing of spells on perishable writing surfaces or their destruction during the

Parallel,' pp. 272–275; and Bhayro, 'An Aramaic Magic Bowl for Fertility.' For a broader analysis, see Bohak, 'Conceptualizing Demons.'

18 These bowls have now been collected and analyzed as a group by Levene, *Jewish Aramaic Curse Texts*. My statistics are based on his discussion, *ibid.*, p. 1. And cf. Saar, 'A Study in Conceptual Parallels.'

19 For the erotic bowls, see Saar, 'An Incantation Bowl'; for the economic bowl, see Levene and Bhayro, 'Bring to the Gates.'

20 For a case in point, see Baron, *Social and Religious History*, VIII, p. 283, note 21: 'The relative paucity of erotic incantations emanating from the Jews of Nippur and elsewhere (Montgomery's text, No. 28, p. 213, invoking the aid of the goddess of love Dlibat evidently was of pagan origin) testifies to the strong hold of the regnant Jewish ethics over the popular masses and their miracle-working agents even in the obscure realm of sex.' For Montgomery's Bowl 28, see below, note 103.

21 For 'black' magic in late-antique Palestine, cf. Alexander, '*Sefer ha-Razim*'; and Bohak, 'Magical Rotuli.'

magical ritual (e.g., by burning or washing in water), and so they left no archaeological traces.[22]

Thus, I would suggest that rather than being the central sphere of Jewish magical activity in late-antique Mesopotamia, the bowls represent just one type of magical activity, but the type which produced long-lasting remains, whereas all other types left far fewer remains or none at all.[23] But this suggestion raises two related questions: (a) What do we know about the other magical practices known to and used by the Jews of Sasanian Babylonia? And: (b) What other Jewish magical texts from Sasanian Babylonia do we currently have and may we hope to find in the future? The present paper is an attempt to answer these two questions, by surveying some of the possible sources of evidence pertaining to the Jewish magical texts and practices of late-antique Mesopotamia, apart from the bowls. In what follows I shall not try to offer a full analysis of each textual corpus, but I will endeavor to raise the basic questions, point to some pertinent examples and note where further research is still needed. Moreover, as many of the relevant texts have never been published, it is my hope that the survey offered here will encourage the edition and closer analysis of these neglected sources.

Babylonian Jewish Magic in the Babylonian Talmud

The most obvious starting point for any attempt to complement the image of Sasanian Jewish magic emerging from the Aramaic incantation bowls is the Babylonian Talmud. Here we are dealing with a large body of evidence that has much to tell us about the magical practices and spells known to, taught by and sometimes even used by the rabbis of late-antique Mesopotamia.[24] Surveying all this evidence would be out

22 Note, however, a lead amulet on which the spell was written in ink, published by Geller, 'More Magic Spells,' pp. 331–334; if authentic, it could provide one more point of entry into late-antique Babylonian Jewish magic. Another relevant item is the amulet from Afghanistan (see below, note 75), which probably dates to the tenth century, and whose authenticity is hardly in doubt.

23 And note Shaked, '*Dramatis Personae*,' who highlights the differences between the magic bowls and Geniza magical texts, and stresses, on p. 366, that 'the bowls do not reflect the whole range of magical practices used in the Babylonian environment at the time.'

24 For broad surveys of rabbinic magic and a more extensive bibliography, see

of the question here, and as the magical practices and recipes found in the Babylonian Talmud have often been studied, we may merely note two of their most important features. First, here we find numerous examples of medicinal magic, including the use of many types of amulets and the recitation of many types of spells, and some examples of anti-demonic and anti-witchcraft practices – but very little aggressive magic, no erotic magic whatsoever and very little divinatory magic. Second, most of the magical activity recorded in the Babylonian Talmud is transmitted and enacted orally; there are only a few references to the writing down of magical spells as a part of the ritual process,[25] confirming our suspicion that the Jews of Sasanian Babylonia utilized many magical practices that involved only the oral recitation of spells, without writing them down. These practices also involved the manipulation of various objects, the binding or slaughtering of animals and the burial (or hanging) of magical objects at crossroads, in cemeteries and at the entrance to one's home. Thus, the Talmud complements the evidence supplied by the bowls in terms not only of the goals sought by those who had recourse to magic, but also of the rituals enacted in order to attain those goals.

As has often been noted, the Babylonian Talmud never refers to the practice of writing down spells on clay bowls, and it seems unaware of this practice, whose apogee probably postdates the time of its redaction.[26] And yet, numerous motifs appear both in the Babylonian Talmud and in the Aramaic incantation bowls, including specific rabbinic, demonic and angelic figures, shared legal and liturgical formulae, similar uses of

Blau, *Das altjüdische Zauberwesen*; Goldin, 'Magic of Magic'; Harari, 'The Sages and the Occult'; Geller, 'Deconstructing Talmudic Magic'; and Bohak, *Ancient Jewish Magic*, pp. 351–425.

25 For these exceptions, see BT *Baba batra* 73a (sailors writing on wooden staffs); BT *Yoma* 84a (a spell to be written on hyena-skin); BT *Pesaḥim* 111b (two rabbinic disciples writing amulets); BT *Gitin* 67b ('Why do you need to know the demon's name? To write the proper amulet'). The Talmud also refers to books of magic (e.g., BT *Ḥullin* 13a), but these were books owned by non-Jews or laypersons, and not by the rabbis themselves.

26 The Babylonian Talmud (BT *Ḥullin* 84b, *Baba metsia* 29b) is aware of the existence of 'a sorcerers' cup' (כסא דחרשין) but attributes this knowledge to the Palestinian Rabbi Yohanan, and the ensuing discussion shows that it is not the inscribed clay bowls that the rabbi had in mind.

biblical verses and a pervasive fear of demons and witchcraft.[27] More specifically, there are some interesting overlaps between the spells found in the incantation bowls (and not found on the metal amulets from late-antique Palestine, Egypt, Italy and so on) and those recommended by the Babylonian Talmud, thus showing that both textual corpora share some of the magical know-how of late-antique Babylonian Jewish society. These parallels have never been collected systematically, but useful starting points have been provided in several earlier studies.[28] In what follows, I wish to point to one such parallel, which has not yet been studied, and note its potential significance.

In BT *Shabbat* 67a, a discussion of the mishnaic dictum (Mishna *Shabbat* 6:10) that one may not carry (as an amulet) the egg of a locust, the tooth of a fox or a nail from a crucifixion, because these are 'ways of the Amorites,' soon leads to a dictum by Rabbi Ḥiyya bar Abin (a Babylonian *amora* of the third generation) that two specific first aid practices are not to be included under this umbrella term for forbidden practices. First, if a fishbone got stuck in someone's throat, those next to him should place a bone of the same kind on his head and say: 'One, one, went down, swallowed, swallowed, went down, one, one.'[29] Second, for a fishbone (stuck in one's throat), one should say: 'You were stuck in like a needle and you were locked up like a shield, *shia shia*' (ננעצתה כמחט וננעלתה כתריס שייה שייה).[30] The first of these spells

27 For some of these, see Ten-Ami, 'Rabbinic Motifs'; Manekin Bamberger, 'Jewish Legal Formulae'; Shaked, Ford and Bhayro, *Aramaic Bowl Spells*, pp. 22–23, 53–55, 103–104; Bhayro, 'Divorcing a Demon'; and Elman, 'Saffron, Spices, and Sorceresses.' For the rabbis who are mentioned in the bowls, see Shaked, 'Rabbis.'

28 See Segal, *Catalogue*, p. 74; Müller-Kessler, *Die Zauberschalentexte*, p. 45; Bohak, 'Babylonian Incantation Bowls,' p. 258; Mishor, 'Hebrew,' p. 224; Shaked, Ford and Bhayro, *Aramaic Bowl Spells*, p. 55; and Manekin Bamberger, 'An Akkadian Demon.'

29 The same magical practice, but without the spell, is found in Tosefta *Shabbat* 7:21 (ed. Zuckermandel, p. 119), and in *Testament of Solomon* 18, and is attributed by Pliny, *NH* 28.49, to the Magi. This parallel has often been noted; and see Blau, *Das altjüdische Zauberwesen*, p. 76; and Veltri, 'The "Other" Physicians,' p. 51.

30 The most important manuscripts, as recorded in the Henkind Databank of the Saul Lieberman Institute, read: בגעצתה כמחט מנעלתה כתריס שייה שייה (Munich 95); ננעצתא כמחט ננעלתא כתריס שיא כשיאה (Oxford, Opp. Add. 23); (ניגע צתא) [נינעצתא] כמחט נינעלתא כתריס שרא שיאה שיאה (Vatican 108); נינעצתה במחט נינעלתה

is characterized by a chiastic structure (A, A, B, C, C, B, A, A), which in this case clearly is intended mimetically to encourage the bone that went down the throat to go back up again and join its fellow bone on the patient's head.[31] As far as I know, no parallel to this spell has thus far been found in any of the published Aramaic incantation bowls, but the chiastic structure is well attested both in the Aramaic bowls (as we shall see in one of the following examples) and in other spells recommended by the Babylonian Talmud.[32] However, the second spell is paralleled in several bowls, where it appears as דעלת כימחט דעס ביתרוס, or על כל דמחט דעלת כימחט דעס כיתרוס, or ועץ מחץ כיתרם ... כיתרם מחץ ועץ דמחט כל על, or דעלת כימחט רססת כיתרס שוא פשנוש.[33] The last of these examples might even be a partial parallel to the sequence שייה שייה at the end of the talmudic spell, and in all of them we find clear parallels to the Talmud's ננעצתה כמחט וננעלתה כתריס, even though these parallels are not identical with the talmudic spell, or with each other.[34]

Reading all these parallels, one is struck by the fact that the talmudic spell is both coherent and context-specific, whereas those of the bowls are not. In the talmudic spell, most of the text, with the exception of the last two words, makes perfect sense (which definitely is not true of all the spells recommended by or recorded in the Babylonian Talmud), and this sense accords well with its intended use as a spell against a fishbone that got inserted into the throat like a needle and got locked up in there like a shield. In the bowls, on the other hand, the text of this spell makes

כתריס (שיחשיאה)[שייאה שייאה] (Westminster College, Talm. II, 2 [Geniza]). Rashi *ad loc.* interprets the last two words as meaning 'Go down, go down.' The *'Arukh* of R. Nathan b. Yehiel gives them as שיה שיה and interprets them as deriving from the Aramaic root שוח, 'to melt'; see Kohut, *Aruch Completum*, VIII, p. 47.

31 See also Bar-Ilan, 'Between Magic and Religion,' pp. 394–396.

32 The clearest example being the spell הוית דפקיק, דפקיק הוית, for which see Shaked, Ford and Bhayro, *Aramaic Bowl Spells*, p. 55.

33 See, respectively, Faraj, *Coppe magiche*, pp. 52–53, Bowl 4 (IM 148241), l. 7; Shaked, Ford and Bhayro, *Aramaic Bowl Spells*, p. 75, JBA 7 (MS 2053/12), ll. 13–14; *ibid.*, p. 266, JBA 61 (MS 2053/214), l. 7. See also *ibid.*, p. 254, JBA 57 (MS 2053/36), l. 8. The same formula is found in some unpublished bowls whose texts were shared with me by Dan Levene.

34 However, the readings of the bowls are complicated by the indistinguishability, in many of them, of the letters *yod* and *waw*, *bet* and *kaph*, and *samekh* and final *mem*. Thus, these parallels may be closer than what their editors' readings might lead us to believe.

no sense at all, changes from one bowl to the next and is appended to the bowls' main texts as a small appendage. Moreover, the sequence is given in Hebrew, and when the texts of the Aramaic incantation bowls shift from Aramaic to Hebrew, this usually is because they are citing pre-existing Hebrew textual units – from the Hebrew Bible, the Mishna or the Jewish liturgy, from what we now know as the Hekhalot literature and so on – which were originally transmitted in Hebrew. Finally, the word תריס, 'shield,' is a loanword from Greek (*thyreos*) that appears frequently in tannaitic sources, and while it is attested elsewhere in the Babylonian Talmud, it might point to a Palestinian origin of the entire spell.[35] Thus, we seem to have a Hebrew spell that was originally intended to help people who got fishbones stuck in their throats and that may have come to Babylonia from Palestine. In the bowls, it has nothing to do with fish or bones and appears mainly as a 'space filler,' a short formula intended to complement the longer spells that already were inscribed upon the bowl but did not suffice to fill its surface with text.

To sum up our brief discussion of the Babylonian Talmud, we may note that it is an extremely important source for the study of Babylonian Jewish magic and an excellent aid in placing the magic of the bowls in its wider social and religious contexts. On the one hand, there are enough overlaps between the bowls and the talmudic spells to assure us that they reflect the same world and stem from the same cultural environment. These overlaps still deserve a much closer scrutiny in order to highlight both the textual parallels and the contextual resemblances and differences between the two corpora, but enough has already been achieved to give us a sense of the terrain. On the other hand, the Babylonian Talmud complements the data provided by the bowls in many important ways and sheds much light on magical aims and practices that are unattested, or only partly attested, in the bowls. But even when we combine the data provided by these two major

35 Since Rabbi Ḥiyya bar Abin visited Palestine (see Hyman, *Toldoth tannaim ve'amoraim*, II, pp. 439–441), it is possible that he brought this spell with him, and that it is of Palestinian Jewish origin. That some spells of Palestinian Jewish origin found their way to the bowls is made clear by the example of the Semamit-*historiola*, for which see Naveh and Shaked, *Amulets and Magic Bowls*, pp. 188–197; Elitzur-Leiman, 'An Aramaic Amulet'; and Ford, 'New Light from Babylonia on the Story of Smamit.'

textual corpora, we cannot help feeling that large parts of late-antique Babylonian Jewish magic still lie beyond our grasp.

A Brief Note on Method

Before turning to the Jewish magical texts of later periods in search of the remains of late-antique Babylonian Jewish magic, a methodological issue must be raised: None of the evidence discussed below was found in Babylonia, nor is it preserved in late-antique manuscripts (since none from the region has survived); it comes from medieval and even later Jewish manuscripts, which we assume to contain copies of copies of much earlier texts. But this raises a grave question – reading a Jewish magical text found in medieval and later Jewish manuscripts, how would we know that it is of late-antique Babylonian origins? One criterion is linguistic, but it is problematic, because of the tendency of medieval Jewish scribes to 'normalize' Aramaic texts in line with the Aramaic of the Babylonian Talmud and of Targum Onqelos, which they knew so well.[36] Such processes are much more pronounced in the magical texts, which are non-canonical and intended for practical use, so that their language was constantly 'updated,' modified or even changed to the contemporary vernacular. As a rule, we may note that the magical instructions were far more likely to be modified than the incantations themselves (the copyists' assumption being that the instructions should be as clear as possible, but the incantations might lose their power if modified), but even the latter were corrupted, 'corrected,' modified and translated during their long transmission history. Thus, a linguistic analysis of later Jewish magical texts in search of earlier Babylonian Aramaic forms is not *a priori* useless, but it is not very probative either. Moreover, some Aramaic spells may even be medieval compositions. We know that Jews were writing new texts in Aramaic in the Middle Ages, with the Zohar as our best example (on which we shall say more in a moment) and the *Sidre deshimmusha rabba*, a mystical-magical text edited and analyzed by Gershom Scholem, as an even more pertinent example.[37] Even the presence of Babylonian vocalization in a

36 For this process, as seen in non-magical texts, see the classic statement by Kutscher, *Studies*, pp. 2 and 12–15.

37 For this phenomenon, see Rapoport-Albert and Kwasman, 'Late Aramaic';

manuscript of Jewish magic is no proof of the Babylonian origin of its recipes. Below, we shall note a magical booklet from Damascus that displays some Babylonian vocalization, but right next to it we could place Cairo Geniza magical texts with Babylonian vocalizations, texts whose magical recipes show no sign of a specifically Babylonian origin.[38]

A second and related problem is that once the Babylonian Talmud became the central text of medieval Jewish culture, its own magical spells and recipes became widely known to many medieval Jews. Interestingly, they did not have a great impact on the Jewish magical tradition, which had many other sources from which to draw its spells and recipes, but occasionally we do find spells and recipes that drew at least some of their inspiration from the Babylonian Talmud.[39] Moreover, there are cases where the reliance on talmudic precedents led to the creation of new spells that in some way resemble those of the Babylonian incantation bowls. Note, for example, the following passage in the Zohar, which retells the story of the creation of the woman out of the primordial human being, how Lilith was incensed by that development, and:

> ערקת היא לימא, וזמינא לאבאשא בני עלמא. אסוותא להאי, בההיא שעתא דאזדווג
> בר נש באתתיה, יכוין לביה לקדושה דמאריה, ולימא הכי, עטיפא בקטפא אזדמנת,
> שארי שארי, לא תעול ולא תנפוק, לא דידך ולא בעדבך, תוב תוב, ימא אתרגישא,

Mopsik, 'Late Judeo-Aramaic'; and Tal, 'The Role of Targum Onqelos.' For the *Sidrei*, see Scholem, 'Sidrei.'

38 See, for example, Oxford, Bodleian Heb. e 74.21 (for which see the brief note in Yeivin, *The Hebrew Language Tradition*, I, p. 236); and Schäfer and Shaked, *Magische Texte*, III, no. 69 (= T-S AS 142.13 + T-S NS 317.18). All three Geniza fragments come from the same manuscript, which is characterized by the Babylonian vocalization of some of its 'magic words,' but the magical recipes display no special affinity with the Babylonian Jewish magical texts of late antiquity.

39 As one example, I note the sequence שברירי ברירי רירי ירי רי י, which appears in BT *'Avoda zara* 12b and *Pesaḥim* 112a in a recipe against temporary blindness (for the Akkadian origin of the term *shabriri*, and for magical rituals against it, see Stol, 'Blindness,' and Geller, 'Akkadian Medicine,' p. 107). The same sequence appears in medieval and modern manuscripts of Jewish magic and is often used in contexts that have nothing to do with blindness. See, for example, Barel, 'Rav-Pe'alim,' p. 223, where it is used against epilepsy and to exorcize a demon.

גלגלוי ליך קראן, בחולקא קדישא אחידנא, בקדושה דמלכא אתעטפנא. ולחפיא ליה לרישיה ולאתתיה עד שעתא חדא, וכן בכל זמנא, עד תלת יומין לקליטה, דכל הרכבה דלא קולטת לתלת יומין, תוב ליתא קולטת.

She fled to the sea and is present to harm the people of the world. The cure for this – at that hour when a man copulates with his wife, he should turn his heart to the holiness of his Master and say thus: 'The one who is wrapped in bed-linen is present; loosen, loosen; you shall not come in and not come out; it is neither yours nor of your share (?). Return, return, the sea is stormy, its waves are calling you; to the holy garment I cleave, in the holiness of the King I wrap myself.' And he should cover his head and that of his wife for one hour, and thus at every time, up to three days from the moment of the reception (of the sperm in the womb), since every combination that does not receive (pregnancy) within three days, does not receive any more.[40]

Comparing this spell with those of the bowls, we may note the duplication of some words (תוב תוב, שארי שארי) and especially the structure of 'by X I did A (בחולקא קדישא אחידנא), by Y I did B (בקדושה דמלכא אתעטפנא),' both well attested in the Jewish Babylonian Aramaic bowls. And yet, there is no need to assume that the composer of this recipe had any direct or indirect knowledge of the bowls or their spells, since both features are well attested in the Babylonian Talmud as well.[41] We already noted above the sequence שייה שייה, which may have served as a source of inspiration for the Zohar's שארי שארי (loosen, loosen).[42] We may also note such a talmudic spell as במישרא דכרתי חבטיה בלועא דחמרא

40 Zohar III, 19a. The translation is my own, but I used the Hebrew translation of the incantation in Scholem, *Elements*, p. 152. For a brief discussion of this incantation, see Cohen-Alorro, 'Magic and Sorcery,' pp. 110–111. On pp. 319–320, note 24, Cohen-Alorro adduces an Akkadian parallel to this incantation and refers to the spells against Lilith in Babylonian incantation bowls.

41 Scholem, in his own copy of the Zohar, wrote of this spell that 'its composer is the very author of the (Zoharic) pericope on Leviticus, as emerges from its language and its contents' (לעניין הלחש: המחבר הוא בעל פרשת ויקרא עצמו כפי שיוצא מלשונו ותוכנו). See Scholem, *Sefer haZohar*, V, p. 2244.

42 Moreover, such formulae are common in many magical traditions, and see the formula שרא שרא גבר, 'Release, release a man,' in a Nabatean magical text published by Naveh, 'A Nabatean Incantation,' p. 113. I am grateful to Ortal-Paz Saar for this reference.

חטרתיה, 'in a bed of leeks I hit it, with the mouth of an ass I pounded it' (*Shabbat* 67a), as a source of inspiration for the second formula.[43] In light of such precedents, we can see why the Zohar's own spell may resemble the bowls in some striking ways, but this resemblance is not necessarily due to any historical continuity from the bowls to the world of the Zohar.

In light of these considerations, we cannot merely count on a general resemblance of language, or on some phenomenological similarities between the bowl-spells and those of later Jewish magical texts, as proof of historical continuity. We need much sounder criteria. One sound criterion for deciding about the 'Babylonian-ness' of other Jewish magical texts is a comparison thereof with the Babylonian incantation bowls, especially when we find in them parallel motifs and parallel formulae that are not attested in other Jewish magical texts, such as those from late-antique Palestine or from the Babylonian Talmud, or those found in other magical traditions (except, of course, Mandaic and Syriac magical texts, which often are of Babylonian origin themselves). In such cases, we may also use our extensive knowledge of Palestinian Jewish magic and of the Greco-Egyptian magical tradition, which had such an impact upon Palestinian Jewish magic but had only a minor impact on the Babylonian incantation bowls, to highlight those aspects of the bowls that are typical of them and of them alone.[44] When such elements re-emerge in later Jewish magical texts, these texts are likely to be copies of copies of texts that go back to late-antique Mesopotamia.

One possible application of this criterion would be to search in later Jewish magical texts for those long spells and *historiolae* that are known to us from the Babylonian incantation bowls and are unattested in late-antique Palestine. Below, we shall note some striking examples of such continuity, but also their rarity. Another application would be to search outside the Babylonian incantation bowls for words and technical terms that are extremely typical of the bowls' vocabulary and are unattested in Palestinian Jewish magic. Most useful in this regard are terms and

43 And the Zohar's description of Lilith as עטיפא בקטפא may have been influenced by the reference to חומרתא דקטיפתא, 'amulet of *qeṭifta*,' in BT *Shabbat* 57b.

44 For the continuity of Palestinian Jewish magic from Late Antiquity to the Middle Ages, which is much easier to demonstrate, see Naveh, 'A Good Subduing'; idem, 'On Ancient Jewish'; and Bohak, 'Jewish Magical Tradition.'

names borrowed from the Persian language, such as זרני, דנחיש, דיוי, בגדנא, איספנדס and פתיכרי, as these are *a priori* unlikely to have had much of an impact on Palestinian Jewish magic.[45] But to this short list we may add a much longer list of Aramaic and Hebrew terms that are typical of the bowls (some of which go back to Akkadian, but others do not), including especially the many different categories of demons, such as זכיא, בני איגרי, אשלמתא, שקופתא, שלניתא, ענקתא, מבכלתא, לטבי, ירורי, חטפיתא, חומרי זידניתא and so on, as well as the many personal names of the demons and liliths attested in the bowls, including פלחס, פלחדד, אביטור and so on.[46] To this list, which reflects the highly developed demonology of Babylonian Jewish magic, we may add the Babylonian gods, who occasionally appear in the Babylonian Jewish magical texts, especially in lists of the seven planets – שמיש וסין ונבו ודליבת וביל ונריג וכיון.

Of course, when compiling such a list we must recall that once one of these words is found in a text that is of a Palestinian and late-antique origin, it must be excluded, which is why we must strike off our list terms like עינא בישא, שידא, חרשין בישין or עובדין תקיפין, not to mention סטנין or מזיקין, all of which are typical of both Palestinian and Babylonian Jewish magical texts. Similarly, words that are found in the Hebrew Bible or the Babylonian Talmud should not be on our list, which is why we should exclude Ashmedai, even though he has a Persian name, and Lilith, in spite of her Babylonian origins, and why a single appearance of Bel or Keiwan does not necessarily tell us much about a text's provenance. And, as with every such set of 'textual markers,' we must note that it is not always easy to distinguish between real appearances of a certain word and mere phantoms, as when a corrupt word or a *vox magica* accidentally resembles one of the words in our list. Thus, the more such 'markers' we find in any given text, and the more we can be certain that they are indeed our words and not some random flukes, the more likely the text itself is to be of Babylonian origin or to preserve older Babylonian material.[47]

45 For these terms, see Shaked, 'Bagdâna,' and idem, 'Popular Religion.'

46 To date, no attempt has been made to catalogue all the demons that appear in the Aramaic bowls, and the most detailed survey remains Montgomery, *Aramaic Incantation Texts*, pp. 70–83. For a useful comparandum, see Furlani, 'I nomi delle classe.'

47 One more feature that seems typical of Babylonian Jewish magic and sometimes

To these 'textual markers' we could, at least in theory, add a list of 'iconographical markers,' that is, features of the bowls' peculiar iconography (especially the appearance of the demons and the different manners by which they are bound) for which we could search in later Jewish magical texts.[48] However, such an analysis would not get us very far, since later Jewish magical texts rarely have a pictorial component, and when they depict demons, these depictions resemble those of Muslim magical texts and greatly differ from those of the Aramaic incantation bowls.[49] Similarly, one could examine the magic signs that occasionally appear in the bowls and usually differ from the typical *characktêres* of Greco-Egyptian and Palestinian Jewish magic, and search for similar signs in later Jewish magical texts.[50] However, I know of no attempt to assemble the relevant data from all the published (and well photographed!) bowls, without which no such research could be carried out.

Another important criterion is the appearance in later Jewish magical texts of themes and practices that seem typical of non-Jewish Mesopotamian magic, and especially of the older Babylonian magical tradition.[51] This tradition seems to have had relatively little impact on the Babylonian incantation bowls, although the exact nature of this impact is still being debated by scholars, and the publication of more bowls might shed additional light.[52] However, in looking for older Babylonian magical elements that entered the Jewish magical tradition,

emerges in later Jewish magical texts is the first-person *historiola* (for which see Shaked, Ford and Bhayro, *Aramaic Bowl Spells*, pp. 15–17). However, I know of no attempt to classify the *historiolae* found in the 'Western' and 'Eastern' branches of late-antique Jewish magic and to isolate those features that are found exclusively in the 'Eastern' branch.

48 For the bowls' iconography, see Vilozny, 'Between Demons and Kings'; eadem, 'Lilith's Hair'; eadem, *Lilith's Hair*; and cf. Lesses, 'Image and Word.'

49 For one striking example, see the image from T-S Ar. 51.95, reproduced in Baker and Polliack, *Arabic and Judaeo-Arabic Manuscripts*, Plate 21.

50 For the *charaktêres*, see Bohak, 'The *Charaktêres*,' with further bibliography.

51 The same applies to the Persian magical tradition, which, unfortunately, is not well documented.

52 And see Müller-Kessler, 'Die aramäische Beschwörung'; Oelsner, 'Incantations in Southern Mesopotamia'; Geller, 'Tablets and Magic Bowls'; idem, 'Magic Bowls'; Gabbay, 'King of the Demons'; Bhayro, 'The Reception'; Levene, Marx and Bhayro, 'Gabriel is on Their Right'; Ford, 'Ancient Mesopotamian Motif'; and Wasserman, 'Old-Babylonian.'

we must always keep in mind that similar traditions and practices may have existed outside Babylonia as well.[53] Their presence in the Jewish magical tradition may therefore be due to non-Babylonian influences and thus tell us little about their ultimate origins. Of course, the more specifically-Babylonian a certain text or practice is, the more likely it is to have entered the Jewish magical tradition in late-antique Mesopotamia.

With these guidelines in mind, we may approach the sources, which include more than a thousand magic-related fragments from the Cairo Geniza and many hundreds of non-Geniza manuscripts of Jewish magic, some of which are hundreds of pages long. In what follows, I shall try to make two separate inroads into this vast territory. First, I shall look for longer Jewish magical texts that may be identified as coming from Sasanian Babylonia, or as displaying some Babylonian features. Next, I shall look for single Jewish magical recipes, found in manuscripts from the Cairo Geniza and elsewhere, that may be identified as stemming from late-antique Babylonian Jewish origins, even though they are found in collections of magical recipes with recipes of many different origins. I shall end with a brief evaluation of the results and some suggestions for further research.

Jewish Magical Texts of Mesopotamian Provenance

Reading through the dozens of Aramaic and Hebrew magical texts transmitted in medieval and later Jewish manuscripts (most of which have never been properly edited), we are soon forced to conclude that the search for magical texts that are likely to be of a late-antique Babylonian Jewish origin proves to be extremely complex. On the one hand, some of the magical texts may securely be attributed to other geograph-

53 I note, in this context, the interesting book by Daiches, *Babylonian Oil Magic*. Noting that the practice of gazing at oil-stains for the purpose of divination is attested in Mesopotamia and is well known to the Babylonian Talmud, Daiches goes on to edit and analyze early modern and modern manuscripts of Jewish magic where such practices may be found. His book contains much valuable data on modern Jewish magic, but it is entirely irrelevant to the study of Jewish magical texts of Babylonian origin, especially as the practice of oil-gazing for divination is extremely common in the Greek magical papyri as well and probably entered the Jewish magical tradition from several different directions.

ical and historical contexts and especially to late-antique Palestine or to the Jews of the Middle Ages, living under either Muslim or Christian rule. Thus, to give a few examples, a text such as *Sefer harazim* is so deeply influenced by the Greco-Egyptian magical tradition, and so full of Greek loanwords, as to assure us of its Palestinian origins and of its date some time in the Early Byzantine period, prior to the Muslim conquest.[54] Its Palestinian origins are further confirmed by its immense popularity in the Cairo Geniza, which as a rule tends to preserve Palestinian materials much more than Babylonian ones (as may be seen, for example, from the study of the *piyyutim*).[55] A Palestinian origin may also be postulated for *Shimmush Tehillim* (Use of the Psalms), which is written in Palestinian Jewish Aramaic, displays some Greek loanwords and is also well attested in the Cairo Geniza.[56] Similarly, the text called *Sheva' ma'alot* (The seven grades) is written in Palestinian Jewish Aramaic and displays many borrowings from the Greco-Egyptian magical tradition, and it may thus be classified as Palestinian, even though it is not as well represented among the Geniza fragments.[57]

While these texts stem from late-antique Palestine, other Jewish magical texts clearly date to the Middle Ages. This applies, for example, to the texts of astral magic that are found both in the Cairo Geniza and in non-Geniza manuscripts, which tend to be of a Muslim origin and to have reached the Jewish world either directly from Arabic or through intermediaries in other languages.[58] Likewise, a text like *Segullot 'or hanaḥash* (The properties of snakeskin) is a medieval Hebrew translation (or rather, a set of several different translations) of a Latin text called *Experimenta duodecim Johannes Paulini* (The twelve experiments of

54 For *Sefer harazim*, see Margalioth, *Sepher Ha-Razim*; Morgan, *Sepher Ha-Razim*; and Rebiger and Schäfer, *Sefer ha-Razim*.

55 For the Geniza fragments of *Sefer harazim*, see Rebiger and Schäfer, *Sefer ha-Razim*, I, pp. 1–16, 121*–201*.

56 See Rebiger, *Sefer Shimmush Tehillim*; for some of the Geniza fragments, see Schäfer and Shaked, *Magische Texte*, III, nos. 78–84.

57 For this text, which deserves a fuller study, see Schäfer and Shaked, *Magische Texte*, II, no. 26 (= T-S K 1.35 + T-S K 1.48), 2b/1–28; *ibid.*, no. 27 (= T-S K 1.74), 1a–1b; and MS NYPL 190, in Bohak, *A Fifteenth-Century Manuscript*, I, pp. 195–198; II, pp. 153–155.

58 For a pertinent example, see Burnett and Bohak, 'A Judaeo-Arabic Version.'

Johannes Paulinus), which itself is said to have been translated from Arabic.[59] Other examples of these processes could easily be adduced.[60]

If some books of Jewish magic display clear signs of a Palestinian or medieval provenance, others prove much harder to pin down. I note, for example, that both *Sefer hayashar* (The Book of the righteous) and *Sefer hamalbush* (The Book of the wearing [of the divine name]) are written in Hebrew and are likely to be of late-antique origin, but they do not provide any clear signs of either Palestinian or Babylonian provenance.[61] In both cases, only a small part of the relevant textual evidence has received any scholarly attention, and the question of their provenance has hardly even been discussed. Thus, it is possible that a closer examination of each of these texts would yield sounder conclusions about their likely provenance, but it also is quite possible that we will not have a clear answer even if and when such analyses are carried out.

Thus, we are left with some Jewish magical texts that clearly have little to do with late-antique Babylonia, and some whose provenance is not really known. But we also have some texts that are likely to go back to late-antique Babylonia, and of these, four merit special attention: the *Ḥarba deMoshe*, the *Pishra deRabbi Ḥanina ben Dosa*, the *Havdala deRabbi Aqiba* and some versions of *Sefer haqevitsa*.[62] Let us look

59 For this text, see my brief comments in Bohak, 'Rabbanite Magical Texts,' pp. 26–27, with further bibliography. In the future, I hope to devote a separate study to this text.

60 And see Shaked, 'Jewish Magical Literature'; Leicht, 'Legend of St. Eustachius'; Bohak, 'Catching a Thief'; Mesler, 'The Three Magi'; and Saar, 'A Genizah Magical Fragment.'

61 For both texts, see Wandrey, *Das Buch des Gewandes*. See also the book known as *Sefer Adam*, recently edited in Rebiger and Schäfer, *Sefer ha-Razim*, as '*Sefer ha-Razim* II.' It, too, displays no clear sign of its ultimate origins.

62 Another book that must have been of Babylonian Jewish origin is *Raza rabba* (The Great secret), which one Karaite author described as רזה רבה פי קצת סבע סמואת ומלאיכה ופרורים ודיוים ולטבין וירורין בגיר אלעדד, '*Raza rabba*, on the history of the seven heavens, and angels, and *paror*s, and *dev*s, and no-good-ones and *yaror*s without number.' For this passage, see Mann, *Texts and Studies*, II, p. 82. Unfortunately, *Raza Rabba* is no longer extant, and Scholem's attempts to reconstruct it from Ashkenazi citations of a Hebrew book with a similar name (see Scholem, *Origins of the Kabbalah*, pp. 106–123) were not successful. That we have yet to find this book only shows how little we really know about the Jewish magical texts of late-antique Babylonia and how much room is left for further research.

at each of these more closely and assess the evidence for its possible provenance.

(a) *Ḥarba deMoshe*

One obvious, but problematic, starting point for our quest is the *Ḥarba deMoshe* (The Sword of Moses). Since the text is first mentioned by Hai Gaon in his famous responsum on the uses of divine names, written ca. 1000 CE, we may perhaps assume that this is a Babylonian Jewish text, going back a few centuries before Hai's own time.[63] But the *Ḥarba deMoshe* is only preserved in very late manuscripts that clearly are corrupt, with only a few earlier Geniza fragments, covering only a part of the text.[64] As we now have it, the text of the *Ḥarba deMoshe* clearly presents some Babylonian components, but it also has some obviously Palestinian elements, including materials derived from the Greco-Egyptian magical tradition.[65] A close analysis of all the evidence has led Yuval Harari to conclude that the *Ḥarba deMoshe* combines both Palestinian and Babylonian elements and that its final redaction was in Palestine.[66] As with all such source-critical analyses, certainty on these issues is beyond our reach, but the fact that the *Ḥarba deMoshe* is not the most reliable witness for the study of Babylonian Jewish magic in late antiquity seems incontrovertible. We shall return to this issue below.

(b) *Havdala deRabbi Aqiba*

A somewhat less problematic example is provided by the *Havdala deRabbi Aqiba* (Rabbi Aqiba's *havdala*), a text that is modelled on the

63 For Hai's responsum, see Emanuel, *Newly Discovered*, pp. 124–146; the reference to the *Sword of Moses* and the citation of its *incipit* are on p. 131. The text of the *Sword of Moses* was first identified and edited by Moses Gaster, from a manuscript in his possession; and see Gaster, *Sword of Moses*.

64 For a newer edition, based on MS Sassoon 290, see Harari, *Ḥarba deMoshe*; for a recent translation, see idem, 'The Sword of Moses'; for the Geniza fragments, see idem, 'Geniza Fragments.'

65 For some pertinent examples, see Rohrbacher-Sticker, 'From Sense to Nonsense'; see further Bohak, *Ancient Jewish Magic*, pp. 175–179.

66 See Harari, *Ḥarba deMoshe*, pp. 52–53; idem, 'The Sword of Moses,' pp. 65–67.

standard rabbinic *havdala* ritual (intended symbolically to 'separate' the sacred from the profane at the end of the Sabbath) but transforms it into an apotropaic ritual to ward off demons, cure 'bound' (i.e., impotent) husbands, 'open the heart' (i.e., improve one's memory and learning abilities) and so on. It was edited from several manuscripts by Gershom Scholem, who published it with a detailed introduction and commentary.[67] Here, too, there is no doubt that some textual units go back to Babylonian Jewish magic, including long lists of demons known to us exclusively from the Babylonian incantation bowls and clearly Mesopotamian in origin, and one first-person *historiola* that clearly belongs in the world of the Babylonian incantation bowls and finds partial parallels in some of the published ones.[68] But the *Havdala deRabbi Aqiba* also includes many Hebrew sections that display no clear affinity with what we find in the bowls, and it is not clear that the whole composition is of a Babylonian origin or a late-antique date. Scholem noted some of the Babylonian elements and argued for either a Babylonian or a south Italian origin of the final text, and for a date in the Gaonic period.[69] But he also stressed that this text seems to have been assembled from several different sources and that some of its adjurations display the impact of the Greco-Egyptian magical tradition.[70] Hannu Juusola offered a more detailed linguistic analysis and concluded that the text presents both 'Eastern' and 'Western' features, and that, like the *Ḥarba deMoshe*, it, too, must have had a complex redaction history.[71] Thus, both the contents and the language argue for a Babylonian origin for parts of this text, but probably not for all of it; that it is only rarely found among the Geniza fragments might provide further support for the assumption of a Babylonian-Jewish origin, but it could also support

67 Scholem, 'Havdala.'

68 For the long list of demons' names, see *ibid.*, pp. 258–262 (= pp. 160–164 of the revised reprint), and Scholem's numerous references in his commentary to the appearance of many of these demons in the Babylonian incantation bowls. For the *historiola*, see *ibid.*, pp. 262–265 (= pp. 164–167) (for the partial parallels, see BM 135563, edited in Segal, *Catalogue*, as 049A, and re-edited in Morgenstern, 'Notes'), and cf. the 'Enochic' *historiola* in pp. 270–272 (= pp. 171–173).

69 For Scholem's view of the text's likely origins, see *ibid.*, pp 245–246 (= p. 148).

70 See, for example, *ibid.*, pp. 252 (= p. 154) and 267 (= p. 168).

71 Juusola, 'Notes on the Aramaic Sections.'

a southern Italian origin, in accordance with Scholem's intuitive suggestion.[72] Thus, we find ourselves once again, as in the case of the *Ḥarba deMoshe*, with a text that preserves some elements of late-antique Babylonian Jewish magic but probably does not stem in its entirety from that geographical and historical context.

(c) Pishra deRabbi Ḥanina ben Dosa

If both the *Ḥarba deMoshe* and the *Havdala deRabbi Aqiba* leave us wishing for more conclusive results, the *Pishra deRabbi Ḥanina ben Dosa* (The Spell-loosener of R. Ḥanina ben Dosa), an anti-witchcraft spell that is about two or three pages long, seems much less problematic.[73] This text, which has been edited only once, from a faulty manuscript, is surprisingly well attested; it is found in at least nine Geniza fragments and in quite a few later manuscripts, including some twentieth-century amulets.[74] The late-antique Babylonian origin of this text is made quite clear not only by its Babylonian Aramaic dialect, but also by the fact that it continues in a tradition of much older Babylonian anti-witchcraft rituals (especially some of the features of the Maqlû texts) and 'Judaizes' them by turning the gods' names into angel names. The Babylonian nature of this text is further highlighted by the list of demons and dangers with which it opens, which closely resembles those of the magic bowls; by the close parallel between its closing formula and a formula used in circumcision rituals in Babylonian Jewish prayer books (*siddurim*); and by the close parallel between one of its adjura-

72 The only securely identifiable Geniza fragment of the *Havdala deRabbi Aqiba* of which I am currently aware is T-S NS 326.51; for other possible fragments, see Schäfer, *Geniza-Fragmente*, G16 (=T-S NS 322.21) and G18 (= Bodleian Heb. e 107.10). For a find that could modify our view of the *Havdala*, but might be a modern forgery, see Hamilton, 'A New Hebrew-Aramaic Incantation,' with Bohak, *Ancient Jewish Magic*, p. 158.

73 For a brief introduction to the *Pishra*, see Bohak, 'Pishra.'

74 See Michelini Tocci, 'Note e documenti,' pp. 101–106. For a published Geniza fragment, see Schäfer and Shaked, *Magische Texte*, II, no. 22 (= T-S K 1.144 + T-S K 21.95T + T-S K 21.95P), 1a/1–1b/9. For a fifteenth-century manuscript, see NYPL 190 (on which more below), in Bohak, *A Fifteenth-Century Manuscript*, I, pp. 229–231; II, pp. 187–189. For a twentieth-century amulet that utilizes the *Pishra* text, see Vukosavović, *Angels and Demons*, p. 126.

tions and a section of an Aramaic amulet from Afghanistan.[75] As far as I can see, its text remained remarkably stable throughout its long transmission history and bears no clear marks of later, medieval interpolations.

Like the vast majority of the incantation bowls, the *Pishra*, too, is an apotropaic, anti-witchcraft spell, and most of its contents are rather repetitive, consisting mainly of the names of the respective angels who would loosen an aggressive magic act performed against the spell's potential user on each day of the week, each day of the month and so on.[76] But one section also lists all the different types of aggressive magical acts that might have been performed against the potential user and thus gives us a glimpse of the world of aggressive magic in late-antique Babylonia, as known to the *Pishra*'s composers.[77] Of course, much of this aggressive magic may have been utilized by non-Jewish magicians and witches, and it thus is not necessarily relevant to the study of the aggressive magical texts and practices of the Jews of Sasanian Babylonia, but in at least one case we can probably show that an aggressive magical practice known to the composers of the *Pishra* was indeed used by Jews as well. It occurs in the section that says: ואם בחספא וסילוי עבדו ליה כיבמשיאל ישרי ויפשר ליה, 'And if with clay / potsherd and thorns they worked (witchcraft) upon him, Kivmashiel will release and loosen him.'[78] This is a rather vague reference, but it

75 I hope to deal with these issues at greater length elsewhere. For the amulet from Afghanistan (whose reading can be improved in light of this parallel), see Shaked, 'A Jewish Aramaic Amulet.' It must be noted, however, that the study of the *Pishra* is partly complicated by the fact that a text with similar logic is found on an unpublished amulet, deciphered by Joseph Naveh, Shaul Shaked and Ada Yardeni, which clearly is of Palestinian Jewish origins.

76 This list of angelic names enjoyed a life of its own in later Jewish magic, and appears, for example, in MS New York JTSA 8114 (IMHM F 11305), part 2, fols. 4v–6r.

77 Such listings sometimes appear in the bowls, too. See the brief discussions in Morony, 'Magic and Society,' pp. 99–100, and Levene, *Jewish Aramaic Curse Texts*, pp. 12–16. A full survey of such listings in all the published bowls and their comparison with those of the *Pishra* remains a scholarly desideratum.

78 I cite the text from MS NYPL 190 (on which more below), in Bohak, *A Fifteenth-Century Manuscript*, I, p. 229; and II, p. 187. All the other copies of the text I examined differ only with regard to the angel's exact name, which is irrelevant to the present discussion.

is tempting to compare it with the detailed instructions provided by the *Ḥarba deMoshe* in one of its aggressive magical recipes:

> אם בעית למקטל אינש סב טינא מן תרי כיפי נהרא ועביד צלמא וכת׳ עליה שמיה וסב ז׳ סלוין מן דיקלא צויא ועביד קשתא דחוסקניאתא במיני דסוסיא ואחית צלמתא בגו צרתא ומתח צלוי בקשתא ושדי בה ואמור על כל סלוא מן אקדתס ועד פרסוסי יתחבל פ׳ב׳פ׳ וי׳ת׳ד׳ מ׳נ׳ך׳.

> If you wish to kill a person, take mud from the two banks of the river and make a figurine and write his name on it. And take seven thorns from a withered date palm and make a bow of *huskaniata* wood and strands of horse hair and put the figurine in a cloth bag and stretch the thorns in the bow and shoot it (the figurine) and say over every thorn from *'QTDS* until *PRSWSY* may N, son of N, be injured, and he will be removed from you.[79]

The preparation of mimetic figurines (what we might call 'voodoo dolls') to represent the aggressive ritual's intended victims is, of course, an almost universal practice, but the instruction to take mud from the two banks of the river is far from common and finds a close parallel in older Babylonian magical praxis.[80] And the use of palm-thorns (סילוי) as arrows with which to shoot the clay figurine is also very specific and fits extremely well with the *Pishra*'s reference to an aggressive magical ritual carried out by means of clay (חספא) and palm-thorns (סילוי). Thus, we seem to be seeing the same magical practice, or two close variants thereof, once from the aggressive side and once from the apotropaic side.

(d) Some Versions of Sefer haQevitsa

Sefer haqevitsa (the Book of gathering [of demons]) is a text, or a cluster of texts, written in Judeo-Arabic, Hebrew and Aramaic, whose aim is to gather demons to a certain place, to adjure them and thus to make

79 I cite the text from Harari, *Ḥarba deMoshe*, p. 42, and the translation from idem, 'The Sword of Moses,' p. 89, with minor modifications. The corrupt textual sequence ויתדמנך at the end of the recipe might be derived from דמך, in which case the translation would be: 'and he shall be laid low.'

80 See Geller, 'Mesopotamian Love Magic,' p. 132.

them subservient to the adjuring practitioner. Both the aim and the praxis involved, as well as the names of some of the demons adjured, point to a strong Arabic-Muslim influence on this body of texts.[81] And yet, the texts seem to incorporate some older materials, including demons who are known to us exclusively from the Babylonian Jewish magical tradition of late antiquity. Note, for example, the appearance, in one published Geniza fragment of this literature, of the demons שפטין ... וסטנין וברקו[תא] ופגעא ופלגא ודחלולי ימא ודחלו[לי] ליליא ... ורוחא דיתבא בליבא ... ורוח כומרי ורוח פתכרי ואסתרתא ... ולוטבין בישין ... מיני דנחוש ... מיני איגרי ... ומיני טולי ומיני דיקלי ... וכל זיקין ומזיקין and so on.[82] All these demons find clear parallels in the bowls (in some cases, in slightly different spellings), and their clustering here is far too thick to be a mere accident. Moreover, in another Geniza fragment the demons are adjured:

> ותבואו מארבע רוחות השמים ותביאו לי עמכם את המלכה ששמה ארגז בת קטט דיתבא על נהרות מיטרא[83] דפרת היא וכל חייליה ... שלא יקרא (!) אתכם מה שה יקרא[84] בגוגרום מדינתא אתר דמתקלין תמן כל שדין וכל רוחין באתון נורא יקידתא.
>
> And you shall come from the four directions and bring to me with you the queen whose name is Argaz daughter of Qaṭaṭ, who sits on the rivers ??? of the Euphrates, she and all her soldiers ... so that you will not suffer the same fate as what happened in the town GWGRWM,[85] the place where all demons and spirits are burnt in a furnace of blazing fire.[86]

The geographical reference to the Euphrates would not suffice to identify this text as building on older Babylonian materials, but the reference to

81 As was noted long ago by Scholem, 'Bilar'; and idem, 'Some Sources.'

82 Schäfer and Shaked, *Magische Texte*, II, no. 54 (= T-S NS 322.29), 1a/6–1b/11. Other published Geniza fragments of this text, such as *ibid.*, I, no. 6 (= T-S K 1.1) display no Babylonian features, and the same is true of many unpublished fragments.

83 In JTS 3513.11, the reading is מישרא.

84 Lege: מה שקרה.

85 Or, 'inside (בגו) the town GWRM.' I am grateful to James Nathan Ford for this suggestion.

86 T-S NS 307.6, with a parallel in JTS 3513.11. Parts of this text (but not those that interest us here) are paralleled in Schäfer and Shaked, *Magische Texte*, III, no. 66 (= T-S AS 142.15 + T-S NS 246.14), 1b/11–34.

the demoness ארגז בת קטט is extremely revealing. Not only is this type of personal name for a demon extremely common in Babylonian Jewish magic (including אגרת בת מחלת, mentioned in BT *Pesaḥim* 112b), but this specific name appears in two bowls, as ארגז בת קסס.[87] And while I have not yet been able to identify the town GWGRWM (or GWRM) and the story about the place where demons are burnt, I suspect that it is in the Babylonian incantation bowls, or in earlier Babylonian magical texts, that the answer to this crux shall be found.[88] Be this last point as it may, some older Babylonian Jewish sources seem to lurk behind at least some of the medieval *Qevitzah* texts, so popular among Jews in the Muslim but also in the Christian world from the Middle Ages onwards.

Looking at the results of the above enquiries, we may note that they are mixed. On the one hand, there is no doubt that the *Ḥarba deMoshe*, the *Havdala deRabbi Aqiba* and the *Pishra deRabbi Ḥanina ben Dosa* have at least some components that go back to Babylonian Jewish magic of the Sasanian period. In and of itself, this conclusion should suffice to convince us that late-antique Babylonian Jewish magic was not a dead-end street, and that the fact that the production of Aramaic magic bowls ceased some time in the seventh or eighth centuries does not mean that the Babylonian Jewish magical tradition completely died out at that time. On the contrary, we may conclude that there were many other forms of Jewish magical activity in Sasanian Babylonia, and that the instructions for some of these activities kept on being transmitted and were incorporated into texts such as the *Havdala*, the *Ḥarba* and the *Pishra*. We may even conclude that some of the longer spells inscribed upon the bowls kept on being transmitted even after such bowls were

87 See Gordon, 'Aramaic and Mandaic Magical Bowls,' Bowl H (p. 87), l. 8; Shaked, Ford and Bhayro, *Aramaic Bowl Spells*, JBA 55 (=MS 1928/1), l. 3. Another female demon who seems to re-emerge in later Jewish traditions is Buznai, daughter of Zanai Lilith, who is found in some bowls (see especially Müller-Kessler, 'The Story of Bguzan-Lilit'), and who appears in a midrashic text in T-S C 1.3 (ed. Ginzburg, 'Hagadot qetu'ot,' pp. 66–67) as פיזנא and as אפיזנא בת פיזנאי לילית, as was first noted by Shaked, 'Popular Religion,' p. 112.

88 For an illuminating parallel, see bowl MS 1927/9, ll. 5–6: שבילכי אם לא תשני אירמי יתיכי לחצקר חצב גובא אתר דירמן שידייא כולהון, 'If you do not change your path, I will cast you into HẒQR HẒB, the pit, the place (into which) all demons are cast.' The text was published in Shaked, 'Form and Purpose,' p. 27, and the reading was corrected by Matthew Morgenstern. I am grateful to James Nathan Ford for bringing this parallel to my attention.

no longer being produced, and several spells probably were woven into the *Havdala deRabbi Aqiba*. As we shall soon see, this conclusion gains much support from the evidence provided by individual recipes transmitted in medieval and later Jewish magic.

Jewish Magical Recipes of Mesopotamian Provenance

When we move from the rather limited inventory of longer Jewish magical texts to the thousands of Jewish magical recipes preserved individually or in larger compendia in hundreds of Geniza fragments and non-Geniza manuscripts, we find ourselves in a similar situation as before. On the one hand, some of these magical recipes may securely be attributed to late-antique Palestine, while others are demonstrably medieval in origin and often borrowed from Muslim or Christian sources.[89] On the other hand, a vast majority of the relevant recipes are quite 'timeless' in nature, and it is difficult to ascribe them to specific chronological or geographical places of origin. Thus, the search for magical recipes whose ultimate origins lie in late-antique Babylonia is tantamount to searching for a few needles in the proverbial haystack. And yet, such needles may be identified, as we shall see from the following few examples.

(a) The first example is perhaps the clearest evidence currently available for the continuous transmission of the spells found in Aramaic magic bowls.[90] It is found in a Geniza fragment, HUC 1029, probably dating to the twelfth century, where we find traces of two magical recipes, one of which is formulated as a *get* (a deed of divorce) for the demoness Lilith. Not only is the practice of writing deeds of divorce for the demons extremely popular in Babylonian Aramaic bowls (and even in some Syriac and Mandaic bowls), but the text of the Geniza fragment closely parallels one of the commonest variants of the divorce deed found on the bowls.[91] In this case, there is no doubt that the medieval recipe is directly based on a spell originating in Sasanian Babylonia, but it also

89 And see above, notes 58–60.
90 For a fuller discussion of this example, see Levene and Bohak, 'Divorcing Lilith.'
91 In addition to the bowls cited in the paper mentioned in the previous note, we may now note this spell's appearance in Shaked, Ford and Bhayro, *Aramaic*

seems quite clear that this spell was not very popular in the Middle Ages, since this is the only Geniza fragment of which I am aware that preserves it, and I have not yet found it in any non-Geniza manuscripts of Jewish magic.

To this example of direct continuity, one or two more examples may be added of long spells that appear both in unpublished bowls and in published magical texts from the Cairo Geniza.[92] In addition, several other published Geniza magical spells and recipes have some parallels in the bowls or are likely to be of late-antique Babylonian origins.[93] Surveying all these fragments would be out of the question here, but the number of potential candidates is quite small, making it clear that most of the published magical recipes from the Cairo Geniza are not likely to be of a Babylonian Jewish origin.

(b) Turning from the published Geniza magical texts to the unpublished ones, we find ourselves in a similar situation, with only a few recipes that are likely to be of a Babylonian Jewish origin. One such case is T-S Misc. 34.22, a parchment bifolium inscribed in several different hands, all dated by Edna Engel to the tenth century. It contains a Judeo-Arabic commentary on Deuteronomy 2 and 3, an elaborate drawing of a menorah, labelled מנרת שפטים, and – on a page probably left blank in the original manuscript – two magical recipes:

לאהבה בשם גבריאל ומיכאל ורפאל וח?[סדיאל? ו...] / אתון ה׳ מלאכין דימממניין
על גנין[94] ו... / [ ]ומזומן לה בהיך אסא ב׳א׳ל׳ה׳א׳ רב?. דבר ... א? / וחזוא

Bowl Spells, JBA 15 (MS 1927/43), 19 (MS 2053/132), 24 (MS 2053/251) and 62 (MS 2053/242).

92 These examples are studied in a forthcoming publication by James Nathan Ford.

93 See Kwasman, 'Demon of the Roof,' for a cluster of Babylonian demons found in a recipe in Schäfer and Shaked, *Magische Texte*, I, no. 2 (= T-S K 1.56) and *ibid.*, no. 20 (= T-S K 1.147). Another published Geniza fragment that is likely to preserve magical recipes of Babylonian-Jewish origin is Mosseri Ia 26.2 (published by Goitein and Friedman, *Abraham ben Yijû*, pp. 418–421), a collection of magical recipes apparently copied by Abraham ben Yijû in Aden; recipe no. 4 contains an interesting first-person *historiola*, and a reference to דנהש, who is probably identical with דנחיש, for whom see Shaked, 'Bagdâna,' pp. 520–522, and Müller-Kessler, 'Dan(ḥ)iš.' See also Shaked, 'An Early Geniza Fragment,' for a fragment that is unique and therefore harder to classify.

94 Lege: גנון.

לפ׳ב׳פ׳ תשתחן ותשתגר ותשבב נשגי ממללה / בפומה ולישנה ביני ספוותה תפול פ׳ב׳פ׳ תחות / פ׳ב׳פ׳ כיטינא תחות עבדיה כי בסתרקיך תחות גבׄרא / מ?ריה בשם אה אה יה וה יה קדוש קדוש יי׳ צב׳ / מל׳ כל הא כבודו שריר וקיים קי׳[95] ג׳ טאס?י[96] דאסא / וזמניה על שמה ואמור על כל חד וחד ז׳ זמ׳ והב לה ת.[97]

שילוח אש אנה גולגלתא אנא גלגולתא כ?ם ו?הנ?ם / כם והנם אנא והנם אנה והנם אשבע לכי ו?מ?נ?א? לכי? / .ד רום סטנא בישא דיתיב על תלת מאה ושיתין סטנִין/ איזיל ואפיל אש על פ׳ב׳פ׳ אימ׳ ולליתה יקיד ולא / יתטפי מיניה עד דאנה אצבי ויהי העם כמת[אוננים] / כוליה כ׳ת׳ על ביעתא ברת יומא וקבר על / בביה.

For love:[98] In the name of Gabriel and Michael and Raphael and H[asdiel? and ...], you five angels who are appointed over (the) bridal chamber and ???, and is prepared for her by this by this[99] myrtle, by the great God who created (?) [charm?] and grace to NN, may she be inflamed, heated up and enkindled, may her speech become confused in her mouth, and her tongue (become confused) between her lips, may NN fall under NN like clay under its worker, like a mattress[100] under the hero, its master. In the name of ’H ’H YH WH YH ‘Holy holy holy the Lord of Hosts, the whole earth is filled with his Glory’ (Isa 6:3). Firm and established. Take (?) three leaves (?) of myrtle and prepare it (i.e., them) on her name, and say on each one seven times and give her. The End.

(For) sending fire:[101] I, skull,[102] I, skull, KM WHNM KM WHNM ’N’ WHNM ’NH WHNM, I adjure you and I beswear you, D RWM the evil Satan, who sits upon three hundred and sixty Satans. Go and let fall upon NN a fire, burning by night and day, and it shall

95 Lege: קח?; in any case, the meaning should be ‘take.’
96 Lege: טרפי? Or maybe טאסי, ‘foils’ → ‘leaves’?
97 Perhaps תם or תמת.
98 For Jewish erotic magic, see Saar, *Jewish Love Magic*.
99 The duplication is probably a result of scribal dittography.
100 For the Persian loanword ביסתרקא, ‘bedding, mattress, carpet’, see Sokoloff, *Dictionary*, p. 204.
101 This type of aggressive action of sending fire or fever against someone is extremely common; see, for example, Naveh and Shaked, *Magic Spells and Formulae*, G16 (= T-S K 1.91 + K 1.117), p. 7, l. 1; Schäfer and Shaked, *Magische Texte*, III, no. 56 (= T-S Ar. 44.26), 1b/3; *ibid.*, no. 60 (= T-S K 1.120), 1a/4, 10.
102 For the use of human skulls in late-antique Jewish magic, see Levene, ‘Calvariae Magicae.’

not be extinguished from him until I desire (so). 'And the people com[plained]' (Num 11:1) in its entirety. Write (all this) on a day-old egg and bury it at his gate.

Several factors argue for a Babylonian Jewish origin of these two recipes. In the first recipe, in addition to some Babylonian Aramaic forms such as נשגי, the separation of the preposition כי from the subsequent noun (כי בסתרקיך) and the Persian loanword בסתרקיך, 'mattress,' we may note that the formula תשתחן ותשתגר ותשבב is closely paralleled in one of the erotic bowls published by Montgomery.[103] Another formula, נשגי ממללה בפומה ולישנה ביני ספוותה, is partly paralleled in a bowl published by Shaked, where the damages caused by the spirit that afflicts the poor targets include ומשגשא לישנה בפומה, 'and it confuses her tongue in her mouth.'[104] And in the second recipe, the spell is partly paralleled by a similar formula found in the Damascus magical recipe book to which we shall soon turn.[105] All this does not amount to a clear proof of a Babylonian Jewish origin, but it certainly makes such an origin very plausible.

To this example, several others may be added of unpublished Geniza magical spells and recipes that display some sign of a Babylonian Jewish origin.[106] And yet, the total number of such recipes seems

103 See Montgomery, *Aramaic Incantation Texts*, Bowl 28, ll. 1–2 (p. 213): לשמיה דאנור .. בר פרכוי דנישתיחן ונישתגר ונישתבב בתר אחת בת נבאזך (Montgomery reads the second verb as ונישתנר). A similar but much longer series of verbs appears in an unpublished Geniza fragment, JTS 3320.7. For other parallels, see Levene, *Jewish Aramaic Curse Texts*, p. 85 (VA 2492), ll. 2–3: נישחנוניה ונישבבניה ונירדוניה ונישגרוניה, and cf. *ibid*., p. 118 (039A), l. 13, and p. 81 (VA 3381), l. 16.

104 See Shaked, 'Peace Be upon You,' p. 207 (Bowl M1, ll. 11–12).

105 See below, note 107. The spell there reads גולגולתא גפנם וני?סגף / א?שבעית עלך נורדפיס סטנא דתיזיל / [ות]פ?יל אשתא על פ׳ב׳פ׳, 'Skull, GPNM WNYSGP, I have adjured you, NWRDPYS the satan, that you shall go and cast fire upon NN.'

106 I note, for example, T-S K 1.67, where one finds the sequence ויתנצל מן נחי..א ומן ממללתה / ומן כל חרשין בישין ועובדין / תקיפין ומן רוחי בישתה וחומרי / זנייתה, 'and he shall be saved from ??? and from (evil) words and from all evil sorceries and powerful (magical) actions, and from evil spirits and fornicating (or זידניתה, 'evil,' which is the common formula in the bowls) amulet spirits.' This amulet was written for Nûmeir bar Qûbîha, the same individual for whom the spell in T-S K 1.26 (Schäfer and Shaked, *Magische Texte*, II, no. 45) was written – a spell which, as noted by James Nathan Ford, also displays clear parallels with the bowls. T-S Misc. 10.90 bears the title (written

exceedingly small, given the large number of magical texts from the Cairo Geniza, and the presence there not only of magical spells and recipes whose late-antique Palestinian provenance is quite clear, but even of a Babylonian Jewish text like the *Pishra deRabbi Ḥanina ben Dosa*.

(c) From the Cairo Geniza we may turn to a very curious find, namely, a booklet with magical recipes, possibly dating to the eleventh century, found by Bruno Violet in the Geniza of the famous Mosque in Damascus.[107] In this case, both the Aramaic dialect and some of the specific parallels with the bowls argue for a Babylonian Jewish origin, and the Damascene provenance of the booklet itself certainly could support such a hypothesis. Moreover, very little in this booklet is derived from or influenced by the Greco-Egyptian magical tradition or by Christian or Muslim magic. Thus, while there is no way of accurately measuring the 'antiquity' or 'Babylonian-ness' of each of its recipes, we seem to have here a good starting point for the study of Babylonian Jewish magic as it survived, and was perhaps also modified, in the Early Islamic period, in a region not far removed from Babylonia.[108] What is perhaps most interesting about this find is that the booklet's magical recipes have few clear parallels among the many thousands of magical recipes found in the Cairo Geniza or in non-Geniza manuscripts, which might show that while the Babylonian Jewish magical tradition survived the Muslim conquest, its remains kept on fading into oblivion in subsequent centuries, apart from the few exceptions surveyed here.

(d) From the Jewish Geniza of Cairo and the Muslim Geniza of Damascus we move to non-Geniza manuscripts of Jewish magical recipes – that is, to manuscripts that normally do not date from before the thirteenth or fourteenth centuries. This vast field has never even been

in a strange script!) קמיעות מבחנות מבבל, 'tested amulets from Babylonia,' but the recipes themselves do not seem particularly Babylonian. JTS 3753.9–10 has an interesting *historiola* about Mt. Hermon and a demon, which might be of Babylonian Jewish origin.

107 See Bohak and Morgenstern, 'A Babylonian Jewish Aramaic Booklet.'

108 One obvious modification is the translation of some of the instructions, which must originally have been written in Aramaic, into Judeo-Arabic, a phenomenon that is extremely well attested in the magical recipe books from the Cairo Geniza as well.

charted, let alone studied in greater depth.[109] I therefore limit myself to a single manuscript that I know well: NYPL 190 (formerly Sassoon 56), a fifteenth-century compendium of magic and Kabbalah produced in an unknown location (but certainly somewhere in the Arabic-speaking world), of which I have prepared a complete critical edition.[110] In this manuscript, recipe no. 124 ('For the evil eye') on pp. 111–112 displays clear signs of the Babylonian Jewish origins of at least some of its components, the clearest of which is the following formula:

> אשבעית עליכון כל חרשין בישין וכל / עובדין תקיפין בשם סלגס סליגס אדרקס אדריקס נקיקיאל קבניאל / אתון מלאכיא קדישיא דממנן על חרשין בישין ועל עובדין תקיפין / ובישין עבידו לפ׳ בן פ׳ פשרתא ואסותא אם חרשי יהודאי עבידו לה / פשרו[111] ופשרו לה אם חרשי ארמאי עבידו לה פשרו ופשרו לה אם חרשי / טיאעי עבידו לה פשרו ופשרו לה אם חרשי פרסאי עבדו לה פשרו ופשרו / לה ואם במיא ובמילחא צתרי במיכלא ובמשתיא וכל לבושא וכסויא וכל / מדעם מאית בעלמא עבדו לה פשרו ופשרו ותהא ליה אסותא א׳א׳א׳ סלה.

> I adjure you, all evil sorceries and all powerful (magical) deeds, in the name of SLGS SLYGS 'DRQS 'DRYQS NQYQY'L QBNY'L, you holy angels who are appointed over evil sorceries and powerful and evil (magical) acts, accomplish for NN a spell-loosening and a healing. If Jewish sorcerers performed (witchcraft) upon him, loosen[112] and loosen him; if Aramean sorcerers performed (witchcraft) upon him, loosen and loosen him; if Ṭayya'ei sorcerers performed (witchcraft) upon him, loosen and loosen him; if Persian sorcerers performed (witchcraft) upon him, loosen and loosen him. And if with water and salt ??? in food or drink and any garment and covering and any dead thing in the world they performed (witchcraft) upon him, loosen and loosen (him), and may there be health for him, A(men) A(men) A(men) Sela.[113]

109 For some useful starting points, see Trachtenberg, *Jewish Magic and Superstition*; Benayahu, '*Shoshan yesod ha'olam*'; Scholem, *Kabbalah*, pp. 182–189; and Harari, 'Jewish Magic.'

110 See Bohak, *A Fifteenth-Century Manuscript*.

111 Here and in what follows, the original formula must have been שרו ופשרו ליה.

112 The original text must have read 'release and loosen him' – see the previous note.

113 NYPL 190, in Bohak, *A Fifteenth-Century Manuscript*, I, pp. 155–156; II, p. 112, ll. 19–26.

Three different arguments may be adduced to support the late-antique Babylonian Jewish origins of this spell. The first is that the last section closely resembles in its logic and phraseology the *Pishra deRabbi Ḥanina ben Dosa*, even if the specific aggressive magical activities mentioned here are not mentioned in the *Pishra*. The second is the geographical and chronological logic of the references to Jews, Arameans (which may mean nothing more than 'Gentiles'), Persians and Ṭayya'ans (i.e., pre-Muslim Arab tribesmen), the latter being well known from the Babylonian Talmud. Clearly, whoever composed this spell lived in a time and place where Persians and pre-Islamic Mesopotamian Arabs were the Jews' close neighbors.

But the third and most conclusive argument is that this very formula is attested on one of the Babylonian incantation bowls, where it reads:

> ויבטלון ... חרשין / ארמאין חרשין יהודאין חרשין טיאעין חרשין פרסאין חרשין
> הינדואין חרשין יונאין חרשין די כיתין חרשין / דמיתעבדין בשבעין לישנין.
>
> And there shall be annulled ... Aramean sorceries, Jewish sorceries, Ṭayya'an sorceries, Persian sorceries, Indian sorceries, Greek sorceries, Roman sorceries, sorceries that are performed in (each of the) seventy languages.[114]

The identity between the two spells is quite clear, and the fact that almost a full millennium separates the Aramaic bowl and the manuscript with magical recipes written in the 1460s by a certain Moses, son of Jacob and Marḥaba, proves that at least some Babylonian Jewish magical spells kept on being transmitted even long after the incantation bowls were no longer produced. Unfortunately, it is not easy to tell how much of the fifteenth-century recipe goes back to late-antique Babylonia, but an examination of its other components, and the reconstruction of some unpublished Geniza parallels to them, will no doubt shed more light on this issue. It is also impossible to say whether the fact that this is an Oriental manuscript, produced by an Arabic-speaking Jew who may have lived in or come from one of the large cities of present-day Syria or Iraq, makes it more likely that its producer came across magical

114 See Gordon, 'Aramaic Magical Bowls,' bowl D (p. 328), l. 9. In the original publication, Gordon read טיאעין as שיאעין, 'Shiites,' but he corrected his mistake in idem, 'Aramaic and Mandaic Magical Bowls,' p. 106.

formulae whose origins lie in Sasanian Babylonia. Only after much further research, and detailed studies of many other manuscripts, will the answers to such questions become somewhat clearer.

Conclusions and Desiderata

Having searched for the remains of late-antique Babylonian Jewish magic in several different textual corpora, I may now offer some broader conclusions and note in which areas more research is still needed. First and foremost, we may safely assert that even when all the above-mentioned criteria are used, and the relevant texts are isolated from the vast corpus of medieval and later Jewish magical texts, we would still face a body of sources that suffers from two disadvantages vis-à-vis the bowls. On the one hand, for most of these texts we can never be absolutely sure that they are late-antique and Babylonian in origin, unless we find detailed parallels in thc bowls themselves. Moreover, we can never assume that they present the text in its 'pure' form, whatever that might mean, for we are dealing only with much later copies of copies of whatever original texts may have been in circulation in Sasanian Babylonia.

Going into greater detail, we may note the need for a fuller assessment of the relationship between Babylonian Jewish magic as reflected in the bowls and that reflected in the Babylonian Talmud. To offer such an assessment, we must not only gather all the textual parallels between these two corpora, but also analyze the function and context of each of these parallel units in the bowls on the one hand and in the Talmud on the other. Moreover, we must note especially those areas where the Babylonian Talmud helps us study those facets of ancient Babylonian Jewish magic that are not well represented by the bowls, in order to arrive at a more balanced view of what late-antique Babylonian Jewish magic may have looked like.

A second conclusion that emerges from our survey is that magical texts such as the *Havdala deRabbi Aqiba* or the *Pishra deRabbi Ḥanina ben Dosa* often are easier to identify as Babylonian in origin than individual magical recipes. The reason for this is that such texts were often seen by their copyists as complete units and thus enjoyed a certain degree of textual stability (as may be seen, for example, in the different manuscripts of the *Pishra*), whereas individual recipes were often translated, abridged, simplified or modified in other ways. Thus, the more often a recipe was copied, the less likely it was to retain its original wording and therefore also the markers of its ultimate origins. In this regard, one may note another scholarly desideratum: the re-edition of the *Pishra deRabbi Ḥanina ben Dosa*, and perhaps also of *Sefer hayashar* and *Sefer hamalbush*, in light of new textual evidence, especially from the Cairo Geniza. To this may be added the renewed search for the long-lost *Raza rabba*, which must have enjoyed some circulation in the ninth and tenth centuries, after which it seems to have vanished.

A third conclusion that emerges from our survey is that the bowls' limited spheres of interest inadvertently limit our ability to look for Jewish Babylonian magic in other textual corpora as well. As we saw, when we compile a list of 'textual markers' that are specific to the Babylonian incantation bowls, this list ends up containing mostly the names and classes of the different demons of Sasanian Babylonia. Thus, when we look in later Jewish magical texts, a list of demons found in the *Havdala*, or a specific female demon found in *Sefer haqevitsa*, or a *get* against demons in a fragment from the Cairo Geniza may all securely be identified as building on earlier Babylonian sources. But when we look at erotic and aggressive magical texts from the Cairo Geniza, we find that they have very few precedents among the incantation bowls, and we can therefore point to very few specifically Babylonian 'textual markers.' And, the fewer the comparanda, the less secure we must remain about these recipes' place in the Babylonian Jewish magical tradition, leaving us trapped in a vicious circle, like demons trapped in a bowl.

What all this means is that with the sources currently at our disposal, we are not likely to have a large body of non-bowl texts that can securely be used as evidence for late-antique Babylonian Jewish magic. As noted at the outset, the enormous advantage of the bowls is that they come from Mesopotamia and that they are late-antique objects; none of the other sources at our disposal can be used 'as is' as evidence for late-antique Babylonian Jewish magic, and some of it can only tentatively be classified as Babylonian. At the same time, the fact that we have some non-bowl texts that can securely be seen as later copies and reworkings of Jewish magical texts of Babylonian Jewish origin, and that each of these texts reached us through different channels of transmission, leaves some room for optimism. Once more such sources are identified, published and analyzed, and with the ever-growing corpus of incantation bowls at our disposal, we will be on a much surer footing in our study of late-antique Babylonian Jewish magic.[115]

References

Abousamra, Gaby. 'Une nouvelle coupe magique Araméenne,' in J.-M. Durand and A. Jacquet (eds.), *Magie et divination dans les cultures de l'Orient: Actes du colloque organisé par l'Institut du Proche-Orient Ancien du Collège de France, la Société Asiatique et le CNRS (UMR 7192), les 19 et 20 juin 2008* (Cahiers de l'Institut du Proche-Orient Ancien du Collège de France, 3), Paris: Maisonneuve, 2010, pp. 109–121.

Abousamra, Gaby, and André Lemaire. 'Bol magique avec inscription araméenne,' *Semitica*, 58 (2016), pp. 247–255.

Alexander, Philip S. '*Sefer ha-Razim* and the Problem of Black Magic in Early Judaism,' in Todd Klutz (ed.), *Magic in the Biblical World: From the Rod of Aaron to the Ring of Solomon* (*Journal for the Study of the New Testament* [*JSNT*], Suppl. 245), London: T & T Clark, 2003, pp. 170–190.

Baker, Colin F., and Meira Polliack. *Arabic and Judaeo-Arabic Manuscripts in the Cambridge Genizah Collections: Arabic Old Series (T-S Ar. 1a-54)*, Cambridge: Cambridge University Press, 2001.

Bar-Ilan, Meir. 'Between Magic and Religion: Sympathetic Magic in the World of the Sages of the Mishnah and Talmud,' *Review of Rabbinic Judaism*, 5 (2002), pp. 383–399.

Barel, Gabriel. 'Rav-Pe'alim: Un manuel de médicine populaire de Maroc,' in Issachar Ben-Ami (ed.), *Recherches sur la culture des Juifs d'Afrique du Nord*, Jerusalem: Communauté Israelite Nord-Africaine, 1991, pp. 211–232 (Hebrew).

Baron, Salo W. *A Social and Religious History of the Jews*, I–XVIII, New York: Columbia University Press, 2nd ed., 1952–1983.

115 I am grateful to James Nathan Ford, Marco Moriggi and Ortal-Paz Saar for their many helpful comments on an earlier version of this paper.

Benayahu, Meir. 'The Book *Shoshan yesod ha'olam* by Rabbi Yoseph Tirshom,' in I. Weinstock (ed.), *Temirin*, I, Jerusalem: Mosad Harav Kook, 1972, pp. 187–269 (Hebrew).

Bhayro, Siam. 'An Aramaic Magic Bowl for Fertility and Success in Childbirth: Lisboa, Museu da Farmácia (Lisbon, Pharmacy Museum), Inv. No. 10895,' *Aramaic Studies*, 15 (2017), pp. 106–111.

—. 'Divorcing a Demon: Incantation Bowls and BT Giṭṭin 85b,' in Markham J. Geller (ed.), *The Archaeology and Material Culture of the Babylonian Talmud* (IJS Studies in Judaica, 16), Leiden: Brill, 2015, pp. 121–132.

—. 'The Reception of Mesopotamian and Early Jewish Traditions in the Aramaic Incantation Bowls,' *Aramaic Studies*, 11 (2013), pp. 187–196.

Bhayro, Siam, James Nathan Ford, Dan Levene and Ortal-Paz Saar. *Aramaic Magic Bowls in the Vorderasiatisches Museum in Berlin: Descriptive List and Edition of Selected Texts* (Magical and Religious Literature of Late Antiquity, 7), Leiden: Brill, 2018.

Blau, Ludwig. *Das altjüdische Zauberwesen*, Strassbourg: Trubner, 1898 (repr. Cambridge: Cambridge University Press, 2010).

—. 'Amulet,' in Isidore Singer (ed.), *The Jewish Encyclopedia*, I, New York: Funk & Wagnalls, 1901, pp. 546–550.

Bohak, Gideon. *Ancient Jewish Magic: A History*, Cambridge: Cambridge University Press, 2008.

—. 'Babylonian Incantation Bowls: Past, Present and Future (on *A Corpus of Magic Bowls: Incantation Bowls in Jewish Aramaic from Late Antiquity*, by Dan Levene),' *Pe'amim* 105–106 (2005/6), pp. 253–265 (Hebrew).

—. 'Catching a Thief: The Jewish Trials of a Christian Ordeal,' *Jewish Studies Quarterly*, 13 (2006), pp. 344–362.

—. 'The *Charaktêres* in Ancient and Medieval Jewish Magic,' *Acta Classica Universitatis Scientiarum Debreceniensis*, 47 (2011), pp. 25–44.

—. 'Conceptualizing Demons in Late Antique Judaism,' in Siam Bhayro and Catherine Rider (eds.), *Demons and Illness from Antiquity to the Early-Modern Period* (Magical and Religious Literature of Late Antiquity, 5), Leiden: Brill, 2017, pp. 111–133.

—. 'Dangerous Books: The Hekhalot Texts as Physical Objects,' *Henoch*, 39 (2017), pp. 306–324.

—. *A Fifteenth-Century Manuscript of Jewish Magic: MS New York Public Library, Heb. 190 (formerly Sassoon 56)*, Los Angeles: Cherub Press, 2014 (Hebrew).

—. 'The Jewish Magical Tradition from Late Antique Palestine to the Cairo Genizah,' in Hannah M. Cotton, Robert G. Hoyland, Jonathan J. Price, and David J. Wasserstein (eds.), *From Hellenism to Islam: Cultural and Linguistic Change in the Roman Near East*, Cambridge: Cambridge University Press, 2009, pp. 324–339.

—. 'The Magical Rotuli from the Cairo Genizah,' in Gideon Bohak, Yuval Harari, and Shaul Shaked (eds.), *Continuity and Innovation in the Magical Tradition* (Jerusalem Studies in Religion and Culture, 15), Leiden: Brill, 2011, pp. 321–340.

—. 'Observations on the Transmission of Hekhalot Literature in the Cairo Genizah,' in Ra'anan S. Boustan, Martha Himmelfarb, and Peter Schäfer (eds.), *Hekhalot Literature in Context: From Byzantium to Babylonia* (Texts and Studies in Ancient Judaism [henceforth: TSAJ], 153]), Tübingen: Mohr Siebeck, 2013, pp. 213–229.

—. 'Pishra de-Rabbi Hanina ben Dosa,' in Roger Bagnall, Kai Brodersen, Craige B. Champion, Andrew Erskine, and Sabine R. Huebner (eds.), *The Encyclopedia of Ancient History*, Chichester: Wiley-Blackwell, 2013, IX, p. 5337.

—. 'Rabbanite Magical Texts in Karaite Manuscripts,' *Karaite Archives*, 1 (2013), pp. 17–34.

Bohak, Gideon, and Matthew Morgenstern. 'A Babylonian Jewish Aramaic Magical Booklet from the Damascus Genizah,' *Ginzei Qedem*, 10 (2014), pp. 9*–44*.

Boustan, Ra'anan S. 'The Study of Heikhalot Literature: Between Mystical Experience and Textual Artifact,' *Currents in Biblical Research*, 6 (2007), pp. 130–160.

Burnett, Charles, and Gideon Bohak. 'A Judaeo-Arabic Version of Ṯābit ibn Qurra's *De Imaginibus* and Psuedo-Ptolemy's *Opus Imaginum*,' in Felicitas Opwis and David Reisman (eds.), *Islamic Philosophy, Science, Culture, and Religion: Studies in Honor of Dimitri Gutas*, Leiden: Brill, 2012, pp. 179–200.

Cohen-Alorro, Dorit. 'Magic and Sorcery in the Zohar,' Ph.D. Dissertation, The Hebrew University of Jerusalem, 1989 (Hebrew).

Cook, E.M. 'An Aramaic Incantation Bowl from Khafaje,' *Bulletin of the American Schools of Oriental Research* (*BASOR*), 285 (1992), pp. 79–81.

Daiches, Samuel. *Babylonian Oil Magic in the Talmud and in the Later Jewish Literature*, London: Jews' College, 1913.

Elitzur-Leiman, Rivka. 'An Aramaic Amulet in the Collection of the Bible Lands Museum Jerusalem: A New Version of the Semamit Legend,' in Shmuel Ahituv, Israel Eph'al, Ada Yardeni, and Anat Mandel (eds.), *Joseph Naveh Volume* (Eretz Israel: Archaeological, Historical and Geographical Studies, 32), Jerusalem: Israel Exploration Society, 2016, pp. 4–10 (Hebrew).

Elman, Yaakov. 'Saffron, Spices, and Sorceresses: Magic Bowls and the Bavli,' in Kimberly B. Stratton and Dayna S. Kalleres (eds.), *Daughters of Hecate: Women and Magic in the Ancient World*, Oxford: Oxford University Press, 2014, pp. 365–385.

Emanuel, Simcha. *Newly Discovered Geonic Responsa*, Jerusalem–Cleveland: Ofeq Institute–Friedberg Library, 1995 (Hebrew).

Fain, Tatyana, James Nathan Ford and Alexey Lyavdansky. 'Aramaic Incantation Bowls at the State Hermitage Museum, St. Petersburg,' in L. Kogan, N. Koslova, S. Loesov and S. Tishchenko (eds.), *Babel und Bibel 9: Proceedings of the 6th Biennial Meeting of the International Association for Comparative Semitics and Other Studies*, Winona Lake, IN: Eisenbrauns, 2016, pp. 283–316.

Faraj, Ali H. *Coppe magiche dell'antico Iraq, con testi in aramaico giudaico di età ellenistica*, Milan: Lampi di Stampa, 2010.

—. 'An Incantation Bowl of Biblical Verses and a Syriac Incantation Bowl for the Protection of a House,' in Frederick Mario Fales and Giulia Francesca Grassi (eds.), *CAMSEMUD 2007: Proceedings of the 13th Italian Meeting of Afro-Asiatic Linguistics Held in Udine, May 21st–24th, 2007* (History of the Ancient Near East – Monographs, 10), Padua: S.A.R.G.O.N. Editrice e Libreria, 2010, pp. 205–212.

Faraj, Ali H., and Marco Moriggi. 'Two Incantation Bowls from the Iraq Museum (Baghdad),' *Orientalia*, 74 (2005), pp. 71–82.

Ford, James Nathan. 'The Ancient Mesopotamian Motif of *kidinnu*, "Divine Protection (of Temple Cities and Their Citizens)," in Akkadian and Aramaic Magic,' in Uri Gabbay and Shai Secunda (eds.), *Encounters by the Rivers of Babylon: Scholarly Conversations between Jews, Iranians and Babylonians in Antiquity* (TSAJ, 160), Tübingen: Mohr Siebeck, 2014.

—. 'New Light from Babylonia on the Story of Smamit,' in Shmuel Ahituv, Israel Eph'al, Ada Yardeni and Anat Mandel (eds.), *Joseph Naveh Volume* (Eretz Israel: Archaeological, Historical and Geographical Studies, 32), Jerusalem: Israel Exploration Society, 2016, pp. 149–161 (Hebrew).

—. 'A New Parallel to the Jewish Babylonian Aramaic Magic Bowl IM 76106 (Nippur 11 N 78),' *Aramaic Studies*, 9 (2011), pp. 249–277.

Ford, James Nathan, and Alon Ten-Ami. 'An Incantation Bowl for Rav Mešaršia son of Qaqay,' *Tarbiz*, 80 (2011), pp. 219–230 (Hebrew).

Franco, F. 'Five Aramaic Incantation Bowls from Tell Baruda (Choche),' *Mesopotamia*, 13–14 (1978–79), pp. 233–249.

Frankfurter, David. 'Scorpion/Demon: On the Origin of the Mesopotamian Apotropaic Bowl,' *Journal of Near-Eastern Studies*, 74 (2015), pp. 9–18.

Furlani, Giuseppe. 'I nomi delle classe dei demoni presso i Mandei,' *Rendiconti della Accademia Nazionale dei Lincei, Classe di Scienze morali, storiche e filologiche*, 9 (1954), pp. 389–435.

Gabbay, Uri. 'The King of the Demons: Pazuzu, Bagdana and Ašmedai,' in Wayne Horowitz, Uri Gabbay and Filip Vukosavović (eds), *A Woman of Valor: Jerusalem Ancient Near Eastern Studies in Honor of Joan Goodnick Westenholtz* (Biblioteca del Próximo Oriente Antiguo, 8), Madrid: Consejo Superior de Investigaciones Científicas, 2010, pp. 57–72.

Gaster, Moses. *The Sword of Moses*, London: Nutt, 1896 (also published in *Journal of the Royal Asiatic Society* [*JRAS*], 1896). Repr. in idem, *Studies and Texts in Folklore, Magic, Medieval Romance, Hebrew Apocrypha and Samaritan Archaeology*, I–III, London: Maggs Brothers, 1928 (repr. New York: Ktav, 1971), I, pp. 288–337, and III, pp. 69–103.

Gawlikowski, M. 'Une coupe magique araméenne,' *Semitica*, 38 (1990), pp. 137–143.

Geller, Markham J. 'Akkadian Medicine in the Babylonian Talmud,' in Dan Cohn-Sherbok (ed.), *A Traditional Quest: Essays in Honour of Louis Jacobs* (*Journal for the Study of the Old Testament* [*JSOT*], Supp. 114), Sheffield, 1991, pp. 102–112.

—. 'Deconstructing Talmudic Magic,' in Charles Burnett and W.F. Ryan (eds.), *Magic and the Classical Tradition* (Warburg Institute Colloquia, 7), London: Warburg Institute, 2006, pp. 1–18.

—. 'Eight Incantation Bowls,' *Orientalia Lovaniensia Periodica*, 17 (1986), pp. 101–117.

—. 'Four Aramaic Incantation Bowls,' in Gary Rendsburg, Ruth Adler, Milton Arfa, and Nathan H. Winter (eds.), *The Bible World: Essays in Honor of Cyrus H. Gordon*, New York: Ktav, 1980, pp. 47–60.

—. 'Magic Bowls Belong in Babylonia,' in Jens Kamlah, Rolf Schäfer and Markus Witte (eds.), *Zauber und Magie in Palästina und in seiner Umwelt: Kolloquium des Deutschen Vereins zur Erforschung Palästinas vom 14. bis 16. November 2014 in Mainz* (Abhandlungen des Deutschen Palästina-Vereins, 46), Wiesbaden: Harrassowitz, 2017, pp. 95–106.

—. 'Mesopotamian Love Magic: Discourse or Intercourse?' in S. Parpola and R.M. Whiting (eds.), *Sex and Gender in the Ancient Near East: Proceedings of the 47th Rencontre Assyriolgique Internationale, Helsinki, July 2–6, 2001* (Compte rendu, Rencontre Assyriologique Internationale [CRRAI], 47), Helsinki, 2002, pp. 129–139.

—. 'More Magic Spells and Formulae,' *Bulletin of the School of Oriental and African Studies* (*BSOAS*), 60 (1997), pp. 327–335.

—. 'Tablets and Magic Bowls,' in Shaul Shaked (ed.), *Officina Magica: Essays on the Practice of Magic in Antiquity* (IJS Studies in Judaica, 4), Leiden: Brill, 2005, pp. 53–72.

Ginzburg, L. 'Hagadot qetu'ot,' *Hagoren*, 9 (1922), pp. 31–68 (Hebrew).

Goitein, Shlomo Dov, and Mordechai Akiva Friedman. *Abraham ben Yijû, India Trader and Manufacturer: Cairo Geniza Documents* (India Book, 3), Jerusalem: Ben-Zvi Institute, 2010 (Hebrew).

Goldin, Judah. 'The Magic of Magic and Superstition,' in E. Schussler Fiorenza (ed.), *Aspects of Religious Propaganda in Judaism and Early Christianity*, Notre Dame: University of Notre Dame Press, 1976, pp. 115–147.

Goodenough, Erwin R. *Jewish Symbols in the Greco-Roman Period*, I–XIII, New York: Pantheon, 1953–1968.

Gordon, Cyrus H. 'Aramaic Incantation Bowls,' *Orientalia*, 10 (1941), pp. 116–141, 272–276, 278–289, 339–360.

—. 'Aramaic and Mandaic Magical Bowls,' *Archiv Orientální*, 9 (1937), pp. 84–106.
—. 'Aramaic Magical Bowls in the Istanbul and Baghdad Museums,' *Archiv Orientální*, 6 (1934), pp. 319–334.
—. 'Magic Bowls in the Moriah Collection,' *Orientalia*, 53 (1984), pp. 220–241.
Gorea, Maria. 'Trois nouvelles coupes magiques araméennes,' *Semitica*, 51 (2003), pp. 73–93.
Hamilton, G.J. 'A New Hebrew-Aramaic Incantation Text from Galilee: Rebuking the Sea,' *Journal of Semitic Studies* (*JSS*), 41 (1996), pp. 215–249.
Harari, Yuval. 'Geniza Fragments of the *Sword of Moses*,' *Ginzei qedem*, 10 (2014), pp. 29–92 (Hebrew).
—. *Ḥarba deMoshe (The Sword of Moses): A New Edition and a Study*, Jerusalem: Academon, 1997 (Hebrew).
—. 'Jewish Magic: An Annotated Overview,' *El Prezente: Studies in Sephardic Culture*, 5 (2011), pp. 13*–85* (Hebrew).
—. *Jewish Magic before the Rise of Kabbalah*, Detroit: Wayne State University Press, 2017.
—. 'On the Trail of the Magical Plate from the Yeruham Cemetery: Incantation Bowls from the Ancient World and in Islam,' *Pe'amim*, 103 (2005), pp. 55–90 (Hebrew).
—. 'The Sages and the Occult,' in Shmuel Safrai, Zeev Safrai, Joshua Schwartz, and Peter J. Tomson (eds.), *The Literature of the Sages*, II: *Midrash and Targum, Liturgy, Poetry, Mysticism, Contracts, Inscriptions, Ancient Science, and the Languages of Rabbinic Literature*, Assen: Van Gorcum, 2006, pp. 521–564.
—. 'The Sword of Moses (*Harba de-Moshe*): A New Translation and Introduction,' *Magic, Ritual and Witchcraft*, 7 (2012), pp. 58–98.
Harviainen, Tapani. 'An Aramaic Incantation Bowl from Borsippa: Another Specimen of Eastern Aramaic "Koiné,"' *Studia Orientalia*, 51/14 (1981), pp. 3–28.
Hunter, Erica C.D. 'Manipulating Incantation Texts: Excursions in Refrain A,' *Iraq*, 64 (2002), pp. 259–273.
Hyman, Aaron. *Toldoth tannaim ve'amoraim*, I–III, London, 1910 (Hebrew).
Hyvernat, Henri. 'Sur un vase judéo-babylonien du Musée Lycklama

de Cannes,' *Zeitschrift für Keilschriftforschung*, 2 (1885), pp. 113–148.

Isbell, C.D. *Corpus of the Aramaic Incantation Bowls* (Society of Biblical Literature Dissertation Series, 17), Missoula, MT: Scholars Press, 1975.

—. 'The Story of the Aramaic Magical Incantation Bowls,' *Biblical Archaeologist*, 41 (1978), pp. 5–16.

Jeruzalmi, Isak. *Les coupes magiques araméennes de Mésopotamie*, Paris: Sorbonne, 1963.

al-Jubouri, Bahaa Amer. 'An Aramaic Incantation Bowl in Iraq Museum,' *Sumer*, 56 (2011), pp. 25–30.

—. 'An Aramaic Incantation Text,' *JSS*, 58 (2013), pp. 59–63.

—. 'A New Aramaic Incantation Bowl,' *Semitica*, 57 (2015), pp. 211–216.

Juusola, Hannu. 'Notes on the Aramaic Sections of the Havdalah de-Rabbi Aqiba,' in idem, Juha Laulainen, and Heikki Palva (eds.), *Verbum et Calamus: Semitic and Related Studies in Honour of the Sixtieth Birthday of Professor Tapani Harviainen* (Studia Orientalia, 99), Helsinki: Finnish Oriental Society, 2004, pp. 106–119.

Kohut, Alexander. *Aruch Completum, sive lexicon vocabula et res, quae in libris targumicis, talmudicis et midrashicis continentur, explicans*, I–VIII, Vienna, 1878–1892.

Kutscher, E.Y. *Studies in Galilean Aramaic* (English transl. by Michael Sokoloff), Ramat-Gan: Bar-Ilan University Press, 1976.

Kwasman, T. 'The Demon of the Roof,' in Irving L. Finkel and Markham J. Geller (eds.), *Disease in Babylonia* (Cuneiform Monographs, 36), Leiden: Brill, 2007, pp. 160–186.

Lacau, P. 'Une coupe d'incantation,' *Revue d'assyriologie et d'archéologie orientale*, 3 (1894), pp. 49–51.

Layard, Austen H. *Discoveries in the Ruins of Nineveh and Babylon*, London: John Murray, 1853.

Leicht, Reimund. 'The Legend of St. Eustachius (Eustathius) as Found in the Cairo Genizah,' in Klaus Herrmann, Margarete Schlüter, and Giuseppe Veltri (eds.), *Jewish Studies Between the Disciplines / Judaistik zwischen den Disziplinen: Papers in Honor of Peter Schäfer on the Occasion of his 60th Birthday*, Leiden: Brill, 2003, pp. 325–330.

Lesses, Rebecca. 'Image and Word: Performative Ritual and Material Culture in the Aramaic Incantation Bowls,' in April D. DeConick, Gregory Shaw and John D. Turner (eds.), *Practicing Gnosis: Ritual, Magic, Theurgy and Liturgy in Nag Hammadi, Manichaean and Other Ancient Literature – Essays in Honor of Birger A. Pearson* (Nag Hammadi and Manichaean Studies, 85), Leiden: Brill, 2013, pp. 377–408.

Levene, Dan. 'Calvariae Magicae: The Berlin, Philadelphia and Moussaieff Skulls,' *Orientalia*, 75 (2006), pp. 359–379.

—. *A Corpus of Magic Bowls: Incantation Texts in Jewish Aramaic from Late Antiquity* (The Kegan Paul Library of Jewish Studies), London: Kegan Paul, 2003.

—. *Curse or Blessing, What's in the Magical Bowl?* (Ian Karten Lecture, 2002 = Parkes Institute Pamphlet, 2), University of Southampton, 2002.

—. *Jewish Aramaic Curse Texts from Late-Antique Mesopotamia: 'May These Curses Go Out and Flee'* (Magical and Religious Literature of Late Antiquity, 2), Leiden: Brill, 2013.

Levene, Dan, and Siam Bhayro. "Bring to the Gates ... upon a Good Smell and upon Good Fragrances:' An Aramaic Incantation Bowl for Success in Business,' *Archiv für Orientforschung*, 51 (2005–2006), pp. 242–246.

Levene, Dan, and Gideon Bohak. 'A Babylonian Jewish Aramaic Incantation Bowl with a List of Deities and Toponyms,' *Jewish Studies Quarterly*, 19 (2012), pp. 56–72.

—. 'Divorcing Lilith: From the Babylonian Incantation Bowls to the Cairo Genizah,' *Journal of Jewish Studies* (*JJS*), 63 (2012), pp. 197–217.

Levene, Dan, and James Nathan Ford. '"For Aḥata-de-'abuh Daughter of Imma": Two Aramaic Incantation Bowls in the Vorderasiatisches Museum, Berlin (VA 2414 and VA 2426),' *JSS*, 57 (2012), pp. 53–67.

Levene, Dan, Dalia Marx and Siam Bhayro. '"Gabriel Is on Their Right": Angelic Protection in Jewish Magic and Babylonian Lore,' *Studia Mesopotamica*, 1 (2014), pp. 185–198.

Manekin Bamberger, Avigail. 'An Akkadian Demon in the Talmud: Between Šulak and Bar-Širiqa,' *Journal for the Study of Judaism*, 44 (2013), pp. 282–287.

—. 'Jewish Legal Formulae in the Aramaic Incantation Bowls,' *Aramaic Studies*, 13 (2015), pp. 69–81.

Mann, Jacob. *Texts and Studies in Jewish History and Literature*, I, Cincinnati: Hebrew Union College Press, 1931; II, Philadelphia: Jewish Publication Society, 1935 (repr. of both volumes, New York: Ktav, 1972).

Margalioth, Mordechai. *Sepher Ha-Razim: A Newly Recovered Book of Magic from the Talmudic Period*, Tel Aviv: Yedioth Ahronoth, 1966 (Hebrew).

Mesler, Katelyn. 'The Three Magi and Other Christian Motifs in Medieval Hebrew Medical Incantations: A Study in the Limits of Faithful Translation,' in Resianne Fontaine and Gad Freudenthal (eds.), *Latin-into-Hebrew: Texts and Studies* (Studies in Jewish History and Culture, 39–40), Leiden: Brill, 2013, I, pp. 161–218.

Michelini Tocci, Franco. 'Note e documenti di letteratura religiosa e parareligiosa giudaica,' *Annali dell'Istituto Universitario Orientale di Napoli*, 46 (1986), pp. 101–108.

Mishor, Mordechay. 'Hebrew in the Babylonian Incantation Bowls,' in A. Maman, S.E. Fassberg and Y. Breuer (eds.), *Sha'arei lashon: Studies in Hebrew, Aramaic and Jewish Languages Presented to Moshe Bar-Asher*, Jerusalem: Bialik Institute, 2007, II, pp. 204–227 (Hebrew).

Montgomery, James A. *Aramaic Incantation Texts from Nippur* (Philadelphia University Museum, Publications of the Babylonian Section, 3), Philadelphia: University Museum, 1913 (repr. Cambridge: Cambridge University Press, 2010).

Mopsik, Charles. 'Late Judeo-Aramaic: The Language of Theosophic Kabbalah,' *Aramaic Studies*, 4 (2006), pp. 21–33.

Morgan, Michael A. *Sepher Ha-Razim: The Book of the Mysteries*, Chico, CA: Scholars Press, 1983.

Morgenstern, Matthew. 'Notes on a Recently Published Magic Bowl,' *Aramaic Studies*, 2 (2004), pp. 207–222.

Moriggi, Marco. 'Aramaean Demons in Rome: Incantation Bowls in the Museo Nazionale d'Arte Orientale,' *East and West*, 51 (2001), pp. 205–228.

—. 'Two New Incantation Bowls from Rome (Italy),' *Aramaic Studies*, 3 (2005), pp. 43–58.

Morony, Michael G. 'Magic and Society in Late Sasanian Iraq,' in Scott

B. Noegel, Joel Walker, and Brannon M. Wheeler (eds.), *Prayer, Magic, and the Stars in the Ancient and Late Antique World* (Magic in History Series), University Park: Pennsylvania State University Press, 2003, pp. 83–107.

—. 'Religion and the Aramaic Incantation Bowls,' *Religion Compass*, 1 (2007), pp. 414–429.

Müller-Kessler, Christa. 'Die aramäische Beschwörung und ihre Rezeption in den mandäisch-magischen Texten am Beispiel ausgewählter aramäischer Beschwörungs-formulare,' in Rika Gyselen (ed.), *Charmes et Sortileges, Magie et Magiciens* (Res Orientales, 14), Louvain: Peeters, 2002, pp. 193–208.

—. 'Dan(ḥ)iš: Gott und Dämon,' in Joachim Marzahn and Hans Neumann (eds.), *Assyriologica et Semitica: Festschrift für Joachim Oelsner* (Alter Orient und Altes Testament, 252), Münster: Ugarit-Verlag, 2000, pp. 311–318.

—. 'Eine ungewöhnliche Hekhalot-Zauberschale und ihr babylonisches Umfeld: Jüdisches Gedankengut in den magischen Texten des Ostens,' *Frankfurter Judaistische Beiträge*, 38 (2013), pp. 69–84.

—. 'The Story of Bguzan-Lilit, Daughter of Zanay-Lilit,' *Journal of the American Oriental Society* (*JAOS*), 116 (1996), pp. 185–195.

—. *Die Zauberschalentexte in der Hilprecht-Sammlung Jena, und weitere Nippur-Texte anderer Sammlungen*, Wiesbaden: Harrassowitz, 2005.

—. 'Zauberschalen und ihre Umwelt: Das Schreibmedium Zauberschale,' in Jens Kamlah, Rolf Schäfer and Markus Witte (eds.), *Zauber und Magie in Palästina und in seiner Umwelt: Kolloquium des Deutschen Vereins zur Erforschung Palästinas vom 14. bis 16. November 2014 in Mainz* (Abhandlungen des Deutschen Palästina-Vereins, 46), Wiesbaden: Harrassowitz, 2017, pp. 59–94.

Myhrman, David W. 'An Aramaic Incantation Text,' in *Hilprecht Anniversary Volume: Studies in Assyriology and Archaeology*, Leipzig: J.C. Hinrichs, 1909, pp. 342–351.

Naveh, Joseph. '"A Good Subduing, There is None Like It": An Amulet from Horvat Marish in the Galilee,' *Tarbiz*, 54 (1985), pp. 367–382 (Hebrew).

—. 'A Nabatean Incantation Text,' *Israel Exploration Journal* (*IEJ*),

29 (1979), pp. 111–119 (repr. in idem, *Studies in West-Semitic Epigraphy: Selected Papers*, Jerusalem: Magnes Press, 2009, pp. 209–217).

—. 'On Ancient Jewish Magical Recipe Books,' in A. Oppenheimer, I. Gafni, and D. Schwartz (eds.), *The Jews in the Hellenistic and Roman World* (Menahem Stern Memorial Volume), Jerusalem: Zalman Shazar Institute, 1996, pp. 453–465 (Hebrew).

Naveh, Joseph, and Shaul Shaked. *Amulets and Magic Bowls: Aramaic Incantations of Late Antiquity*, Jerusalem: Magnes Press, 1985.

—. *Magic Spells and Formulae: Aramaic Incantations of Late Antiquity*, Jerusalem: Magnes Press, 1993.

Oelsner, Joachim. 'Incantations in Southern Mesopotamia: From Clay Tablets to Magical Bowls (Thoughts on the Decline of the Babylonian Culture),' in Shaul Shaked (ed.), *Officina Magica: Essays on the Practice of Magic in Antiquity* (IJS Studies in Judaica, 4), Leiden: Brill, 2005, pp. 31–51.

Rapoport-Albert, Ada, and Theodore Kwasman. 'Late Aramaic: The Literary and Linguistic Context of the *Zohar*,' *Aramaic Studies*, 4 (2006), pp. 5–19.

Rebiger, Bill. *Sefer Shimmush Tehillim: Buch vom magischen Gebrauch der Psalmen – Edition, Übersetzung und Kommentar* (TSAJ, 137), Tübingen: Mohr Siebeck, 2010.

Rebiger, Bill, and Peter Schäfer. *Sefer ha-Razim I und II – Das Buch der Geheimnisse I und II*, I–II (TSAJ, 125, 132), Tübingen: Mohr Siebeck, 2009.

Rohrbacher-Sticker, Claudia. 'From Sense to Nonsense, From Incantation Prayer to Magical Spell,' *Jewish Studies Quarterly* (*JSQ*), 3 (1996), pp. 24–46.

Rossell, W.H. *A Handbook of Aramaic Magical Texts*, Ringwood Borough, NJ: Shelton College, 1953.

Saar, Ortal-Paz. 'A Genizah Magical Fragment and Its European Parallels,' *JJS*, 55 (2014), pp. 237–262.

—. 'An Incantation Bowl for Sowing Discord,' *JSS*, 58 (2013), pp. 241–256.

—. *Jewish Love Magic: From Late Antiquity to the Middle Ages* (Magical and Religious Literature of Late Antiquity, 6), Leiden: Brill, 2017.

—. 'A Study in Conceptual Parallels: Graeco-Roman Binding Spells and Babylonian Incantation Bowls,' *Aramaic Studies*, 13 (2015), pp. 24–53.

Schäfer, Peter. *Geniza-Fragmente zur Hekhalot-Literatur* (TSAJ, 6), Tübingen: Mohr, 1984.

Schäfer, Peter, and Shaul Shaked. *Magische Texte aus der Kairoer Geniza*, I–III (TSAJ, 42, 64, 72), Tübingen: J.C.B. Mohr (Paul Siebeck), 1994–1999.

Scholem, Gershom. 'Bilar the King of Devils,' *Jewish Studies*, 1 (1926), pp. 112–127 (repr. in Scholem, *Devils, Demons and Souls* [2004], pp. 9–53) (Hebrew).

—. *Devils, Demons and Souls: Essays on Demonology by Gershom Scholem*, ed. Esther Liebes, Jerusalem: Ben-Zvi Institute, 2004 (Hebrew).

—. *Elements of the Kabbalah and Its Symbolism*, Jerusalem: Keter, 1976 (Hebrew).

—. 'Havdala de-Rabbi Aqiva: A Source for the Tradition of Jewish Magic during the Geonic Period,' *Tarbiz*, 50 (1980/81), pp. 243–281 (repr. in Scholem, *Devils, Demons and Souls* [2004], pp. 145–182) (Hebrew).

—. *Kabbalah*, Jerusalem: Keter, 1974.

—. *Origins of the Kabbalah* (English transl. by Allan Arkush), ed. R.J. Zwi Werblowsky, Philadelphia: Jewish Publication Society, 1987.

—. *Sefer haZohar shel Gershom Shalom*, I–VI, Jerusalem: Magnes, 1992 (Hebrew).

—. 'Sidrei deShimusha Rabba,' *Tarbiz*, 16 (1945), pp. 196–209 (Hebrew).

—. 'Some Sources of Jewish-Arabic Demonology,' *JJS*, 16 (1965), pp. 1–13 (repr. in Scholem, *Devils, Demons and Souls* [2004], pp. 103–115) (Hebrew).

Schwab, Moïse. 'Une coupe d'incantation,' *Revue d'assyriologie et d'archéologie orientale*, 1 (1884–1885), pp. 117–119.

—. 'Coupes à inscriptions magiques,' *PSBA*, 13 (1891), pp. 583–595.

—. 'Deux vases judéo-babyloniens,' *Revue d'assyriologie et d'archéologie orientale*, 2 (1892), pp. 136–142.

—. 'Les coupes magiques et l'hydromancie dans l'antiquité orientale,' *Proceedings of the Society of Biblical Archaeology* (*PSBA*), 12 (1890), pp. 292–342.

Segal, J.B. *Catalogue of the Aramaic and Mandaic Incantation Bowls in the British Museum*, London: British Museum Press, 2000.

Shaked, Shaul. 'Bagdâna, King of the Demons, and Other Iranian Terms in Babylonian Aramaic Magic,' in *Papers in Honour of Professor Mary Boyce* (*Acta Iranica*, 25 = Hommages et Opera Minora, 11), Leiden: Brill, 1985, pp. 511–525.

—. '*Dramatis Personae* in the Jewish Magic Texts: Some Differences between Incantation Bowls and Genizah Magic,' *JSQ*, 13 (2006), pp. 363–387.

—. 'An Early Geniza Fragment in an Unknown Iranian Dialect,' in J. Duchesne-Guillemin, W. Sundermann, and F. Vahman (eds.), *A Green Leaf: Papers in Honour of Professor Jes P. Asmussen* (*Acta Iranica*, 28 = Hommages et Opera Minora, 12), Leiden: Brill, 1988, pp. 219–235.

—. 'Form and Purpose in Aramaic Spells: Some Jewish Themes (The Poetics of Magic Texts),' in Shaul Shaked (ed.), *Officina Magica: Essays on the Practice of Magic in Antiquity* (IJS Studies in Judaica, 4), Leiden: Brill, 2005, pp. 1–30.

—. 'Jewish and Iranian Visions in the Talmudic Period,' in A. Oppenheimer, I. Gafni, and D. Schwartz (eds.), *The Jews in the Hellenistic and Roman World* (Menahem Stern Memorial Volume), Jerusalem: Zalman Shazar Institute, 1996, pp. 467–486 (Hebrew).

—. 'A Jewish Aramaic Amulet from Afghanistan,' in Károly Daniel Dobos and Miklós Köszeghy (eds.), *With Wisdom as a Robe: Qumran and Other Jewish Studies in Honour of Ida Fröhlich* (Hebrew Bible Monographs, 21), Sheffield: Sheffield Phoenix Press, 2009, pp. 485–494.

—. 'Jewish Magical Literature in the Lands of Islam: Notes and Examples,' *Pe'amim*, 15 (1983), pp. 15–28 (Hebrew).

—. 'Jews, Christians and Pagans in the Aramaic Incantation Bowls of the Sasanian Period,' in Adriana Destro and Mauro Pesce (eds.), *Religions and Cultures: First International Conference of Mediterraneum*, Binghamton, NY: Global Publications, Binghamton University, 2002, pp. 61–89.

—. 'Magical Bowls and Incantation Texts: How to Get Rid of Demons and Pests,' *Qadmoniot*, 129 (2005), pp. 2–13 (Hebrew).

—. '"Peace Be upon You, Exalted Angels": On Hekhalot, Liturgy and Incantation Bowls,' *JSQ*, 2 (1995), pp. 197–219.

—. 'Popular Religion in Sasanian Babylonia,' *Jerusalem Studies in Arabic and Islam*, 21 (1997), pp. 103–117.

—. 'Rabbis in Incantation Bowls,' in Markham J. Geller (ed.), *The Archaeology and Material Culture of the Babylonian Talmud* (IJS Studies in Judaica, 16), Leiden: Brill, 2015, pp. 97–120.

—. 'Transmission and Transformation of Spells: The Case of the Jewish Babylonian Aramaic Bowls,' in Gideon Bohak, Yuval Harari, and Shaul Shaked (eds.), *Continuity and Innovation in the Magical Tradition* (Jerusalem Studies in Religion and Culture, 15), Leiden: Brill, 2011, pp. 187–217.

Shaked, Shaul, James Nathan Ford and Siam Bhayro. *Aramaic Bowl Spells* (Magical and Religious Literature of Late Antiquity, 1), Leiden: Brill, 2013.

Sokoloff, Michael. *A Dictionary of Jewish Babylonian Aramaic of the Talmudic and Geonic Periods*, Ramat-Gan: Bar-Ilan University Press, 2002.

Stol, M. 'Blindness and Night-Blindness in Akkadian,' *Journal of Near Eastern Studies* (*JNES*), 45 (1986), pp. 295–299.

Tal, Avraham. 'The Role of Targum Onqelos in Literary Activity During the Middle Ages,' in Holger Gzella and Margaretha L. Folmer (eds.), *Aramaic in Its Historical and Linguistic Setting* (Akademie der Wissenschaften und der Literatur, Mainz, Veröffentlichungen der Orientalischen Kommission, 50), Wiesbaden: Harrassowitz, 2008, pp. 159–171.

Ten-Ami, Alon. 'Rabbinic Motifs in Incantation Bowls from Sasanid Babylonia,' M.A. Thesis, The Hebrew University of Jerusalem, 2001 (Hebrew).

Trachtenberg, Joshua. *Jewish Magic and Superstition: A Study in Folk Religion*, New York: Behrman, 1939 (repr. Philadelphia: University of Pennsylvania Press, 2004).

Veltri, Giuseppe. 'The "Other" Physicians: The Amorites of the Rabbis and the Magi of Pliny,' *Korot*, 13 (1998–99), pp. 37–54.

Vilozny, Naama. 'Between Demons and Kings: The Art of Babylonian Incantation Bowls,' in Julia Rubanovitch (ed.), *Orality and Textuality in the Iranian World: Patterns of Interaction across the Centuries* (Jerusalem Studies in Religion and Culture, 19), Leiden: Brill, 2015, pp. 400–421.

—. *Lilith's Hair and Ashmedai's Horns: Figure and Image in Magic and Popular Art, between Babylonia and Palestine in Late Antiquity*, Jerusalem: Ben-Zvi Institute, 2017 (Hebrew).

—. 'Lilith's Hair and Ashmedai's Horns: Incantation Bowl Imagery in the Light of Talmudic Descriptions,' in Markham J. Geller (ed.), *The Archaeology and Material Culture of the Babylonian Talmud* (IJS Studies in Judaica, 16), Leiden: Brill, 2015, pp. 133–152.

Vukosavović, Filip (ed.). *Angels and Demons: Jewish Magic Through the Ages*, Jerusalem: Bible Lands Museum, 2010.

Wandrey, Irina. *'Das Buch des Gewandes' und 'Das Buch des Aufrechten': Dokumente eines magischen spätantiken Rituals, ediert, kommentiert und übersetzt* (TSAJ, 96), Tübingen: Mohr Siebeck, 2004.

Wasserman, Nathan. 'Old-Babylonian, Middle-Babylonian, Neo-Babylonian, Jewish-Babylonian?: Thoughts about Transmission Modes of Mesopotamian Magic through the Ages,' in Uri Gabbay and Shai Secunda (eds.), *Encounters by the Rivers of Babylon: Scholarly Conversations between Jews, Iranians and Babylonians in Antiquity* (TSAJ, 160), Tübingen: Mohr Siebeck, 2014.

Waterman, Leroy. *Preliminary Report upon the Excavations at Tel Umar, Iraq*, Ann Arbor: University of Michigan Press, 1931.

Wohlstein, Joseph. 'Über einige aramäische Inschriften auf Thongefäßen des königlichen Museum zu Berlin,' *Zeitschrift für Assyriologie*, 8 (1893), pp. 313–340; 9 (1894), pp. 11–41.

Yamauchi, E.M. 'Aramaic Magic Bowls,' *JAOS*, 85 (1965), pp. 511–523.

Yeivin, Israel. *The Hebrew Language Tradition as Reflected in the Babylonian Vocalization*, I–II, Jerusalem: The Academy of Hebrew Language, 1985 (Hebrew).

Holy Relics in Mata Meḥasya

Christians and Jews after the Muslim Conquest of Babylonia

Geoffrey Herman

Christian Response to the Arab Invasion

In Late Antiquity, when the vast majority of Jews and Christians found themselves in either the Sasanian or the Byzantine Empire, the political dynamics between these two religious communities in the respective empires were markedly different. Byzantine Jews found themselves under Christian rulers, their shared biblical heritage a source of friction and suspicion. In the Sasanian Empire, by contrast, it was the Christians who might be regarded with suspicion as co-believers of the Byzantines, and the Jews could hope to be treated as any other religious minority before the crown. On the whole, however, Christianity would flourish in the Sasanian Empire, notwithstanding the occasional Zoroastrian hostility, accentuated in times of conflict with Rome and certainly aided by the perpetual theological bickering that would split Sasanian and Byzantine Christianities along denominational lines.[1] The Sasanian rulers, more often than not, related both to their own Jews and to Christians with the same degree of indifferent pragmatism.[2]

This situation was dramatically undermined in the seventh century, which witnessed the Persian conquest of Jerusalem and of extensive parts of the Byzantine Empire, followed by the return of Byzantine rule

* This article is offered as a token of esteem to my teacher of many years, Shaul Shaked. An earlier version was read on 8 April, 2010, at the conference on 'Identity and Space' held in Ra'anana, Israel, under the auspices of the Israel Historical Society and the Open University of Israel.

1 For an overview of the situation of the Christians in the Sasanian Empire, see Brock, 'Christians in the Sasanid Empire.'

2 A review of the condition of the non-Zoroastrian religious communities under the Sasanians can be found in Herman, *A Prince without a Kingdom*, pp. 39–53.

to these regions and its extension to part of the Sasanian Empire, and then by the Arab conquest of the entire Sasanian Empire and much of its Byzantine counterpart.

For some decades now, scholars have been discussing the effect of these upheavals upon the relations between Jews and Christians,[3] with the focus usually on the Byzantine Empire and the parts of it that were conquered. One incontrovertible outcome was a substantial increase in Christian compositions polemicizing against Jews.[4]

Why the increase? One scholarly approach sees in it a real interaction, reflecting a Christian response to the return of the Jews to the historical arena in the wake of the various events. Others see in it merely a rhetorical development, one-sided and unrelated to real Jews. They view the anti-Jewish literature as a theological phenomenon, a means of coping with the decisive military and political defeat of Byzantine 'imperial' Christianity, first by the Persians and then by the Arabs. Faced with the collapse of the Byzantine imperial dominion, which, for many, represented the victory of Christianity, Christians now turned towards the more familiar traditional foe rather than confront the real, new and sometimes little understood enemy.

One proponent of this approach is Daniel Oster. His book *Roman Defeat, Christian Response, and the Literary Construction of the Jew* (1994), and especially the chapter entitled 'We Are Still Better than You,' intimates that the Christians comforted themselves that despite the new situation under Islam, Christianity still reigned superior in comparison with the Jews. While scholars have dealt with the Byzantine experience, the situation in the Sasanian Empire has hardly been addressed, and that is the topic I shall briefly consider here.

How did Sasanian Jews and Syriac Christianity, particularly Nestorian Christians, respond to the events, and how did those events impact the relationship between these two Sasanian minorities? With respect to the Christians, most scholars agree with Olster that:

> of the three competing Syrian Christian sects, Jacobites, Melkites and Nestorians, it was the Nestorians – who had long experienced

3 See, e.g., Dagron, 'Juifs et Chrétiens'; Déroche, 'La polémique anti-judaïque'; and Cameron, 'Byzantines and Jews.'

4 See Cameron, 'The Eastern Provinces,' pp. 294–295, 301–306. Olster refers to the 'explosion of anti-Jewish texts in the seventh century in the light of this broader cultural response to crisis'; idem, *Roman Defeat*, p. 3.

Persian rule, and for whom the Arab conquest was merely a change of heathen masters – who most successfully accommodated themselves to their new conditions.[5]

This statement, echoing Labourt's memorable retort, 'il importe peu à l'esclave de servir tel ou tel maître,'[6] is essentially correct in its bottom line,[7] but it hardly does justice to the complexity and fullness of the relationship between Nestorian Christianity and the Sasanian Empire. One should, perhaps, more clearly distinguish between impotence and indifference in the face of events.

Eastern Syriac literature was created in the Sasanian Empire in the course of many centuries. Works in the realms of hagiography, martyrdom literature, synodal acts, law and chronicles[8] attest to the efforts invested by Christians in finding acceptance and integration within the Sasanian Empire. Likewise, they reveal Christians' pride in the Sasanian Empire and their efforts to adapt themselves to Persian language and culture. This consciousness probably reached its apogee precisely in the last century of the Sasanian Empire. It is inconceivable that Sasanian Christians were not deeply moved and concerned by the empire's downfall. Some incidences of a more proactive if not enthusiastic Christian response to the arrival of the Arabs can be found, but they belong to later sources and have been understood, with justice, as reflecting a later era.[9] Closer to the period at hand, we hear other

5 Olster, *Roman Defeat*, p. 181. See also Hoyland, *Seeing Islam*, p. 25; Becker, 'Beyond the Spatial and Temporal *Limes*,' pp. 382–387; Fiey, 'The Last Byzantine Campaign'; and Panaino, 'La Chiesa di Persia,' p. 859.

6 Labourt, *Le Christianisme*, p. 246.

7 But in view of the many early sources that attest to the Nestorian appreciation of the religious world of the Arab conquerors, it is certainly problematic to assume that they considered them heathens. See, e.g., Brock, 'Syriac Views'; and Cahen, 'Note sur l'accueil.'

8 It is neither possible within the confines of this article nor, I believe, necessary to provide full evidence for this statement. The following, however, are examples. For hagiography, the account of Mar Augin conveys a positive relationship with the Sasanian Empire; in the realm of martyrology, we have the martyrdom of Mar Qardagh, for which see Wiessner, 'Christlicher Heiligenkult'; and Walker, *The Legend*. For the synod proceedings, see Chabot, *Synodicon orientale*; and for law, see Sachau, *Syrischer Rechtbücher*. The chronicle to be considered below is an apt case of Nestorian–Sasanian symbiosis.

9 See the examples provided by Gerö, 'Only a Change of Masters,' p. 46. Even Christian sources a little closer chronologically – such as the epistles by the Nestorian patriarch, Timothy I; the chronicle of John of Phenak; and eighth

voices. In the immediate aftermath of the Muslim conquest, we find the Catholicos abandoning the capital, Meḥoza, after it was captured by the Arabs,[10] and a bishop mourning the 'dead kingdom.'[11]

We are faced with a similar situation with regard to Jewish history for this period, although, after the completion of the Babylonian Talmud and before the arrival of the Geonic literature, the paucity of source material is even more acute. Here, too, later sources depict an enthusiastic reception of the newcomers. However, we cannot give too much credence to a brief report, found in Sherira Gaon's tenth-century epistle, that the gaon Mar Isaac, followed by 90,000 Jews of Pērōz Shābūr, received 'Alī ibn Abī-Ṭālib with open arms.[12] From the perspective of the tenth century, what else would the Jews have done? Another Jewish episode that has been set in the era of the Muslim conquest concerns the founder of the post-Sasanian Exilarchate, Bustanay. However the historical reality behind the Bustanay story also remains unclear.[13] Sherira Gaon himself confessed that the sequence of the leadership of the Mata Meḥasya academy from the final decades of Sasanian rule until the year 689 CE was not at all clear to him. He blamed the political upheavals and the strong hand of the Exilarchate.[14]

and ninth-century Syriac chronicles – cannot be said with any confidence to reflect the era of the conquest itself; cf. Brock, 'Syriac Views,' pp. 11–13. The opposite is true, too. The late traditions of Tha'ālibī (ed. Zotenberg, p. 748, ll. 1–2) and Ferdosi (ed. Mohl, VII, p. 484, ll. 498ff) that Christian monks took care of Yazdgird III's burial are to be rejected. See Gerö, 'Only a Change of Masters,' p. 45. On the legal status of non-Muslims in the period following the Muslim expansion see Levy-Rubin, *Non-Muslims*.

10 Guidi, 'Un nuovo testo,' p. 31.

11 ܡܠܟܘܬܐ ܡܝܬܬܐ, ed. Duval, *Išō'yahb III*, ep. C7, p. 237. Morony, in *Iraq*, pp. 343–346, reviews this era of transition, when 'the relationship established between the Nestorian Church and the Sasanian state by the end of the Sasanian period was broken as a result of the Islamic conquest' (p. 343). As Gerö observes in 'Only a Change of Masters,' p. 45, the Anonymous chronicle published by Guidi (see further below) sees the Arab invasions as Divine punishment for the wrongs of the Byzantines but does not accuse the Persians of any wrongdoings that brought about the Arab victories.

12 Lewin, *Igeret Rav Sherira Gaon*, p. 101.

13 On this episode see Gil, 'The Babylonian Encounter.' See now my own study on this topic, 'Back to Bustanay: The History of a Legend.'

14 Lewin, *Igeret Rav Sherira Gaon*, p. 105. On the Sasanian Exilarchate see Herman, *A Prince without a Kingdom*.

A short story in a contemporary local Christian chronicle sheds some light on this period and in particular on the relations between Jews and Christians. I believe it deserves more attention than it has received.[15]

The Anonymous Syriac Chronicle

The story I wish to consider is taken from a Nestorian chronicle written in Syriac, probably composed shortly after 660 CE.[16] The name of the author is not provided, nor is there a colophon. Published by Ignazio Guidi at the end of the nineteenth century,[17] it has been called 'Guidi's/the anonymous chronicle' or, sometimes, the 'Ḥuzestan Chronicle,' in accordance with the view that it was composed there.[18]

The chronicle bears the title 'Some events from the Ecclesiastical and Secular Annals, from the death of Hormizd the son of Xusrō until the end of the Persian kingdom.' Though it actually continues a little further, this is a fairly accurate description of the contents, which comprise episodes from the political history of the Sasanian Empire, interwoven with lengthy pieces of particular interest to Christians. Thus, beyond the depictions of historical events, which concern Persian national history and seem to be devoid of any Christian tone, it elaborates upon Yazdīn, a wealthy Christian layman who was highly influential in the royal court; the Christian wives of the Persian king; Christian religious leaders; and the ecclesiastical leadership. It appears to have two parts: a redacted

15 Although discussed in Obermeyer, *Die Landschaft*, pp. 289–290, this episode receives only a passing reference in Neusner, *A History*, p. 21, and is not mentioned in Oppenheimer, *Babylonia Judaica*. Joachim Jeremias seeks to integrate this source into his broader theory of ancient Jewish veneration of holy relics; see idem, 'Drei weitere Spätjüdische Heiligengräber,' pp. 99–101.

16 This is the view of S. Brock in idem, 'Guidi's Chronicle,' but earlier, in his 'Syriac Sources for Seventh Century History,' p. 23, he had placed it between 670 and 680 CE, agreeing with Nöldeke ('Die von Guidi herausgegebene syrische Chronik,' p. 3), who set it around 670 CE. Hoyland (*Seeing Islam*, p. 185) dates it to the 660s, noting that there is no clear reference to any event after 652 CE.

17 The printed text is based on MS Borgia syr. 82, a modern copy (1891) of an old manuscript preserved in the Near East (probably MS Alqosh 169, of the fourteenth century). An important early German translation with brief commentary was provided in Nöldeke, 'Die von Guidi herausgegebene syrische Chronik.'

18 For an attempt to identify the author as Elias of Merv, see Nautin, 'L'auteur.' Cf. Gerö, 'Only a Change of Masters,' p. 45, note 8.

chronicle, which begins from around 590 CE, and disparate episodes appended at the end.[19] However, terminological inconsistencies reveal that even the beginning section combines a number of diverse sources that have been molded together by an author or redactor.

Our story appears towards the end of the chronicle. The text refers to the Arab conquest and then narrates the death of the Catholicos, Ishō‘yahb II, and the election of a new incumbent, Mar-Emmeh. Having suitably introduced Mar-Emmeh, reviewed his qualities and noted that he was honored by the Ishmaelite leaders, the chronicle relates the following story:[20]

ܐܡܪܝܢ ܕܝܢ ܕܩܪܝܬܐ ܚܕܐ ܐܝܬ ܕܐܝܬܝܗ ܕܝܗܘܕܝܐ ܟܠܗ. ܘܣܝܡܐ ܒܝܬ ܡܚܘܙܐ
ܠܚܝܪܬܐ. ܘܫܡܗ ܡܛܐܡܣܝܐ. ܘܟܕ ܥܒܪ ܗܘܐ ܒܚܕ ܡܢ ܝܘܡܝܢ ܐܣܟܘܠܝܐ ܚܕ
ܬܡܢ. ܐܚܕܗ ܚܕ ܡܢ ܒܢܝ̈ ܙܩܘܦܐ ܘܐܥܠܗ ܠܒܝܬܗ. ܘܙܒܢܐ ܠܐ ܙܥܘܪܐ ܐܣܪܗ
ܕܢܛܚܢ ܒܗ ܪܚܝܐ. ܗܝܕܝܢ ܒܦܘܩܕܢܐ ܕܡܠܟܐ ܐܫܬܕܪ ܒܙܩܘܦܝܐ ܚܕ ܠܗܝ ܩܪܝܬܐ
ܒܣܘܥܪܢܐ ܡܕܡ. ܘܒܡܦܪܢܣܘܬܐ ܕܐܠܗܐ ܥܠ ܥܙܪܐ ܒܗ ܒܒܝܬܐ. ܘܟܕ ܚܙܝܗܝ ܗܘ
ܐܣܟܘܠܝܐ ܐܙܠ. ܘܐܚܕܗ ܗܘ ܒܙܩܘܦܝܐ ܠܒܪܗ ܕܒܝܬܐ. ܘܟܠܐ ܠܗ ܟܠܗ ܥܕܪܐ.
ܘܐܡܪ ܠܗ. ܕܐܢ ܥܒܕ ܐܢܬ ܠܝ ܗܕܐ ܫܡܠܘܬܐ. ܟܠܐ ܐܢܐ ܠܟ ܥܠ ܫܡܫܬܐ
ܡܫܬܪܬܐ. ܘܣܡܝ ܠܗ ܕܒܚܬܐ ܒܒܝܬܗ. ܕܫܡܫܝܢ ܗܘܘ ܒܗ ܦܪܨܘܦܝܗܘܢ ܕܗܠܝܢ ܚܢܦܐ
ܘܣܓܕܘܗܝ، ܘܗܕܐ ܕܗܘ ܐܣܟܘܠܝܐ ܐܠܗܐ ܦܪܨܘܦܗ. ܐܝܟ ܕܬܬܐ ܟܠܐ ܫܡܫܬܐ
ܕܦܪܨܘܦܝܗܘܢ ܕܛܥܝܐ܀ ܡܬܐܡܪܐ ܕܒܚܕ ܡܢ ܝܘܡܝܢ. ܟܕ ܐܙܠ ܗܘ ܡܪܐܡܗ ܡܢ
ܡܚܘܙܐ ܠܚܝܪܬܐ. ܐܫܬܡܥܠ ܠܗ ܒܩܘܬܐ. ܒܗ ܒܗܝ ܩܪܝܬܐ. ܘܟܕ ܕܫܠܛܗܘܢ
ܕܟܠܗ ܠܐܝܣܘܪܐ ܙܟܐ ܡܟܠܗܘܢ.

They say that there is a town that is entirely of Jews. And it is situated between Meḥoza and Ḥirta,[21] and its name is Matamasia.[22] And when, one day, a disciple passed through there, one of the sons of the crucifiers[23] seized him and brought him into his house. And for not a short time he bound him to have him grind the mill.

19 For a brief description, see Nautin, 'L'auteur'; and Brock, 'Guidi's Chronicle.'

20 Guidi, 'Un nuovo testo,' p. 32.

21 Al-Ḥira.

22 This is *senza dubio* Mata Meḥasya (cf. Guidi, 'Un nuovo testo,' p. 27), as was assumed by Nöldeke and others. On the vocalization of מחסיה, cf. Schechter, *Saadyana*, p. 63, who brings the reading מַחְסֵיָה, based on the vocalization in Jeremiah 32:12 and 51:59; and the Yemenite and Baghdadi traditions. See, too, the discussion in Obermeyer, *Die Landschaft*, p. 289, note 1, and the further references there.

23 The reference is to Jews.

Now upon royal command a certain Christian was sent to that town on some business matter, and through Divine providence, he entered and dwelled in that house. And when that disciple saw him he cried out. And that Christian [visitor] seized the master of the house, and he revealed all the truth, and he said to him. 'If you forgive me this folly, I shall reveal to you a special [hidden] treasure.' And he showed him the place in his house where the corpses of the youths, Hananya and his companions, were placed. And the reason that God had guided this disciple was so that the treasure/tomb of the corpses of the blessed ones might be revealed.

It is said that one day when that Mar-Emmeh was travelling from Meḥoza to Ḥirta, he received lodgings in that self-same town, and on account of their fear of him they received him with great honor.

A Special Treasure

In light of the great interest in holy relics among the Christians of Late Antiquity, these bones are a 'special treasure.' The identity of Hananya, Mishael and Azariah, both as eunuchs – typological monks – and as martyrs, is the key to their special status in early Christianity. However, Hananya and his companions had a unique symbolic value for *Sasanian* Christians: They belonged to the local biblical scene. With the Book of Daniel set in Babylonia, they were *indigenous* biblical heroes.[24]

24 The importance of the Book of Daniel for Christianity is well known, and the story of the three youths in the fire is an important episode within it. See the survey essay by Yarbro Collins, 'The Influence of Daniel.' Christians continued to retell the tale of the furnace with new players; see, e.g., Evagrius, *Ecclesiastical History*, Book IV, §36 (ed. Whitby, *Ecclesiastical History*, pp. 241–242, and esp. p. 242, note 117, for further references). In the Pethion-Adurhormizd-Anahid Syriac martyr cycle we find the prayer: 'Show also now, Lord, your great power, as you showed it to Hananyah, Mishael and his holy companions'; *Acta Martyrum Syriacum* (ed. Bedjan), II, p. 616, ll. 18–19. On the importance of Daniel in the eastern tradition, see Van Rompay, 'Impetuous Martyrs,' pp. 373–375. Another sixth-century Syriac work, *Acts of Mar Mari* (sections 23–24), has its hero, Mar Mari, reenact entry into a furnace as a contest between Christianity and worshippers of fire in the city of Seleucia. They are explicitly identified as Magi in the later Arabic translation, *Liber Turris*.

Uncovering the Biblical Past

The first avenue in exploring this source will, then, be the geographical context. The story may be understood as part of a quest to discover and emphasize the area's biblical past.[25] The practice of identifying local places and cities mentioned in the Bible was widespread among both Jews and Christians.[26] Indeed, Christians had been adopting local Jewish geographical traditions in Palestine from the earliest times.[27] Jews had identified a number of biblical sites in the southern region of Babylonia, where this story is set: the valley of Dura; the valley of dry bones; Daniel's tomb.[28] Special benedictions were fixed to be recited when passing places where biblical miracles had occurred, such as the lions' den from the Book of Daniel or the midrashic furnace of Ur Casdim.

Babylonian Jews were no less interested in Hananya and his companions than their Christian neighbors. Their miracle was evoked in the fixed prayers and also finds mention in an incantation formula against fever.[29] Sites near the city of Babylon were connected to the miracles of Hananya and his companions by Babylonian rabbis, particularly those living in the region, such as Rav Hamnuna and Rav Ashi, an important rabbi associated specifically with Mata Meḥasya, which lies close to biblical Babylon. One wonders whether we might be approaching historical *realia*.

Might the Christian story connect to an existing tradition, perhaps of local Jewish provenance, regarding the burial site of Hananya and his companions? As with many other Christian traditions from that period and earlier, the Jews are perceived as possessing reliable information on the biblical past. The Christians seek to extricate the biblical heritage of Babylonia from the Jews and appropriate it for themselves. Claiming to

25 On the most pronounced tendency of biblicization of Syriac Christianity, Assyrianization, see Becker, 'Ancient Near East.' On the use of the Assyrian imagery see Harrak, 'The Assyrian is the Rod of My Hand.'

26 The targums replaced the biblical names of places with the names of contemporary cities and places that they believed to be the same. Ephrem also identified contemporary cities with places named in Genesis. For the Jewish sources, see Gafni, 'Local Patriotism,' pp. 64–66.

27 Eusebius's *Onomasticon* is one of the more prominent examples of this phenomenon.

28 BT *Sanhedrin* 92b.

29 BT *Shabbat* 67a. Cf. the discussion in BT *Pesaḥim* 117a–118a of the miraculous salvation of Abraham and the three youths while in the furnace.

be the legitimate heirs of the biblical legacy, the Christians succeed in acquiring secret information on an important holy biblical site.

Supply and Demand

And yet, the Christian discovery of the youths' tomb in the midst of the Babylonian Jewish community starkly contradicts a Jewish tradition, preserved in the Babylonian Talmud, according to which they migrated soon after their miracle to Palestine, where they are buried.[30]

It also contradicts not a few Christian traditions. Nestorian Christians were discovering in the seventh century in Mata Meḥasya what other Christians had apparently already found in the fifth, when they successfully recovered the three youths' remains from Nebuchadnezzar's palace in Babylon or, according to another version, from Ctesiphon.[31] Were we to believe all our sources, these earlier excavations had emptied the tomb completely of its contents – a few times. Depending on which version one prefers – and there are several, including one in Greek, two in Armenian and a Georgian version (based on a different Armenian version), many going back to Syriac originals – the relics were discovered during the reign of Warahrān Gōr (420–438).[32] They were removed intact and complete, body and head miraculously reunited, and they were now safely deposited with the Christians.[33] On their current location there is some discrepancy among the sources. It is either in Kolt'n in Armenia; or in a monastery in Babylonia; or in the church of St. Romanus in Constantinople; or under the tomb of St Daniel the Stylite near Antioch; and a hand was on permanent loan to the patriarch in Alexandria, who displayed it with

30 BT *Sanhedrin* 93a. Cf. the tradition in *ibid.* 92b that the people revived by Ezekiel married, went to Palestine and bore children. The twelfth-century Jewish travelers Benjamin of Tudela (Adler, *The Itinerary*, pp. 68*, 45) and Petahya of Regensburg (Grünhut, *Die Rundreise des R. Petachjah*, p. 17), however, knew of the tomb still in Babylonia in the vicinity of the tomb of Ezekiel, not far from Mata Meḥaysa.

31 For a summary of these sources and detailed bibliography see Fox, 'Life of Daniel,' pp. 197–199. I would like to thank my friend Dr. Sergey Minov for a number of valuable references on this subject.

32 For the Armenian sources, see Stone, 'An Armenian Tradition'; Garitte, 'Le texte.' For the Georgian one, which is the most vivid, see Garitte, 'L'Invention'; Fox, 'Life of Daniel,' p. 197.

33 Stone, *Armenian Apocrypha*, pp. 154–155.

great pomp in an Egyptian church in the late sixth century.[34] A tenth-century liturgical calendar for the festal year celebrates two separate deposits of the bones in Jerusalem, on the Mount of Olives, also said to have occurred in the fifth century.[35]

The call for yet another discovery of these holy relics precisely in the seventh century may have been spurred by the apocalyptic events of the time. The Book of Daniel was on the mind of many a Christian, and its scheme of the succession of kingdoms led Syriac Christians, in the early years after the Arab conquest, to regard the Arab conquerors as a new kingdom.[36] Christian works focusing on Daniel were composed precisely in the mid-seventh century.[37]

In most of these tomb-discovery accounts, as in our story, the bones had been in the possession of Jews and were stolen or otherwise brought into Christian hands.[38] Our source, however, is the only one that locates the bones in Mata Meḥasya, a rather surprising location. It is a town of moderate proportions – as its very name implies, indeed, 'not quite a village and not quite a city,' as the Babylonian Talmud (BT *Ketubot* 4a) puts it. It does not boast venerable antiquity, like so many other Babylonian cities, and it only appears in the talmudic sources from the fifth century. It also lacks any immediate connection to the relevant biblical stories. The most logical place for soundings would have been the ancient city of Babylon itself, and it was precisely here that some of the Byzantine and Armenian Christian sources made their discoveries.

Yet Mata Meḥasya does not feature in this story by chance. Indeed, the mention of this location reminds us of the difference between the distant

34 Sophronius, *Mir. Cyr. and Joh.*, PG 87 C, cols. 3677B–3680C. This tradition belongs to the second half of the sixth century.

35 See Fox, 'Life of Daniel,' p. 198.

36 See Brock, 'Syriac Views,' pp. 14, 20. The anti-Jewish polemical work known as *Doctrina Jacobi nuper baptizati* is another contemporary work that relates to the kingdom scheme of the Book of Daniel; see Brock, *ibid.*, p. 9.

37 E.g., the Coptic homily on the 'child saints of Babylon,' written in 640 CE; see Hoyland, *Seeing Islam*, p. 121. For an edition, see *Trois Saint Enfants de Babylone*, in De Vis, *Homélies coptes de la Vaticane*, pp. 58–120. The Guidi chronicle, in fact, includes an excursus on Daniel's tomb in Susa and its Christian associations. Miracles are related surrounding an attempt to transfer the bones from Susa in another contemporary work, *The Armenian History attributed to Sebeos*, ed. Thomson, I, pp. 30f, and II, p. 175.

38 According to the Armenian version cited by Stone, 'An Armenian Tradition,' p. 113, Jews preserved them until the Byzantine emperor Leo I (r. 457–474 CE) requested them – from the Persians – and brought them to Constantinople.

western Christian sources, which draw their knowledge of Babylonia from the Bible, and this local contemporary witness. Our story suggests that Mata Meḥasya grew in importance in the late Sasanian era, maybe due to the presence of an important academy there,[39] and it attests not merely to the existence but, more significantly, to the *centrality* of Mata Meḥasya in this murky period. It also indicates that a town that was important as a *rabbinic* center, and had no other known virtues, enjoyed considerable visibility as a center for Babylonian *Jewry* – something that cannot always be assumed.

Mata Meḥasya appears in the story for its symbolic status, representing a Babylonian town that is 'entirely of Jews.'[40] This symbolic value invites us to probe the polemical side of the story and the attitude of the chronicle as a whole with respect to the Jews.

Jews in the Anonymous Syriac Chronicle

Jews are mentioned thrice in the anonymous chronicle: first, in the context of the Persian conquest of Jerusalem; next, in our story, and finally, in a brief episode that follows it almost immediately.

The first story relates that the Jews burned churches during the conquest of Jerusalem[41] and told the Persians that much gold was buried under the burial site of Jesus.[42] Yazdīn revealed the Jewish schemes to the Persians, who punished them severely.[43] The third story, which

39 Obermeyer seeks to harmonize with this Syriac source a statement in BT *Shabbat* 11a, apparently a late gloss, asserting that Mata Meḥasya had been destroyed. However, the testimony of a Cairo Geniza fragment of this Talmud passage, MS Cambridge T-S F2 (2) 13, may render such efforts unnecessary. According to its reading, it says of Rav Ashi: עבדי לה **לבית כנשתא** (ל)[ד]מתא מחסיא דלא חרבה, and even if the words בית כנשתא might be a gloss, they can be said to fit the context; that is, the discussion there refers to the synagogue, not the town.

40 Evidently it was not always viewed as exclusively Jewish. In BT *Berakhot* 17b we find the following statement, attributed to R. Ashi: 'The *people* of Mata Meḥasya (בני מתא מחסיא) are 'stubborn of heart' (Is. 46:12), for they behold the honor of the Torah twice a year, and not one convert has converted from among them.'

41 As Nöldeke ('Die von Guidi herausgegebene syrische Chronik,' p. 26, n. 4) points out, the burning of these churches is ascribed by Eutychius to the Persians themselves.

42 Guidi, 'Un nuovo testo,' p. 26.

43 It bears noting that this account of the part of the Jews in the Persian conquest of Jerusalem, notwithstanding its anti-Jewish hostility and the author's efforts

takes place under the Muslims, describes a messianic uprising of 400 Jews in a Babylonian village called Pallugta. The Jews burned three churches, but a military force sent from Kūfah killed them.[44]

Jews, evidently, appear in this chronicle only in support of its Christian agenda. The three episodes all speak directly of Jews seeking to harm Christians, and in all three the Jews suffer damning blows from the rulers – punishment, death or humiliation.

In the episode under discussion here, while some elements draw upon the broader genre of anti-Jewish writings from the period, including other chronicles, there is nevertheless something rather surprising: It does not celebrate the destruction or conversion of the Jews. Mata Meḥasya continues to be 'entirely of Jews' after the discovery. More striking, perhaps, is that the relics seem to remain in Jewish hands. Unlike the Byzantine versions of the invention and subsequent transfer of the bones to the safety of a Christian mausoleum, here the bones stay put. It is left unclear what the Christians *did* with this new information and how it helped them. There is no sign that Mata Meḥasya became a pilgrimage site for Christians. What significance was there, one might wonder, in telling us that some years later Mar-Emmeh was honored when he happened to pass through?

Post-Conquest Setting

The historical context may provide an answer. One must return to the chronicle as a whole and review its underlying agenda. It stresses the deep involvement of Christians in the Sasanian political arena. Christian integration in the Persian Empire and closeness to the royal court are uppermost in the mind of the author. The chronicle tends to cover up any allusion to conflict and passes swiftly over the uncomfortable periods for Christians, blaming, on occasion, the 'heretics' for any an-

to clear the Persians of culpability in any deliberate anti-Christian acts of violence, differs markedly from the western Christian accounts. As such, it affirms how completely independent of those traditions this chronicle is. A reassessment of the veracity and credibility of all the accounts, not only concerning the details of the alleged Jewish involvement in a massacre of Christians but even regarding the very assertion of such an event, is necessary. For earlier discussions, none of which takes this source into consideration, see, e.g., Jacobs, 'The Lion and the Lamb,' pp. 116–118; and Wilken, *The Land Called Holy*, pp. 203–204.

44 On this episode, see, briefly, Neusner, *A History*, p. 129.

ti-Christian activity by the rulers. Although some scholars, drawing liberally from this chronicle, have inferred the high status of the Sasanian Christians in this era, this image should, perhaps, be nuanced or even treated with skepticism. For instance, the importance of the Magi in the social, political and religious fabric of the empire is entirely dwarfed in the chronicle, which also lacks any *neutral* reference to non-Nestorian Christians.

In light of this, one must pay attention to how the chronicle attributes to the (Nestorian) Christians preferential treatment by the Sasanian kings, and the reverse for the Jews. This comes into play most clearly in its depiction of the conquest of Jerusalem, where Yazdīn influences the Persians against the Jews. In the Mata Meḥasya story, too, the Christian who discovers the kidnapping is on a *royal* mission.

What happens when Islam arrives on the scene? The latter part of the chronicle deals with this period – a time of war, destruction and uncertainty. The chronicle was composed only a few decades after the transition, but the Mar-Emmeh story was even closer, since he was Catholicos in 643–647.

The Mata Meḥasya story aims, in its context, to offer an answer to this question. Immediately before our story, we hear how the Ishmaelites honored Mar-Emmeh – a claim of no small significance in the critical years after the political upheaval. Then comes the Mata Meḥasya episode, consisting of a story set in the Sasanian era with an addition from the period of Mar-Emmeh, immediately after the Arab conquest of Iraq. It suggests that just as the Christians had the upper hand during the Sasanian era, so, too, under Islam. If the Jews honor the Catholicos, this is a sure sign that all is well under Arab rule. The Jews function, then, as a means of affirming the standing of the Christians. Further confirmation of the secure situation of the Christians is provided in the subsequent episode, dealing with the messianic uprising after which Jews who burned churches were killed by an Arab force sent from Kūfah.

This short story about the discovery of holy relics in Mata Meḥasya appears at first glance to be rather naïve. But the key to the story and its message lies in its historical context – the era of crisis immediately after the fall of the Sasanian Empire. As in the regions of the Byzantine Empire that were conquered by the Arabs, in the east, too, Christians were anxious about the new political and religious situation, and here, too, they found solace through comparing their lot with the Jews. Using Mata Meḥasya as a symbol of Babylonian Jewry as a whole, the

Christian author sought to reassure his flock and establish a hierarchy of the oppressed. With this discovery, the Christians appropriated for themselves the biblical heritage of Babylonia and at the same time asserted their superiority over the Jews before the new lords of the land.

References

Adler, Marcus Nathan. *The Itinerary of Benjamin of Tudela*, London: Oxford University Press, 1907.

Becker, Adam H. 'Beyond the Spatial and Temporal *Limes*: Questioning the "Parting of the Ways" Outside the Roman Empire,' in Adam H. Becker and Annette Yoshiko Reed (eds.), *The Ways that Never Parted: Jews and Christians in Late Antiquity and the Early Middle Ages*, Tübingen: Mohr Siebeck, 2003, pp. 373–392.

—. 'The Ancient Near East in the Late Antique Near East,' in Gregg Gardner and Kevin L. Osterloh (eds.), *Antiquity in Antiquity: Jewish and Christian Pasts in the Graeco-Roman World*, Tübingen: Mohr Siebeck, 2008, pp. 394–415.

Bedjan, Paul (ed.). *Acta Martyrum et Sanctorum*, II, Leipzig: Harrassowitz, 1891.

Brock, Sebastian. 'Christians in the Sasanid Empire: A Case of Divided Loyalties,' in Stuart Mews (ed.), *Religion and National Identity* (Studies in Church History, 18), Oxford: Blackwell, 1982, pp. 1–19; reprinted in idem, *Syriac Perspectives*, Chap. 6.

—. 'Guidi's Chronicle,' *Encyclopedia Iranica*, XI, New York: Encyclopedia Iranica Foundation, 2003, p. 383.

—. *Syriac Perspectives on Late Antiquity*, London: Variorum Reprints, 1984.

—. 'Syriac Sources for Seventh Century History,' *Byzantine and Modern Greek Studies*, 2 (1976), pp. 17–36; reprinted in idem, *Syriac Perspectives*, Chap. 7.

—. 'Syriac Views of Emergent Islam,' in G.H.A Juynboll (ed.), *Studies on the First Century of Islamic Society*, Carbondale–Edwardsville: Southern Illinois University Press, 1982, pp. 9–21; reprinted in Fred M. Donner (ed.), *The Expansion of the Early Islamic State*, Farnham: Ashgate Variorum, 2008, pp. 313–330; and in Brock, *Syriac Perspectives*, Chap. 8.

Cahen, Claude. 'Note sur l'accueil des chrétiens d'Orient à l'islam,' *Revue de l'histoire des Religions*, 166 (1964), pp. 51–58.

Cameron, Averil. 'Byzantines and Jews' (review article), *Byzantine and Modern Greek Studies*, 20 (1996), pp. 249–274.

—. 'The Eastern Provinces in the Seventh Century AD: Hellenism and the Emergence of Islam,' in Suzanne Saïd (ed.), *Hellenismos: Quelques jalons pour une histoire de l'identité grecque – Colloque de Strasbourg, 1989*, Leiden: Brill, 1991, pp. 287–313; reprinted in A. Cameron, *Changing Cultures in Early Byzantium* (Variorum CS, 536), Farnham: Aldershot, 1996, Chap. 6.

Chabot, Jean-Baptiste. *Synodicon orientale ou Recueil des synods nestoriens* (Notices et extraits des manuscrits de la Bibliothèque nationale, 31), Paris: Imprimerie Nationale, 1902.

Dagron, Gilbert. 'Juifs et Chrétiens dans l'Orient du VIIe siècle,' *Travaux et Mémoires*, 11 (1991), pp. 17–46.

Déroche, Vincent. 'La polémique anti-judaïque au VIe et au VIIe siècle: Un mémento inédit, les *Képhalaia*,' *Travaux et Mémoires*, 11 (1991), pp. 275–311.

De Vis, Henri (ed.). *Homélies coptes de la Vaticane*, II (Cahièrs de la bibliothèque copte, 6), Louvain–Paris 1990 (reprint; first published Copenhagen 1929).

Duval, Rubens (ed.). *Išō'yahb III Patriarcha: Liber Epistolarum* (CSCO, Scriptores Syri, ser. ii, 64), Paris 1904.

Ferdosi, *Le Livre des rois par Abou'lkasim Firdousi*, ed. J. Mohl, Paris 1876.

Fiey, Jean Maurice. 'The Last Byzantine Campaign into Persia and Its Influence on the Attitude of the Local Populations towards the Muslim Conquerors, 7–16 H/628–36 AD,' in A. Bakhit (ed.), *Proceedings of the Second Symposium on the History of Bilad al-Sham during the Early Islamic Period up to 40 AH/640 AD*, Amman: University of Jordan, 1987, pp. 96–103.

Fox, Robin Lane. 'The Life of Daniel,' in M.J. Edwards and Simon Swain (eds.), *Portraits: Biographical Representations in the Greek and Latin Literature of the Roman Empire*, Oxford: Clarendon Press, 1997, pp. 175–225.

Gafni, Isaiah. 'Expressions and Types of "Local Patriotism" among the Jews of Sasanian Babylonia,' in S. Shaked and A. Netzer (eds.), *Irano-Judaica*, II, Jerusalem: Ben-Zvi Institute, 1990, pp. 63–71.

Garitte, Gérard. 'L'invention géorgienne des Trois Enfants de Babylone,' *Le Muséon*, 72 (1959), pp. 69–100.

—. 'Le texte arménien de l'Invention des Trois Enfants de Babylone,' *Le Muséon*, 74 (1961), pp. 91–108.

Gerö, Stephen. 'Only a Change of Masters? The Christians of Iran and the Muslim Conquest,' in *Transition Periods in Iranian History: Actes du Symposium de Fribourg-en-Brisgau (22–24 Mai 1985)* (Studia Iranica, 5), Paris: Association pour l'avancement des études iraniennes, 1987, pp. 43–48; reprinted in Fred M. Donner (ed.), *The Expansion of the Early Islamic State*, Farnham: Ashgate Variorum, 2008, pp. 125–130.

Gil, Moshe. 'The Babylonian Encounter and the Exilarchic House in the Light of Cairo Geniza Documents and Parallel Arab Sources,' in Norman Golb (ed.), *Judeo-Arabic Studies: Proceedings of the Founding Conference of the Society for Judaeo-Arabic Studies*, Amsterdam: Harwood Academic Publishers, 1997, pp. 135–173.

Grünhut, Lazar. *Die Rundreise des R. Petachjah aus Regensburg*, II, Frankfurt am Main–Jerusalem: J. Kauffmann, 1904.

Guidi, Ignazio. 'Un nuovo testo siriaco sulla storia degli ultimi Sassanidi,' *Actes du huitième Congrès internationale des Orientalistes, Stockholm, 1889*, Leiden, 1891; reprinted in idem (ed.), *Chronica Minora* (CSCO, Scriptores Syri, ser. iii, 4), Paris 1903.

Harrak, Amir. 'Ah! The Assyrian Is the Rod of My Hand!: Syriac Views of History after the Advent of Islam,' in J.J. Van Ginkel, H.L. Murre Van den Berg and T.M. Van Lint (eds.), *Redefining Christian Identity: Cultural Interaction in the Middle East since the Rise of Islam* (Orientalia Lovaniensia Analecta, 134), Louvain: Peeters, 2005, pp. 45–65.

Herman, Geoffrey. 'Back to Bustanay: The History of a Legend,' in idem and Julia Rubanovich (eds.), *Irano-Judaica*, VII, Jerusalem: Ben Zvi Institute, 2018, pp. 315–343.

—. *A Prince without a Kingdom: The Exilarch in the Sasanian Era*, Tübingen: Mohr Siebeck, 2012.

Hoyland, Robert G. *Seeing Islam as Others Saw It*, Princeton: Darwin Press, 1998.

Jacobs, Andrew S. 'The Lion and the Lamb: Reconsidering Jewish-Christian Relations in Antiquity,' in Adam H. Becker and Annette Yoshiko Reed (eds.), *The Ways that Never Parted: Jews and Christians in Late Antiquity and the Early Middle Ages*, Tübingen: Mohr Siebeck, 2003, pp. 95–118.

Jeremias, Joachim. 'Drei weitere spätjüdische Heiligengräber,' *Zeitschrift für die neutestamentliche Wissenschaft*, 52 (1961), pp. 95–101.

Labourt, Jérôme. *Le Christianisme dans l'empire perse sous la dynastie sassanide (224–632)*, Paris: Librairie Victor Lecoffre, 1904.

Levy-Rubin, Milka. *Non-Muslims in the Early Islamic Empire: From Surrender to Coexistence*, New York: Cambridge University Press, 2011.

Lewin, Benjamin M. *Igeret Rav Sherira Gaon* (אגרת רב שרירא גאון), Haifa 1921.

Nautin, Pierre. 'L'auteur de la "Chonique anonyme de Guidi": Élie de Merw,' *Revue de l'histoire des Religions*, 199, (1982), pp. 303–314.

Neusner, Jacob. *A History of the Jews in Babylonia*, V, Leiden: Brill, 1970.

Nöldeke, Theodor. 'Die von Guidi herausgegebene syrische Chronik übersetzt und commentiert,' *Sitzungsberichte der Philosophisch-historischen Classe der Kaiserlichen Akademie der Wissenschaften*, 128/9, Vienna 1893

Obermeyer, Jacob. *Die Landschaft Babylonien im Zeitalter des Talmuds und des Gaonats*, I, Frankfurt am Main: Kauffmann, 1929.

Olster, David M. *Roman Defeat, Christian Response, and the Literary Construction of the Jew*, Philadelphia: University of Pennsylvania Press, 1994.

Oppenheimer, Aharon (in collaboration with Benjamin Isaac and Michael Lecker). *Babylonia Judaica in the Talmudic Period*, Wiesbaden: Ludwig Reichert, 1983.

Panaino, Antonio. 'La Chiesa di Persia e l'Impero sasanide: Conflitto e integrazione,' in *Cristianità d'occidente e cristianità d'oriente (Secoli VI–XI)*, II, Spoleto 2004, pp. 765–785.

Sachau, Eduard. *Syrischer Rechtbücher*, III, Berlin: Georg Reimer, 1914.

Schechter, Solomon. *Saadyana*, Cambridge 1903.

Sophronius, *Miracula sanctorum Cyri et Johannis*, PG 87C, ed. J.P. Migne, Paris: Imprimerie Catholique, 1863.

Stone, Michael E. 'An Armenian Tradition Relating to the Death of the Three Companions of Daniel,' *Le Muséon*, 86 (1973), pp. 111–123.

— (ed.). *Armenian Apocrypha Relating to the Patriarchs and Prophets*, Jerusalem: Israel Academy of Sciences and Humanities, 1982.

Tha'ālibī, 'Abd al-Malik ibn Muḥammad, *Histoire des rois de Perse*, ed. H. Zotenberg, Paris 1900.

Thomson, R.W. *The Armenian History attributed to Sebeos*, Liverpool: Liverpool University Press, 1999.

Van Rompay, Lucas. 'Impetuous Martyrs? The Situation of the Persian Christians in the Last Years of Yazdgard I (419–420),' in M. Lamberigts and P. Van Deun (eds.), *Martyrium in Multidisciplinary Perspective*, Leuven: Leuven University Press, 1995, pp. 363–375.

Walker, Joel T. *The Legend of Mar Qardagh*, Berkeley–Los Angeles–London: University of California Press, 2006.

Whitby, Michael (transl.). *The Ecclesiastical History of Evagrius Scholasticus* (Translated Texts for Historians, 33), Liverpool: Liverpool University Press, 2000.

Wiessner, Gernot. 'Christlicher Heiligenkult im Umreis eines sassanidischer Grosskönigs,' in W. Eilers (ed.), *Festgabe deutscher Iranisten zur 2500 Jahrfeier Irans*, Stuttgart: Hochwacht, 1971, pp. 141–155.

Wilken, Robert. *The Land Called Holy: Palestine in Christian History and Thought*, New Haven, CT: Yale University Press, 1992.

Yarbro Collins, Adela. 'The Influence of Daniel on the New Testament,' in John J. Collins, *Daniel: A Commentary on the Book of Daniel* (Hermeneia: A Critical and Historical Commentary on the Bible), Minneapolis: Fortress Press, 1993, pp. 90–123.

Questions and Answers

A Literary Dialogue between al-Ḥakīm al-Tirmidhī and Ibn al-ʿArabī

Sara Sviri

My respect and admiration for Shaul Shaked and my gratitude to him go back a very long way. He was the supervisor for my Ph.D. thesis on al-Ḥakīm al-Tirmidhī, and years later I learned that I had been his first doctoral supervisee. Along the passage of time, acquaintance and work, I also learned about Shaul Shaked's interest in Ibn al-ʿArabī's elaborate Ṣūfī philosophy. His taking me on as his supervisee all these years ago relates, perhaps, to his erstwhile interest in Islamic mysticism, before he moved on to explore other fields, in particular his groundbreaking work on magic in late antiquity.

In what follows I shall present a literary dialogue between two remarkable mystics whose imprint on Islamic mysticism has been great and enduring: Al-Ḥakīm al-Tirmidhī (= ḤT, d. ca. 900) and Ibn al-ʿArabī (= IʿA, d. 1240). This is a 'virtual' literary dialogue, as, temporally, a gap of over three centuries separates the two. The dialogue is built upon a set of a hundred and fifty-five questions (= the 'questionnaire') set down in the ninth century by ḤT, a Muslim mystic from the central-Asian town of Tirmidh on the shores of the Oxus River.[1] The questionnaire is included in ḤT's magnum opus 'The Way of the Friends of God' (*Sīrat al-awliyāʾ*), also known as 'The Seal of the Friends of God' (*Kitāb Khatm/khātam al-awliyāʾ*).[2]

1 Al-Ḥakīm al-Tirmidhī belongs to a period and place in which the term *ṣūfī* had not yet been established as the conventional designation for a Muslim mystic. The sobriquet *ḥakīm* may be understood in the sense of 'sage' or 'theosophist,' namely, one who pursues wisdom and the knowledge of the divine realm through visions and revelations; see also note 6 below.

2 This work, long thought lost, has been edited twice, by Othmān I. Yaḥyā (= ḤT, *Kitāb khatm al-awliyāʾ*) and by Bernd Radtke (= ḤT, *Kitāb sīrat al-awliyāʾ*). Unless otherwise noted, subsequent references are to Radtke's edition. For ḤT's questions, see *Sīrat al-awliyāʾ*, pp. 20–29, §40; on ḤT, see Sviri, 'Al-Ḥakīm al-Tirmidhī.'

ḤT himself did not offer answers to the questions in his 'questionnaire.' His intention, rather, was to devise a challenging quiz addressed to those claiming to have attained high spiritual states, namely, the ranks of 'God's friends' (*awliyāʾ allāh*), who, to show for it, pretentiously impart esoteric knowledge: 'If you are empty of what we have mentioned and blind with regard to the knowledge thereof,' he remonstrates, 'what business do you have to enter this gateway, only to muddy its pure water!'[3] By refraining from appending answers to his questions, ḤT obviously wished to deny those he rebuked any external informative sustenance. His 'questionnaire' is not part of a didactic program to be rehearsed and regurgitated through learning; the answers to his questions must become known by 'spiritual' means, through revelation.[4] Some three hundred years later, however, ḤT's challenge was taken up by the thirteenth-century Andalusian mystic Ibn al-ʿArabī. In his own magnum opus, 'The Meccan Revelations' (*al-Futūḥāt al-makkiyya*), IʿA unhesitatingly offered his own elaborate answers.[5]

The 'questionnaire' is not the only literary tract that singles ḤT out from his contemporaries. His autobiography, 'The Beginning of the Affair' (*Buduww shaʾn*), is also quite exceptional – short, but replete with intimate anecdotes concerning his quest, his dreams in the course of it and his mystical experiences, the lonely periods he endured, the harsh ascetical practices he took up during the preparatory stages of his path, and his wife's dreams, her own mystical experiences and the close relationship he developed with her through careful noting them down. He occasionally cites her utterances in Persian, apparently their native language, which makes this probably one of the earliest documents after the Muslim conquests in which the Persian language is present, before its subsequent revival. This feature, incidentally, testifies to the authenticity of ḤT's account.

Significantly for the delineation of the formative period of Islamic mysticism, ḤT, although he sees himself as a 'mystic' – namely, as one who has attained esoteric knowledge (*maʿrifa*) by means of revelation (*kashf*) and inspiration (*ilhām*) – does not see himself as *ṣūfī*; rather, *ṣūfī*,

3 See ḤT, *Sīrat al-awliyāʾ*, p. 29, §42.

4 Cf. ḤT's rebuke: 'Is there a greater offence than that of him who collects the words of the Friends verbatim only to muddle them up and make them into stories?' – *ibid.*

5 See Ibn al-ʿArabī, *al-Futūḥāt al-makkiyya* (ed. Beirut), III, Chap. 73, pp. 70–246. Unless otherwise noted, subsequent references are to this edition.

for him, is a pejorative tag for itinerant ascetics who use their austere practices and ragged appearance to show off and gain public sympathy and esteem.[6] Indeed, in later Ṣūfī compilations, ḤT is not always included in the fold.[7] Nevertheless, his teaching on God's Friends (*awliyāʾ allāh*) – the teaching that underlies the 'questionnaire' – was endorsed, taught and elaborated upon by most (if not all) subsequent Ṣūfī adepts, and themes concerning the holy man (*walīy allāh*) in the Ṣūfī tradition can hardly be approached without reference to it, particularly as developed in *Sīrat al-awliyāʾ*.

Two more elements worth mentioning in this short presentation are ḤT's radical ideas concerning language (a word/name bears an intrinsic relatedness to its meaning),[8] and, as will transpire from what follows, his concern with cosmological structures and cosmogonic processes and their significance for the phenomenology of God's Friends. Comparative analyses of these themes may detect echoes of late antique esoteric traditions, but these are not easy to deconstruct and identify with precision.[9] In any case, it can be affirmed that they do not stem from the Hellenistic philosophical tradition, in either its Aristotelian or its neo-Platonic garb.[10]

Indeed, ḤT was no philosopher; some may refer to him as a 'theosophist,' that is, someone whose esoteric knowledge stems from revelations or theophanies.[11] Based on his visionary illumination, he outlined a mystical system in which human anthropology is seen in analogy to 'cosmic geography' – and in this he foreshadows IʿA. ḤT refers to the 'localities' positioned in this 'cosmic geography' by way

6 For the distinction between *ṣūfī* as the conventional term for a Muslim mystic, established in the classical Ṣūfī compilations of the tenth century onwards, and the earlier, pre-compilatory use of this term, see Sviri, 'Sufism: Reconsidering Terms.'

7 ḤT's reception in the classical Ṣūfī tradition seems equivocal: He is absent altogether from al-Sarrāj's *Kitāb al-lumaʿ*. In al-Sulamī's *Ṭabaqāt al-ṣūfiyya*, which does have an entry on him, Jaʿfar al-Khuldī (in his own entry) is quoted as saying, intriguingly: 'I do not consider him as one of the *ṣūfī*s'; *ibid.*, p. 454, s.v. 'Jaʿfar al-Khuldī.'

8 For more on this, see Sviri, 'Words of Power.'

9 See, e.g., Sviri, 'Emergence of the Holy Man.'

10 Cf. Schimmel, *Mystical Dimensions of Islam*, p. 56, and Abrahamov, *Ibn al-ʿArabī*, p. 5. Schimmel's attribution of the title *al-ḥakīm* to Hellenistic philosophy should be seriously reconsidered and revised.

11 See, e.g., Radtke, *Drei Schriften*, "Einleitug," p. 32; also idem, 'Theosophie (*Ḥikma*) und Philosophie (*Falsafa*).'

of traditional terms such as 'the lower heaven' (*al-samāʾ al-dunyā*), 'the house of power' (*bayt al-ʿizza*), 'the inhabited house' (*al-bayt al-maʿmūr*), 'the upper realms' (*ʿilliyyūn*) or 'the Throne' (*al-ʿarsh*). For him, however, these do not derive from an eschatological teaching concerning the lives of the souls in the afterlife, but from a mystical envisioning of the elevated localities (*maḥāll*, *manāzil*) in which the friends of God are positioned according to their ranks (*darajāt*, *marātib*), during their lifetime in this world.[12]

As for Ibn al-ʿArabī, he was born in 1164 in al-Andalus, in the western regions of the Islamic world, and is reckoned one of the most influential mystical philosophers in the Ṣūfī tradition. As with ḤT, there are those who refer to IʿA as a 'theosophist' (*ḥakīm*) and to his revelations as 'theophanies' (*tajalliyāt*).[13] Although, unlike al-Tirmidhī, he does identify himself as *ṣūfī*, he has an axe to grind with the great Ṣūfīs of the past, among them al-Junayd, al-Ḥallāj and al-Ghazālī.[14] But he has some early role models, too, among them Abū Yazīd al-Bisṭāmī, Abū SaIīd al-Kharrāz, Sahl al-Tustarī, Abū Ṭālib al-Makkī and al-Ḥakīm al-Tirmidhī. IʿA's expansive mystical outlook, to which it is hard to do justice in a brief summary, is based on a universal, multi-dimensional cosmology, in which human and sublime hierarchical strata are seamlessly interwoven: The one cannot be sustained without the other. In bridging between the realms, the *awliyāʾ* play a central role. Among IʿA's many writings, two works became most prominent: 'The Gemstones of Wisdom' (*Fuṣūṣ al-ḥikam*) and 'The Meccan Revelations' (*al-Futūḥāt al-makkiyya*). Chapter 73 of the latter includes IʿA's abovementioned answers to ḤT's questions.

Chapter 73 is a pivotal chapter of the *Futūḥāt*, and one of the densest and longest. It deals, in one way or another, with the *awliyāʾ*, who, after the cessation of Prophecy with the death of Muḥammad, make up the spiritual elite of humankind. Its intriguing title can roughly be translated as: 'On the mystical knowledge of the number of secrets which the contemplator attains while [in a state of] direct facing (*muqābala*) and while [in a state of] digression (*inḥirāf*), and the measure of his

12 See, e.g., ḤT, *Sīrat al-awliyāʾ*, pp. 17–18, §35; also idem, *Nawādir al-uṣūl* (ed. Cairo), II, Chap. 242, pp. 319–326, esp. p. 322.

13 See, e.g., Corbin, *Creative Imagination*, pp. 184ff et passim; also Addas, *Quest for the Red Sulphur*, p. 105 et passim.

14 See Abrahamov, *Ibn al-ʿArabī*.

digression from direct facing.'[15] IʿA alludes in it to an essential aspect of 'friendship with God' (*wilāya*): the ability of the *awliyā*ʾ to grasp God by transcending the implicit dichotomy, not to say dualism, that may be inferred from God's polar attributes (e.g., Merciful, *raḥmān*, vs. Vehement, *dhū al-shidda*). Such transcendence is the Friends' 'direct facing' (*muqābala*). Their ranks, or nearness to God, are determined by the measure of their direct vision of God as a 'Coincidence of Opposites.' The 'perfect man' (*al-kāmil*) is he who holds the opposites together.[16]

As is his custom, IʿA pithily packs into his titles compound notions and ideas which require voluminous elaborations. The unraveling of these dense titles is at times facilitated – and at others obfuscated – by the verses that follow them. Attentive reading of the Proem to Chapter 73 discloses the recurring motif of 'number' (*ʿadad*), as IʿA tirelessly marks the numerical quantities of entities that make up the human and

15 See IʿA, *al-Futūḥāt al-makkiyya* (ed. Beirut), III, Chap. 73, p. 3: *Fī maʿrifat ʿadad mā yuḥṣalu min al-asrār lil-mushāhid ʿinda 'l-muqābala wal-inḥirāf wa-ʿalā kam yanḥarifu min al-muqābala*. I am grateful to Dr. Salman Bashier for reading this work with me. According to my understanding of Bashier's reading, *muqābala* relates to the ability of the Perfect Man (*al-insān al-kāmil*) to face and hold in unison God's polar attributes, while *inḥirāf* relates to digression from such direct facing. Thus, he who attains perfect *muqābala* can hold together the apparent contradiction between relating to God's total transcendence (*tanzīh*) and relating to Him in anthropomorphic terms (*tash-bīh*). Indeed, a few paragraphs after the Proem at the beginning of the chapter, IʿA writes: 'In your heart and in your worship, you are required to face these two relations; do not deviate from them, if you are perfect' (*wa-anta 'l-maṭlūb bil-tawajjuh bi-qalbika wa-bi-ʿibādatika ilā hātayni 'l-nisbatayni fa-lā taʿdilu ʿanhumā in kunta kāmil*[an], *ibid.*, p. 6). Furthermore, '*muqābala* or *in-ḥirāf*, both are in respect of the Divine imaginary descent (*al-tanazzul al-ilāhī al-khayālī*), expressed in the Prophet's saying: "Worship God as if you see Him"; this is *muqābala* towards the Worshipped. Digression (*inḥirāf*) from it is either by upholding God's transcendence (*tanzīh*) – this is the digression of the theologians (*inḥirāf al-mutakallimīn*); or by restricted anthropomorphism (*tashbīh maḥdūd*) – this is the digression of the anthropomorphists (*inḥirāf al-mujassimīn*). The perfect ones are those who hold both things together (*wal-kummal hum ahl al-qawl bil-amrayn*).' *Ibid.*

16 See *ibid.*, p. 6: والكامل هو الجامع بين هاتين النسبتين; and cf. *ibid.*, I, Chap. 24, p. 447: 'Pertaining to this, Abū Saʿīd al-Kharrāz said: "God is only known by being the conjoiner of opposites (*mā ʿurifa allāh illā bi-jamʿihi bayna al-ḍiddayn*)"; then he recited, "He is the First and the Last, the Outer and the Inner" [Q. 57:3].' Many references to Abū Saʿīd and this dictum are scattered throughout IʿA's works.

heavenly universes. His quantitative references, in the Proem and in the rest of the chapter, point to the letters of the alphabet, Qurʾānic *sūras*, celestial spheres, angels, geographical zones, prophets and, last but not least, the *awliyāʾ*, as he calculates the sum total of the varieties of holy men and women who make up the spiritual hierarchy. Rather than shedding light on the title, the Proem remains a veritable riddle, reminding one of the compact, enigmatic style of, say, the Hebrew "Book of Creation" (*Sefer Yetsira*), which also revolves, among other things, around the notion of numbers and counting (*sefira*).[17]

In his detailed account of the categories of people who make up the spiritual hierarchy, IʿA, basing himself on references culled from canonical literature, deals at length with the different types and ranks of holy men and women (*awliyāʾ*). All of them, in one capacity or another, are representatives (*nuwwāb*) of the four ever-living messengers (*rusul*) without whom the world (*al-dunyā*) cannot subsist: Idrīs, Ilyās, ʿĪsā and al-Khaḍir. These four messengers (*sic*!), comprising one 'Pole' (*quṭb*), two Imāms and one 'Stake' (*watad*),[18] comprise a mostly invisible spiritual company that inhabits the highest echelons of the human hierarchy and binds the worlds together. The *awliyāʾ*, knowingly or unknowingly, are guided and protected by the four. IʿA analyzes their typological attributes in detail and, like ḤT before him, locates them on the 'cosmic map.'[19] Obviously, such attention to the mapping of the spiritual hierarchy is something that IʿA shares with ḤT.[20]

What, then, is IʿA's indebtedness to ḤT, and what is the relevance of ḤT's implicit teaching in the 'questionnaire' to Chapter 73 of the *Futūḥāt*? In a clear statement, at the end of his long account (67 pages in the 1994 edition) of the categories of *awliyāʾ*, IʿA explicitly refers to ḤT's 'questionnaire' and proclaims his intent to offer answers to all of its 155 questions:

17 Some other similarities to *Sefer yetsira* can be discerned, but this requires a separate study.

18 For discussions concerning these and other terms pertaining to the ever-present spiritual hierarchy, see, e.g., Massignon, *Essay on the Origins*, p. 92; Schimmel, *Mystical Dimension of Islam*, pp. 199ff; and Karamustafa, *Sufism*, p. 42.

19 See *al-Futūḥāt al-makkiyya* (ed. Beirut), III, pp. 8ff et passim.

20 For IʿA's indebtedness to ḤT's radical teaching in *Khātam al-awliyāʾ* see, e.g., Chodkiweicz, *Seal of the Saints*; also Friedmann, *Prophecy Continuous*, pp. 76, 78.

> In respect of the false claims (*daʿāwiya*) which, formerly and currently, have been widely articulated in this [Ṣūfī] path, the Imām, the possessor of perfect mystical perception (*ṣāḥib al-dhawq al-tāmm*), Muḥammad ibn ʿAlī al-Tirmidhī al-Ḥakīm, isolated (*jarrada*) one hundred and fifty-five questions [for the sake of] examination and testing (*tamḥīṣ wa-ikhtibār*). The answers to these questions are known only to those who have attained them by means of mystical perception and experience (*dhawq*^an^ *wa-shirb*^an^); for they cannot be attained by mental reflection (*al-naẓar al-fikri*) or by logical requirements (*ḍarūrāt al-ʿuqūl*). They can only be attained by means of divine revelation on an invisible plane in one manifestation or another (*fa-lam yabqa illā an yakūna ḥuṣūluhā ʿan tajallin ilāhiyyin fī ḥaḍra ghaybiyya bi-maẓhar min al-maẓāhir*). … This section of this book seeks to clarify and explain these questions (*wa-hādhā al-bāb min hādhā al-kitāb mimmā yaṭlubu īḍāḥ tilka al-masāʾil wa-sharḥahā*).[21]

And, indeed, in the following 175 pages, IʿA diligently engages in answering ḤT's questions one by one.[22] We shall confine ourselves to the first three (or four – see below) questions, in the hope that they will suffice as pointers to the typological affinity between the two mystics as well as to their shared original perspectives concerning the *awliyāʾ*.

In itself, this is a remarkable occurrence of 'intertextuality' in the field of Islamic mystical writings, not only because of the sheer curiosity of a correspondence that bridges three centuries, but because it affords us insight into the multifaceted nature of Islamic mystical wisdom. With respect to ḤT in particular, such insight may help us delineate with greater finesse the varieties of early teachings during the formative period of Islamic mysticism. Typologically speaking, IʿA could certainly have found in ḤT a like-minded mystic, or theosophist (*ḥakīm*), whose mystical perception (*dhawq*) stemmed – as did his own – from genuine divine revelation (*fatḥ, kashf, tajallī*). By means of such perception, both ḤT and IʿA penetrated the mysteries not only

21 IʿA, *al-Futūḥāt al-makkiyya* (ed. Beirut), III, pp. 70–71; see also *ibid.*, p. 28 (towards the end of §76 in IʿA's classification): 'After all this, I shall mention the questions which pertain to this topic and to the Friends; questions the answers to which in total only the Perfect Friend knows (*lā yaʿrifuhā bil-majmūʿ illā al-walīy al-kāmil*). The Imām Muḥammad ibn ʿAlī al-Tirmidhī al-Ḥakīm is he who had alerted attention (*nabbaha ʿalā*) to these questions and had asked them as a test for the pretentious ones (*ikhtibār*^an^ *li-ahl al-daʿwā*).'

22 *Ibid.*, pp. 71–246.

of the human psyche and heart, but also of the transcendent hierarchy of the *awliyāʾ*. This hierarchy, according to both of them, exists, had existed and will continue to exist at every point and moment throughout human history; it does not pertain to the afterlife alone. Positioned in specific localities (*manāzil*, *marātib*, *maḥāll*) within the celestial geography, the ubiquitous existence of the *awliyāʾ* upholds 'this world' (*al-dunyā*) and belongs to it. Thus, though both ḤT and IʿA do not exclude eschatological themes concerning the afterlife from their teachings, their main concern is with the binding together of the two seemingly separated worlds.

The first question that ḤT formulates in *Sīrat al-awliyāʾ* concerns the number of the stations of the Friends of God.[23] For both visionaries, number represents order, hierarchy and relationship, and it signifies the correspondence and relationship between the different strata (*manāzil*) in the cosmic order. Thus, for example, a few passages before commencing his answers, IʿA writes: 'Generally speaking, for each thing in the world that is defined by a number, there exists an equivalent number of God's men by whom God protects this thing.'[24] Phenomena in this scheme are, therefore, not isolated or disconnected; neither are they regarded in terms of genera or species alone. Each thing counts and is protected in its own right, and the protectors are God's men, precisely those about whom ḤT asks. Hierarchy and order thus also entail service, accomplishment of a certain function in the vast gamut of phenomena. This is worship, *ʿubūdiyya*, in its strictest sense.

In the same passage, IʿA goes on to say: 'In this chapter we have [so far] mentioned the men who are defined at all times by a specific number. Let us mention [now] those who are not defined at all times by a specific number, whose number rather increases or decreases.'[25]

23 Note that in Yaḥyā's edition (ḤT, *Kitāb khatm al-awliyāʾ*), the order of the questions concurs with that found in the *Futūḥāt* – the first question being about the *number* of the *awliyāʾ* and the second about the position of their stations (*ayna manāzil al-awliyāʾ*); in Radtke's edition (ḤT, *Kitāb sīrat al-awliyāʾ*), however, the order is reversed – first the *where*, then the *number*. Note, too, that IʿA refers to ḤT's book by the title given by Yaḥyā, *Khatm al-awliyāʾ*, rather than that given by Radtke, *Sīrat al-awliyāʾ*; see, e.g., *al-Futūḥāt al-makkiyya* (ed. Beirut), I, Chap. 24, p. 447.

24 IʿA, *al-Futūḥāt al-makkiyya* (ed. Beirut), III, p. 28: *wa-bil-jumla fa-mā min amr maḥṣūr fī al-ʿālam fī ʿadad mā illā wa-li-llāh rijāl bi-ʿadadihi fī kull zamān yaḥfaẓu allāh bihim dhālika al-amr.*

25 *Ibid.*: *wa-qad dhakarnā min al-rijāl al-maḥṣūrīn fī kull zamān fī ʿadad mā alladhīna lā yakhlū al-zamān ʿanhum … fal-nadhkur min rijāl allāh alladhī-*

For example, there must always be three hundred men who follow the model (literally: 'the heart') of Adam (*thalāthumiʾa nafs ʿalā qalb Ādam ʿalayhi al-salām fī kull zamān lā yazīdūna wa-lā yanquṣūna*).[26] The same goes for the ever-present group of forty people who follow the model of Noah, and so on.[27] As for those who are present at all times but do not have a specific number, among them are, for example, the *malāmiyya* – the people of blame; the *fuqarāʾ* – those who own nothing; the *ṣūfiyya* – the Ṣūfīs, those who possess excellent virtues (*makārim al-akhlāq*); the *zuhhād* – those who turn their back on worldly things; and so on.[28]

The detailed listing of the many groups and ranks of God's men finally leads to the section of the answers proper. To the first of ḤT's questions, 'What is the *number* of the stations of the Friends' (*kam ʿadad manāzil al-awliyāʾ*), IʿA offers a rather prodigious number in response, followed by the complex mathematical calculations by which it is derived. According to him, 'the [total] number of the spiritual stations attained by the *awliyāʾ* in the realms of mystical knowledge (*fī ʾl-maʿārif*) is two hundred and forty-eight thousand.'[29] What is at stake here is not the unlikelihood of such a number and the associated calculations being part of ḤT's 'vision,' but the 'theophanic' method that such a doctrine requires and the epistemological authority by which it is expounded by both ḤT and IʿA – an authority that overrides traditional dogmas, conventional formulae and philosophical doctrines.

ḤT's second question is: 'Where are the stations of the people of proximity?' (*ayna manāzil ahl al-qurba*).[30] Having challenged his readers with an unanswered question regarding the quantity of the spiritual stations, ḤT moves on to intriguing them with a question concerning space – cosmic space. Clueless, his readers are left to ponder ḤT's question about the where of the people of 'proximity' (*qurba*), perhaps in reference to their positioning vis-à-vis God's presence.

na lā yakhtaṣṣūna bi-ʿadad khāṣṣ yathbutu lahum fī kull zamān bal yazīdūna wa-yanquṣūna.

26 IʿA explains that 'to follow the model (*ʿalā qalb*) of an elevated personality' means 'to turn about in the realms of divine knowledge in the way in which that personality turned about (*yataqallabūna fī al-maʿārif al-ilāhiyya taqallub dhālika al-shakhṣ*),' *ibid.*, p. 15.

27 *Ibid.*, p. 16.

28 *Ibid.*, pp. 28ff.

29 *Ibid.*, pp. 71ff.

30 Following the order in Yaḥyā's edition; see above, note 23.

Had the readers been able to glimpse Iʿ A's answer, they would have learnt that the elevated station of the 'people of proximity is what allows them to conjoin their earthly lives with the hereafter (*wa-ʿlam anna manzil ahl al-qurba yuʿṭīhim ittiṣāl ḥayātihim bil-ākhira*),[31] and that in this location (*maqām*), humans (*al-bashar*) meet the angelic retinue (*al-malaʾ al-aʿlā*).'[32] In his answer, IʿA refers several times to al-Khaḍir, the ever-living messenger, which probably suggests that this location, to him, is the space in which the elevated ones – also called *al-muqarrabūn*, which, by the way, can also relate to a class of angels (as in Q. 4:172) – travel to and fro beyond the limits of the two worlds, beyond life and death.

The third question, which may be combined with the fourth, invokes a curious expression. ḤT asks about a special category of holy men who have surpassed a space which he names *ʿasākir* (armies, hosts, troops, camps). What is this space? But first, how, precisely, is the question formulated? For the conscientious philologist, a textual quandary presents itself, for there are three different readings at our disposal: In Radtke's edition, the text reads *wa-ayna alladhīna* ***jāzū*** *al-ʿasākir*: 'Where are those who went beyond the camps?' Yaḥyā's edition reads ***jāwazū***, which, semantically, amounts more or less to the same thing. However, IʿA seems to have read *inna alladhīna* ***ḥāzū*** *al-ʿasākir bi-ayy shayʾin* ***ḥāzū***?: 'Those who have attained the camps, by what have they attained them?' That this must have been his reading is corroborated by his use of the infinitive form ***ḥiyāza*** in the question he goes on to ask: *wa-mā maʿnā* ***ḥiyāzatihim*** *lahum*: 'what is the meaning of their attaining them?' IʿA's reading is upheld not only by the 1414/1994 Beirut edition of the *Futūḥāt*, but also by the Cairo critical edition of 1408/1988, edited by none other than Othmān Yaḥyā – the editor of ḤT's *Khatm al-awliyā*ʾ.[33] Indeed, orthographically, it is easy to confuse Arabic ج (j) and ح (ḥ), and, semantically, both 'go beyond' and 'attain' are reasonable in the context of a question about something reached at or even surpassed. We can therefore accept either of these readings as asking about the whereabouts of those elevated ones who have reached, or gone beyond, or attained, the 'camps' (*ʿasākir*).

But what does ḤT mean by 'camps'? IʿA seems as puzzled as we modern readers may be. He starts his answer by claiming, somewhat

31 IʿA, *al-Futūḥāt al-makkiyya* (ed. Beirut), III, p. 74.

32 *Ibid.*, p. 73.

33 IʿA, *al-Futūḥāt al-makkiyya* (ed. Yaḥyā), XII, p. 69.

apologetically, that 'since the enquirer has sent off his question with no lexical definition or contextual evidence, the one who answers has to resort to the meaning applied to it in his own vocabulary.'[34] Then, searching for its meaning in conventional lexical usages, he concludes that *ʿasākir* refers to 'actions committed with exertion, determination and strenuous efforts' (*shadāʾid al-aʿmāl wal-ʿazāʾim wal-mujāhadāt*). The semantic field of this word, therefore, appears to be strength, force and power (*shidda*), which IʿA associates with the divine name of the King (*al-malik*). And since, according to him, 'those who have attained the *ʿasākir*, attained them by assimilating to the divine name "the King,"' therefore they, too, may be associated with what pertains to Kingship and be thus referred to as 'tremendous' (*shadīd*).[35] Holy men, apparently, assimilate not only with a divine space but also with the divine name that pertains to it.

IʿA goes on to explain the term in conjunction with Qurʾānic verses which, although they do not provide any reference for *ʿasākir*, do refer to the notion of God's armies by a different term, *junūd*: for example, Q. 74:31 (*wamā yaʿlamu* ***junūda*** *rabbika illā huwa*), and Q. 37:173 (*wa-inna* ***jundanā*** *lahum al-ghālibūn*). IʿA identifies these divine armies with, among others, the terrible wind, *al-rīḥ al-ʿaqīm*, that destroyed the tribe of ʿĀd (Q. 51:41), the stone-throwing birds, which, according to traditional exegesis, had helped the Quraysh warriors ward off the Ethiopian army that invaded Mecca in the year of the Prophet Muḥammad's birth (Q. 105:3–4: *wa-arsala ʿalayhim ṭayr^an abābīl tarmīhim bi-ḥijārat^in min sijjīl*). These armies (*ʿasākir*) operate, he explains, only by God's direct command; they are His helpers in His combat against offenders, transgressors and reprobates.

Those of the spiritual hierarchy who attain this tremendous space assimilate with the mighty name of the King and thereby acquire the power to face the adversaries with force, be they God's adversaries or the adversaries of their coreligionists and associates. Imbued with the power of that space, which ḤT had named *ʿasākir*, and with the name *al-Malik*, they themselves become empowered and perform forceful acts. The *ʿasākir*, therefore, are also the mighty helpers from among the *awliyāʾ* who represent and execute God's kingly designs. Finally, IʿA

34 IʿA, *al-Futūḥāt al-makkiyya* (ed. Beirut), III, p. 74.

35 *Ibid.*: *fa-ḥāza hāʾulāʾi al-ʿasākira bil-takhalluq bi-smihi al-malik, fa-inna al-malik huwa alladhī yūṣafu bi-annahu yaḥūzu al-asākira, wal-malik maʿnāhu ayḍ^an al-shadīd.*

implies that when these 'helpers' accomplish their combative function in this mighty position, they attain the divine names *in toto*: 'When they accomplish this, they attain God's "camps," which are His names, for His names are His camps.'[36] Thus, inspired by ḤT's question, IʿA's answer takes us via lexical and Qurʾānic references (*shawāhid*) on a linguistic and literary tour that elucidates his own cosmic vision of a dynamic, militant aspect of the Divine Kingship, in which elevated holy men who have assimilated with the divine names perform mighty acts in the worlds above and below.

Let us now go back to the originator of this question. The notion of divine armies referred to as *ʿasākir* or *junūd* also occurs in other works by ḤT. I shall adduce a few passages that refer explicitly to the *ʿasākir* and may assist us in clarifying its sense in the context of ḤT's vision of this position in the ladder of spiritual hierarchy.

For ḤT, spiritual attainments, first and foremost, are associated with and conditioned by the perfecting of ethical and psychological qualities, and with the process by which the seeker after truth succeeds in abating the power of his 'self' (*nafs*) and allowing his 'heart' (*qalb*) to become the center of his quest for spiritual perfection. In this process, the sincere seeker, the would-be *waliyy*, becomes increasingly convinced of his inherent failings and helplessness. Such conviction arises from scrupulous and dispassionate self-observation, which becomes the hallmark of the distinction that ḤT makes between two types of *awliyāʾ*: the lesser ones, whom he names *ṣādiqūn*, versus the truly elevated ones, whom he names *ṣiddīqūn*. The first lot, in spite of their diligence and exertion, remain within the domain of the 'self.' They rely on their own efforts (*jahd*, *mujāhada*) and good deeds (*aʿmāl al-birr*) and are oblivious to the hidden dangers inherent in the *nafs*. For the *nafs* – what in modern parlance we might call 'ego' – ascribes everything, including effort and good deeds, to itself. Consequently, according to ḤT, the *ṣādīqūn* cannot reach the highest ranks of the spiritual hierarchy. These are reserved for the *ṣiddīqūn* alone, those who relinquish the efforts of the self when they realize that without God's help and mercy they will forever be left prey to its mischief. In *Sīrat al-awliyāʾ*, a few passages after the end of his questionnaire, ḤT describes the state of the *waliyy* who is rescued by God's mercy from being trapped in the confines of the *nafs* and lifted up to a very high position in God's proximity:

36 *Ibid*, p. 75: *fa-idhā taḥaqqaqū dhālika ḥāzū ʿasākir al-ḥaqq allatī hiya asmāʾuhu subḥānahu idh asmāʾuhu taʿālā ʿasākiruhu.*

> When God looks at him and has mercy on him, He lifts him up in the blink of an eye from the position of the 'sincere just ones' (*min maḥall al-ṣādiqīn*) to the position of the 'eminent holy ones' (*ilā maḥall al-ṣiddīqīn*); from 'the house of power' (*bayt al-ʿizza*) in 'the lower heaven' (*al-samāʾ al-dunyā*) to 'the camps around the Throne' (*al-ʿasākir ḥawla al-ʿarsh*).[37]

In this and similar passages, ḤT sheds some light on the mysterious *ʿasākir*. He associates them with the rank of those who have attained an extraordinarily high position 'around God's Throne.' The camps around the Throne are attained by the *ṣiddīqūn* alone, in contradistinction to those who remain in the lesser regions of 'the house of power' in 'the lower heaven.' Note again that ḤT's vision applies to the living *awliyāʾ*. This is no afterlife reward, but the attainment of the eminent men of God during their lifetime.

Digressing for a moment to IʿA's answer to the third-cum-fourth question, one may wonder to what extent IʿA had or did not have access to ḤT's entire corpus – beyond the questionnaire. As the above and similar passages show, ḤT himself might have relieved him of the perplexity to which he admits at the beginning of his answer (see above). Fortunately for us modern readers, databases of Arabic sources reveal some helpful references by which we may follow and encode ḤT's idiosyncratic use of *ʿaskar*/*ʿasākir*. The following are culled from his Ḥadīth compilation, 'The Rare or Precious Traditions' (*Nawādir al-uṣūl*).[38] Here is what we find, e.g., in Chapter (*aṣl*) 275, entitled 'God's Worshippers Are Rescued by Four Things' (*Ghiyāth al-ʿibād fī arbaʿin*):

> When their limbs become invigorated to fulfill God's commands and their selves become obedient and submissive to God, then, when they turn to the Qurʾān, they make the [invocation] *bismi allāh al-raḥmān al-raḥīm* ('in the name of God the Compassionate and Merciful') their knowledge of the Qurʾān's 'camp' (*ʿaskar*). For the Qurʾān is counted as (*bi-manzilat*) an army (*jund*) and a camp [of warriors] (*ʿaskar*) in which there are all kinds of weapons, battle

37 ḤT, *Sīrat al-awliyāʾ* (ed. Radtke), §45, pp. 31–32.

38 I refer to the two editions available to me – neither of which is the critical edition: the Istanbul edition of 1294/1877 (incidentally, this volume was given to me years ago by Shaul Shaked) and the Cairo edition of 1408/1988.

> tools and provisions by which to fight the Inclination (*al-hawā*), the Self (*al-nafs*) and the Adversary (*al-ʿaduww*), in order to destroy their stratagems (*makāyid*).[39]

In the same vein as IʿA's aforementioned analysis of the term *ʿasākir*, we detect here a recognition of the martial aspect of the spiritual quest. But the vision of the Qurʾān as part of these divine armies also entails a sense of the help and succor provided by God's armies to the seeker in his battle with his inner, personal adversaries. As we have seen, for ḤT, divine help and succor are essential to the 'attainment' of the *awliyāʾ*.

A second passage takes us back to ḤT's cosmic geography and offers an additional perspective on the position of the *ṣiddīqūn* therein. In Chapter 245 of *Nawādir al-uṣūl*, entitled 'Seeking Protection from Hypocrisy' (*al-taʿawwudh min al-nifāq*), ḤT writes:

> Inasmuch as [the worshipper in the act of prayer] may throw an external glance at his place among creatures, he may also throw his inner glance at the rank which has been ordained for him (*ilā al-maqām alladhī ruttiba lahu*), if he is one of the people of rank (*in kāna min ahl al-martaba*) …. The ranks of the *ṣiddīqūn*, according to their classes, are within the [bounds of God's] Throne (*al-ṣiddīqūn marātibuhum min al-ʿarsh ʿalā aṣnāfihim*): a camp under the Throne (*ʿaskar dūna al-ʿarsh*), a camp on the Throne (*wa-ʿaskar ʿalā al-ʿarsh*) and a camp in the Kingship (*wa-ʿaskar fī al-malakūt*). The choicest ones are positioned in front of Him in the Kingdom of Kingdoms (*wal-khāṣṣa fī mulk al-mulk bayna yadayhi*),[40] and this is where the glances of their hearts abide (*fa-abṣār qulūbihim hunāka*).[41]

Our pursuit of ḤT's *ʿasākir* allows us, finally, to draw a more complete map of the celestial regions where the *awliyāʾ* reside. Indeed, for both ḤT and IʿA, the celestial realms are filled with holy men – some lesser, some greater. There is hierarchy wherever one looks. The lesser *awliyāʾ*, the *ṣādiqūn*, occupy the lower ranges of the celestial realm, such as 'the house of power' in 'the lower heaven.' Above them is the abode of the greater *awliyāʾ*, the *ṣiddīqūn*. They, too, are arranged in ranks according

39 Ed. Istanbul, p. 401 = ed. Cairo, II, p. 578.

40 For IʿA's acknowledgement of ḤT's originality in devising the concept of *mulk al-mulk*, see *al-Futūḥāt al-makkiyya* (ed. Beirut), I, Chap. 24, p. 444.

41 Ed. Istanbul, pp. 317–318 = ed. Cairo, II, p. 346.

to their various classes – a hierarchy within the hierarchy, as it were. But whatever their class, the *ṣiddīqūn* belong to God's armies, organized in camps on the peripheries of the divine Throne: some beneath it, some upon it and some even farther beyond, in the very proximity of God, in the Kingdom of Kingdoms.

Conclusion

According to both Ḥ T and Iʿ A, human beings, analogously with cosmic geography, exhibit a hierarchical structure built on the principle of spiritual excellence. The two structures – human anthropology and cosmic geography – are not only analogous, they are intertwined. The greater the human perfection, the higher the position of its bearer on the cosmic ladder. Cosmic-spiritual geography is to be distinguished from eschatological geography. Though the notions of paradise and hell, reward and punishment, the afterlife and this lowly life – part and parcel as they are of the Islamic creed – are not dismissed, the teaching of the spiritual hierarchy barely engages with them. It engages, rather, with spiritual attainments and the cosmic positions they merit, realized by certain exemplary men and women during their earthly lives.

ḤT spoke in questions; IʿA speaks with answers. Needless to say, the latter are IʿA's and reflect his own 'theosophy,' which is not necessarily ḤT's. Would ḤT concur with IʿA's answers? A search for ḤT's possible answers, derived from a purposeful reading of his many writings – as we did regarding the *ʿasākir* – may yield different ones. Nevertheless, rather than reflecting dependence of the later writer on the earlier one, the unilateral 'dialogue' between them highlights the conceptual correspondence between two like-minded mystics who, although widely separated in time and inspired by different sources, invite us to place them together within a special typology of Islamic mysticism. A fuller literary and historical comparison may show the differences between the two sages, but it cannot obscure the similar tenor of their perspectives. This similarity allows us to identify within the Ṣūfī tradition, from its early phases, a specific type of theophanic, revelatory mysticism, focused on the nexus and analogy of cosmic and spiritual hierarchies and revealed in the countless phenomena that make up the seen and unseen multiverses within which we live.

References

Abrahamov, Binyamin. *Ibn Al-ʿArabī and the Sufis*, Oxford: Anqa, 2014.

Addas, Claude. *Quest for the Red Sulphur: The Life of Ibn ʿArabī* (English transl. by Peter Kingsley), Cambridge: Islamic Texts Society, 1993.

Chodkiewicz, Michel. *Seal of the Saints: Prophethood and Sainthood in the Doctrine of Ibn ʿArabī* (English transl. by Liadain Sherrard), Cambridge: Islamic Texts Society, 1993.

Corbin, Henry. *Creative Imagination in the Ṣūfism of Ibn ʿArabī* (English transl. by Ralph Manheim), Princeton: Princeton University Press, 1981.

Friedmann, Yohanan. *Prophecy Continuous: Aspects of Aḥmadī Religious Thought and Its Medieval Background*, Berkeley, CA: University of California Press, 1989.

al-Ḥakīm al-Tirmidhī, Muḥammad b. ʿAlī. *Drei Schriften des Theosophen von Tirmiḏ*, ed. Bernd Radtke, Beirut–Stuttgart: Franz Steiner Verlag, 1992.

—. *Kitāb khatm al-awliyā*ʾ, ed. Othmān I. Yaḥyā, Beirut: Al-Maṭbaʿa al-kāthūlīkiyya, 1965.

—. *Kitāb sīrat al-awliyā*ʾ, in idem, *Drei Schriften* (ed. Radtke), pp. 1–134.

—. *Nawādir al-uṣūl fī aḥādīth al-rasūl*, Istanbul, 1294/1877.

—. *Nawādir al-uṣūl fī aḥādīth al-rasūl*, I–II, eds. Aḥmad ʿAbd al-Raḥīm al-Sāʾiḥ and al-Sayyid al-Jamīlī, Cairo: Dār al-adyān lil-turāth, 1408/1988.

Ibn al-ʿArabī, Muḥyī al-Dīn Abū ʿAbd Allāh Muḥammad ibn ʿAlī. *Al-Futūḥāt al-makkiyya*, I–IV, Beirut: Dār al-fikr, 1414/1994.

—. *Al-Futūḥāt al-makkiyya*, I–XIII, ed. Othmān I. Yaḥyā, Cairo: Al-Dār al-miṣriyya al-ʿāmma lil-kitāb, 1972–1990.

Karamustafa, Ahmet T. *Sufism: The Formative Period*, Edinburgh: Edinburgh University Press, 2007.

Massignon, Louis. *Essay on the Origins of the Technical Language of Islamic Mysticism* (English transl. by Benjamin Clark), Notre Dame, IN: University of Notre Dame Press, 1997.

Radtke, Bernd. *Drei Schriften des Theosophen von Tirmiḏ* – see al-Ḥakīm al-Tirmidhī, *Drei Schriften des Theosophen von Tirmiḏ* (ed. Radtke).

— 'Theosophie (*Ḥikma*) und Philosophie (*Falsafa*): Ein Beitrag zur Frage der *ḥikamt al-mašriq/al-išrāq*,' *Asiatische Studien*, 42 (1988), pp. 156–174.

Schimmel, Annemarie. *Mystical Dimensions of Islam*, Chapel Hill: University of North Carolina Press, 1975.

al-Sulamī, Abū ʿAbd al-Raḥmān Muḥammad b. al-Ḥusayn. *Ṭabaqāt al-ṣūfiyya*, ed. Johannes Pedersen, Leiden: E.J. Brill, 1960.

Sviri, Sara. 'The Emergence of the Holy Man in Early Islamic Mysticism: The Myrtle in a Muslim Woman's Dream and Its Late Antique Echoes,' *Journal of Semitic Studies*, 61/2 (Autumn 2016), pp. 463–495 (available at: doi: 10.1093/jss/fgw025, accessed 10 July, 2018).

—. 'Al-Ḥakīm Al-Tirmidhī,' in Muhammad A.S. Abdel Haleem and Mustafa A.A. Shah (eds.), *The I.B. Tauris Biographical Dictionary of Islamic Civilization*, London: I.B. Tauris (in press).

—. 'Ṣūfism: Reconsidering Terms, Definitions and Processes in the Formative Period of Islamic Mysticism,' in G. Gobillot and J.-J. Thibon (eds.), *Les maîtres soufis et leurs disciples IIIe–Ve siècles de l'hégire (IXe–XIe S.)*, Beirut: Presses de l'ifpo, 2012, pp. 17–34.

—. 'Words of Power and the Power of Words: Mystical Linguistics in the Works of al-Ḥakīm al-Tirmidhī,' *Jerusalem Studies in Arabic and Islam*, 27 (2002), pp. 204–244.

The Medieval Persian Author on Guard

In Defense of Authorship

Julia Rubanovich

At the beginning of the eighth/fourteenth century, the famous vizier and prolific writer Rashīd al-Dīn Faḍl-Allāh (ca. 645–718/ca. 1247–1318) issued extensive and carefully elaborated regulations concerning his charitable trust (*vaqf*), Rabʿ-i Rashīdī in Tabriz.[1] Written down in a manuscript dated 1 Rabīʿ al-avval 709/August 9, 1309, mostly in Rashīd al-Dīn's own handwriting, these regulations, which their author entitled *al-Waqfiyya al-Rashīdiyya bi-khaṭṭ al-wāqif fī bayān sharāʾiṭ umūr al-waqf wa-ʾl maṣārif* ('Rashīd's charitable trust [recorded] in the handwriting of the endower, explaining the conditions of the matters of the charitable trust and expenditures'), became known as *Vaqf-nāma-yi Rabʿ-i Rashīdī* ('The Letter [concerning] the charitable trust of the Rabʿ-i Rashīdī').[2]

* This article was written as part of the joint project 'The Borders of Text: Prefaces, Epilogues, and the Emergence of Authorship in Medieval Middle Eastern Literature' (in cooperation with Dr Miriam Goldstein), funded by the Israel Science Foundation (Grant no. 1476/11). The transliterations for Persian and Arabic follow the system adopted in the *International Journal of Middle Eastern Studies* (*IJMES*), with the following modifications: No difference between Persian and Arabic is made in transliterating ض، ذ، ث, *tāʾ marbūṭa* and the *nisba* ending, and they are rendered according to the transliteration for Arabic. Arabic words used in the context of a Persian text are transliterated as Persian.

1 On the generalities of the *vaqf* institution, see Peters, 'Waḳf'; in Persia, see Lambton, 'Waḳf.' On the reconstruction of the architectural layout of the Rabʿ-i Rashīdī, the endowments it incorporated, its inner structure and the organizational principles according to which it was supposed to be governed, see the most up-to-date and comprehensive study by Birgitt Hoffmann (Hoffmann, *Waqf*, pp. 101–239). See also Blair, 'Ilkhanid Architecture and Society.'

2 Throughout this article, I use the truncated Persian title *Vaqf-nāma*. The *Vaqf-nāma* was initially compiled in five copies; see Mīnuvī and Afshār[1], *Vaqf-nāma*,

In a part of this document, Rashīd al-Dīn provided detailed stipulations concerning his rich written theological, historical and scientific legacy.[3] He minutely specified the conditions (*sharāʾiṭ*) and precautions to be taken for the sake of conserving and distributing his numerous compositions, which he unified into a single volume (*jild wāḥid*) 'so that his admonitions would rest for those after him' (*li-yabqā tadhkiratan minnā li-man baʿdanā*).[4] Of tremendous size, the volume, entitled *Jāmiʿ taṣānīf al-Rashīdī* ('Compendium of Rashīd's compositions'),[5] contained two versions of each and every composition Rashīd al-Dīn had ever written, with those composed in Arabic translated into Persian, and vice versa. In this way, Rashīd al-Dīn sought to guarantee that both Arabic- and Persian-speaking audiences would benefit from his legacy.[6] The volume, together with disparate copies of his works, was to be deposited and kept in the 'great mausoleum' (Pers. *gumbad-i buzurg*; Arab. *al-qubba al-ʿaẓīma*), a part of the mosque in the Rabʿ-i Rashīdī main complex (*rauḍa*), which, among other functions, accommodated

Preface, p. 16. See *ibid.* for a facsimile of the original document, preserving all the extant folios in Rashīd al-Dīn's handwriting, and Mīnuvī and Afshār², *Vaqf-nāma*, for the critical edition.

3 This section of the *Vaqf-nāma* is known at least in three versions: (1) A Persian version incorporated in the original *Vaqf-nāma* of 709/1309. See Mīnuvī and Afshār¹, *Vaqf-nāma*, pp. 293–296; and Mīnuvī and Afshār², *Vaqf-nāma*, pp. 237–240; for a partial English translation, see Thackston, *Classical Writings*, pp. vii–viii. (2) A Persian version, dated 713/1313–1314, which, although close to the first one, is incomplete, garbled and contains miscopyings. See Mīnuvī and Afshār¹, *Vaqf-nāma*, pp. 325–344 (f. 327 is mistakenly identified by the editors as part of the version, however it belongs elsewhere); and Mīnuvī and Afshār², *Vaqf-nāma*, pp. 240–241. (3) A version in Arabic placed at the beginning of a manuscript comprising Rashīd al-Dīn's theological works, his *al-Majmūʿa al-Rashīdiyya* (see below, note 9). The Arabic version is cited in full in Quatremère, *Histoire*, pp. cxlvii–clxxv, and partially translated into French, *ibid.*, pp. cxxxii–cxlv; cf. also Browne, *Literary History*, pp. 78–79. My discussion is based on all three versions.

4 Quatremère, *Histoire*, pp. cxlviii (Arabic text) and cxxxiii–cxxxiv (French translation). Unless stated otherwise, translations are mine.

5 *Ibid.*, pp. cxlix (Arabic text) and cxxxvi (French translation). Quatremère's translation of the title is slightly misleading. Cf. Browne, *Literary History*, p. 77. See also below, note 9.

6 … *likay yaʿumma nafʿuhu al-ʿarab wa-ʾl-ʿajam*; Quatremère, *Histoire*, pp. cxlviii (Arabic text), cxxxiv (French translation).

the manuscript room.[7] Rashīd al-Dīn further stipulated concerning the manuscripts of his works:[8]

> (1) Every year, two new copies – one in Arabic, the other in Persian – of specific works should be made;[9] they were to be faithfully transcribed from the master-copy (*nuskhat-i aṣl*) kept in the 'mausoleum' (*gumbad*) of the Rabʿ-i Rashīdī and collated with the original, lest they be corrupted by mistakes or slips of the pen (*ghalaṭ-u taṣḥīf*). The copying should be executed under the close supervision of the responsible superintendent *(mutavallī*), who should see to the completeness of the copy and the physical materials on which it is made: the best paper, of a very large –Baghdadian – size (*qaṭʿ-i ḥāl-i Baghdādī*),[10] bound in leather or its equivalent. The *mutavallī* was also responsible for selecting the best scribes, possessing beautiful and legible handwriting (*khaṭṭ-i nīkū va pāk*) and able to work speedily and competently.[11]

7 On this part of the complex, see Hoffmann, *Waqf*, pp. 194–204 and p. 122, fig. 6.

8 The following stipulations are discussed in Browne, *Literary History*, pp. 77–80; and Hoffmann, *Waqf*, pp. 199–204, albeit in contexts different from that of the present paper.

9 Rashīd al-Dīn goes into minute details regarding the specific works to be transcribed. In the two Persian versions, the number of works to be copied varies. The first Persian version mentions seven titles: *Majmūʿa-yi Rashīdī* ('Rashīd's collection'), comprising four compositions: (1) *Tauḍīḥāt*, or *Tauḍīḥāt-i Rashīdī* ('Rashīd's explanations'; see Storey, *Persidskaja literatura*, I, p. 302); (2) *Miftāḥ al-tafāsīr* ('Key of [Qur'anic] commentaries'); (3) *Sulṭāniyya*, i.e., *Favā'id al-sulṭāniyya* ('Royal gains'), or *al-Mabāḥith al-sulṭāniyya* ('Royal explorations'; see *ibid.*); and (4) *Laṭāyif [al-ḥaqā'iq]* ('Subtleties of truths'). The remaining three works are: *Jāmiʿ al-tavārīkh* ('Collections of histories'); *Āthār-u aḥyā*, or *al-Āthār va al-aḥyā* ('[Book of] monuments and animate beings'); and *Bayān al-ḥaqāyiq* ('Explanation of truths'). The second Persian copy adds to the list: *Taḥqīq al-mabāḥith* ('Exploration of questions,' in several volumes) and *As'ila va ajviba va taʿlīqāt* ('Questions, answers and notes,' in several volumes). The Arabic version is very particular about the exact contents of the seven core works, providing a long *fihrist* and supplementing those seven with three additional compositions on medicine and one on government; see Quatremère, *Histoire*, pp. cxlix–clx.

10 For the parameters of a leaf of the Baghdadian paper, see Hoffmann, *Waqf*, p. 22 and note 6 there.

11 Mīnuvī and Afshār[1], *Vaqf-nāma*, pp. 293–294, 325–326; Mīnuvī and Afshār[2], *Vaqf-nāma*, p. 238; cf. Quatremère, *Histoire*, pp. clxv–clxix.

(2) The transcribed copies were to undergo a ceremony of religious significance: They were to be carried into the principal *ayvān* of the *rauḍa* (*ṣuffa-yi buzurg-i rauḍa*)[12] and placed, one by one, on an elevated stand (*marfaʿ*, possibly a book-rest) between the pulpit (*minbar*) and the prayer-niche (*miḥrāb)*, and a prayer for the author, composed by Rashīd al-Dīn in Arabic, was to be repeated over each copy.[13] In this prayer, Rashīd al-Dīn, referring to himself as Rashīd al-Ṭabīb, asks God's approval for the consecration of a portion of his estate to pious foundations, on the condition that 'from these revenues should be provided sundry copies of these books, so that the Muslims of all lands and of all times may derive profit therefrom.'[14] This prayer was also to be inscribed at the end of each copy, followed by a brief doxology (*ḥamdala*) in Arabic, also formulated by Rashīd al-Dīn himself.[15]

(3) Rashīd al-Dīn stipulates the necessity of a colophon for each transcribed manuscript, to be executed by a *mutavallī* and to include the title of the copied book, the name of the town to which it would be sent on terms of *vaqf*, as well as information regarding the superintendent's relationship (*nisbat*) to the endower (*vāqif*; i.e., Rashīd al-Dīn), generation by generation (*pidar bar pidar*), so that the recipients 'would not forget the endower in [their] prayers' (*tā vāqif-rā dar duʿā farāmūsh nakunand*).[16]

(4) When completed, each transcribed copy was to be submitted to the judges (*quḍāt*) of Tabriz, who, cognizant of Rashīd al-Dīn's

12 For the identification of *ṣuffa-yi buzurg* with the main *ayvān* of the *rauḍa*, see Blair, 'Ilkhanid Architecture and Society,' pp. 69–75.

13 Mīnuvī and Afshār[1], *Vaqf-nāma*, pp. 294, 326; Mīnuvī and Afshār[2], *Vaqf-nāma*, p. 238; cf. Quatremère, *Histoire*, pp. clxix–clxx.

14 Translation in Browne, *Literary History*, p. 78. For the full text of the prayer, see Mīnuvī and Afshār[1], *Vaqf-nāma*, pp. 294, 326; Mīnuvī and Afshār[2], *Vaqf-nāma*, p. 238; cf. Quatremère, *Histoire*, p. clxx. For its full translation, see below.

15 Mīnuvī and Afshār[1], *Vaqf-nāma*, pp. 294–295, 326; Mīnuvī and Afshār[2], *Vaqf-nāma*, pp. 238–239; cf. Quatremère, *Histoire*, p. clxx.

16 Mīnuvī and Afshār[1], *Vaqf-nāma*, pp. 295, 326; Mīnuvī and Afshār[2], *Vaqf-nāma*, p. 239; cf. Quatremère, *Histoire*, p. clxxi. The condition of mentioning the relationship of each superintendent to the endower as a means of the latter's remembrance is connected with the custom of bestowing the office of superintendence of an endowed institution on the endower's offspring; see Thackston, *Classical Writings*, p. viii, note 2.

stipulations, should issue a written and signed certificate (*maktūb*) according to which all the formalities prescribed by the author had been duly carried out. The certificate was to be returned to the superintendent, and only then could the copy be dispatched to a center of learning or a library.[17]

(5) Rashīd al-Dīn goes into great detail regarding the distribution of the copies, prescribing a clear-cut order for their dispatch: Those in Arabic should be sent to lands of the Arabs (*bilād-i ʿarab*), and those in Persian – to Persian lands (*bilād-i ʿajam*), first to the most prominent (or: largest) cities (*muʿaẓẓamtarīn shahr-hā*), then to the prominent (or: large) cities of the second magnitude (*ʿaẓīmtarīn shahr-hā*), as the superintendent sees fit. After dispatch, the copies must be deposited in a *madrasa* in which a teacher (*mudarris*) most renowned in sciences (*ʿulūm*) resides, to be chosen by the decision of judges (*quḍāt*), *imām*s and religious scholars (*ʿulamā*). This will enable interested students (*mutaʿlimmān-ī ki raghbat mīnumāyand*) to read Rashīd al-Dīn's works with that teacher.[18]

(6) Rashīd al-Dīn stipulates free access to individuals who would like to copy or study his works, giving priority to religious law scholars (*fuqahā*). At the same time, he envisages a procedure by which a teacher in a *madrasa* in whose possession the copy is kept would loan it out in return for a deposit (*rahn*). In case the copying is done from the master-copy (*nuskhat-i aṣl*) kept in the *gumbad-i Rabʿ-i Rashīdī*, the copying and examination should be carried out within the confines of the Rabʿ-i Rashīdī alone. The original manuscripts were not to be removed from the precincts. Rashīd al-Dīn also requires that each of the *faqīh*s assigned to the Rabʿ-i Rashīdī make at least one complete copy of his works, in Persian or Arabic, according to their own preference. A scholar who is negligent in copying should be expelled from the premises by the superintendent and replaced with someone more diligent (*har kudām ki dar nivishtan-i ān naqṣa numāyadh va mutavallī-rā maʿlūm shavad ū-rā*

17 Mīnuvī and Afshār[1], *Vaqf-nāma*, pp. 295, 326–328; Mīnuvī and Afshār[2], *Vaqf-nāma*, p. 239; cf. Quatremère, *Histoire*, p. clxxi.

18 Mīnuvī and Afshār[1], *Vaqf-nāma*, p. 295, 328; Mīnuvī and Afshār[2], *Vaqf-nāma*, p. 239; cf. Quatremère, *Histoire*, pp. clxxi–clxxii.

[az] ānjā burūn kunadh va dīgar-ī-rā ba-jā-yi ū naṣb kunad tā dar ān bāb sa‛y numāyadh).[19]

The question of the success, or rather the failure, of Rashīd al-Dīn's measures to secure his writerly legacy is irrelevant to the present discussion. Scholars of the Mongol-Ilkhanid period are well aware of the painfully small number of Rashīd al-Dīn's works that survived.[20] What interests me, as a scholar of medieval Persian literature concerned with the emergence and evolution of the concept of authorship, is his demonstration of a high degree of authorial self-consciousness. In this context, it does not seem fortuitous that most of Rashīd al-Dīn's stipulations concerning his own compositions are patterned after the conditions he stipulated for copying the Qur'ān, in his thirty-volume *Jāmi‛-i Qur'ān-i majīd* and his four- (or more) volume *ḥadīth* collection, *Jāmi‛ al-uṣūl fī aḥādīth al-rasūl* ('Compendium of fundamentals in the sayings of the Prophet'). Among the similarities are the physical dimension of the copies; their placement between the *minbar* and the *miḥrāb* and the utterance of a prayer over them; the colophon with the mandatory mention of Rashīd al-Dīn's name; the certification of the copies by judges; and the order of their distribution.[21] Thus, by extension, Rashīd al-Dīn grants significance to the copying and initiation of his own works, while attempting at the same time to weaken a loaded analogy that might equate his works with the sacred writings.[22]

19 Mīnuvī and Afshār[1], *Vaqf-nāma*, p. 296; Mīnuvī and Afshār[2], *Vaqf-nāma*, pp. 240–241; cf. Quatremère, *Histoire*, pp. clxxiii–clxxiv, clxxii.

20 For a description of the surviving manuscripts of Rashīd al-Dīn's works, see Storey, *Persidskaja literatura*, I, pp. 301–311; on the reasons for the failure of Rashīd al-Dīn's careful planning, see Thackston, *Classical Writings*, pp. viii–x.

21 Mīnuvī and Afshār[1], *Vaqf-nāma*, pp. 166–169; Mīnuvī and Afshār[2], *Vaqf-nāma*, pp. 133–134. For a complete translation of the relevant section, see Hoffmann, *Waqf*, pp. 255–257.

22 The analogy is weakened by what I take to be an intentional separation of the section dealing with the transcription of the Qur'ān and the *ḥadīth* collection from that dealing with Rashīd al-Dīn's works: The former forms an integral part of the *Vaqf-nāma* and is executed in Rashīd al-Dīn's handwriting, while the latter is a kind of appendix written down by an unknown scribe; in it, Rashīd al-Dīn, referring to himself as *īn ḍa‛īf* ('this weak/fallible one'), somewhat apologetically states that he is appending to the end of the *Vaqf-nāma* the conditions concerning his own compositions (*ba-ākhar-i ān ilḥāq mīkunam*: Mīnuvī and Afshār[1], *Vaqf-nāma*, pp. 293, 325; Mīnuvī and Afshār[2], *Vaqf-nāma*, p. 237), which earlier 'fell away from [his] pen' (*az qalam furū-raft*; Mīnuvī and Afshār[1], *Vaqf-nāma*, pp. 293, 325; Mīnuvī and Afshār[2], *Vaqf-nāma*, pp. 237, 241).

Rashīd al-Dīn's profound efforts regarding his compositions, as formulated in the *Vaqf-nāma*, have two principal goals. The first concerns Rashīd al-Dīn's quest for the widest distribution of his works across the Islamic world (Arabic and Persian-speaking), for the sake of disseminating knowledge to scholars and students and also of leaving a memorial *(yādgār)* to himself for posterity.[23] However, the author is well aware of the 'perils' involved in sending his compositions out into the world, potentially resulting in a loss of control over their circulation and risking unauthorized and therefore undesirable modifications, unacknowledged borrowing and sundry misappropriation. To guard his 'progeny' from external menace of this kind, Rashīd al-Dīn devises a range of conditions, meant, on the one hand, to secure his proprietary rights – hence the repeated demand to include his name in the prayer and in the colophons to be attached to every copy – and, on the other hand, to minimize any interference and tampering with his texts. He intends to achieve this goal by creating a single authorized and hence authoritative copy of his works, the above-mentioned *Jāmiʿ taṣānif al-Rashīdī*. Moreover, the very process of copying and collating the copies, their certification by the judges of Tabriz and their consecration in that city's mosque, and finally the bestowing of personal responsibility on all the agents involved in the copying and distribution of his works – from the *mutavallī* in the mosque-library of the Rabʿ-i Rashīdī to *madrasa* teachers in various corners of the Islamic Empire – are intended to ensure a certain degree of authorial control and defense of the works to an author who is himself long gone.

The second principal goal of Rashīd al-Dīn's *Vaqf-nāma* is to resolve the delicate issue of his own creative, authorial individuality vis-à-vis the Creator.[24] The prayer to be recited over the copies in the sacred space between the *minbar* and the *mihrāb*, while confirming Rashīd al-Dīn's authority over his work, points to God as the sole source of authorial inspiration and guidance and as possessing the ultimate agency to accept or reject the author's oeuvre. The full text of the prayer attests to this purpose:[25]

23 The concept of *yādgār* ('memorial, memory, remembrance') is a key concept in the evolution of authorship in medieval Persian literature, both verse and prose. See, e.g., Rubanovich, '*Shāh-nāma* and Medieval Orality,' p. 224; *ibid.*, 'Metaphors of Authorship,' p. 133.

24 Cf. Rubanovich, 'Metaphors of Authorship,' p. 133. See also above, note 22.

25 The translation is drawn from Browne, *Literary History*, pp. 78–79 (with slight modifications).

O God, who reveals the most hidden secrets, and gives knowledge of history and traditions! As You have graciously guided your servant Rashīd the Physician, who stands in need of Your Abundant Mercy, in the composition of these works, which comprise investigations supporting the fundamental dogmas of Islam, and minute researches tending to elucidate philosophical truths and natural laws, profitable to those who meditate on the inventions of Art, and advantageous to such as reflect on the wonders of Creation, even so have You enabled him to consecrate a portion of his estates to pious foundations, on condition that from these revenues should be provided sundry copies of these books, so that the Muslims of all lands and of all times may derive profit therefrom. Accept, O God, all this from him with a favourable acceptance, and cause his efforts to be remembered with thanks, and grant forgiveness for all sins, and pardon all those who shall help to accomplish this good work, and those who shall read or consult these works and put in practice the lessons which they contain. And bestow on him a good recompense, both in this world and the next! Verily You are worthy of fear, yet swift to forgive!

The strong authorial stance of Rashīd al-Dīn and his vehement defense of his intellectual property in the form of a *vaqf-nāma* may have stemmed from his experience as a seasoned administrator involved in all kinds of material property transactions, reinforced by the considerable financial means at his disposal to execute his careful planning.[26] Even more significantly, Rashīd al-Dīn's protective measures might have ensued from the acrid atmosphere at the Ilkhanid court, which was fraught with rivalry and intrigue after the death of Ghāzān Khān in 703/1304 and during the reign of Ūljāytū (r. 703–716/1304–1316), when Rashīd al-Dīn was obliged to share power with other officials, principally Tāj al-Dīn ʿAlī Shāh.[27] Furthermore, in view of the collaborative nature of the work on the *Jāmiʿ al-tavārīkh*,[28] Rashīd al-Dīn may have felt it

26 I would also venture a speculation related to Rashīd al-Dīn's Jewish background: Being a Jewish convert to Islam – which, among other factors, eventually cost him his life – he must have been acutely aware of the perishable status both of his own person and of the products of his life's work. On Rashīd al-Dīn's Jewish roots, see Netzer, 'Rashīd al-Dīn'; Hoffmann, *Waqf*, pp. 61–64.

27 On the basis of a careful reading of sources, Hoffmann provides a graphic and vivid description of envy, rivalry and intrigues among various agents at Ūljāytū's court; see Hoffmann, *Waqf*, pp. 83–89.

28 On this see, e.g., Melville, 'Jāmeʿ al-Tawāri<u>k</u>,' p. 462.

essential to secure authorship of his oeuvre and of the *Jāmiʿ al-tavārīkh* in particular. The assertion of Abū al-Qāsim Qāshānī (= Kāshānī) that he was the real author of the latter composition only strengthens the above supposition.[29]

Whatever the reasons, Rashīd al-Dīn's case clearly reveals the growing awareness among medieval Persian litterateurs, toward the second part of the seventh/thirteenth – early eighth/fourteenth centuries, of the importance of securing proprietary rights to their compositions. Rashīd al-Dīn's example constitutes the pinnacle of that process; to mark its various stages, one must go back to the inception of Neo-Persian literature in the first half of the fourth/tenth century. In what follows, I shall endeavor to map out salient stages in the rise of authorial

29 Qāshānī's claim was widely discussed by modern scholarship in favor of Rashīd al-Dīn's overall authorship. For bibliographical references, see *ibid.*; and Storey, *Persidskaja literatura*, I, p. 321. Qāshānī (d. after 724/1324) was most likely a scribe (*kātib*) and/or a financial official (*ḥāsib*); see, respectively, Zaryāb Khūyī, 'Si nukta,' p. 135, and Storey, *Persidskaja literatura*, III, p. 1396). He assisted his master in compiling some parts of the *Jāmiʿ al-tavārīkh*. In his *Tārīkh-i Ūljāytū*, Qāshānī emotionally and acerbically describes how Rashīd al-Dīn presented Ūljāytū with the *Jāmiʿ al-tavārīkh*, which 'was the composition of this hapless one' (*taʾlīf-u taṣnīf-i īn bīchāra būd*; i.e., Qāshānī); see Hambly, *Tārīkh-i Ūljāytū*, pp. 54 and 240. Qāshānī dwells on the rich gifts and endowments granted to Rashīd al-Dīn, bemoaning his own misery and the unfaithfulness of his master: 'In spite of [his, i.e., Rashīd al-Dīn's] promise [to give a grant] for the composition, he did not grant [even] one *diram* to its composer and compiler, who undertook incredible efforts and successful toil and assembled [the material] for years [*bayt*]: It was I who worked hard, but my master / appropriated it (i.e., my work) under his own name' (... *bā vujūd-i vaʿda ba-taṣnīf yak diram ba-muʾallif-u muṣannif-i ān nadād ki saʿy-i balīgh va jahd-i najīḥ namūda būd va ba-sāl-hā jamʿ karda: ranj man burdam valī makhdūm-i man / ān ba-nām khʷīshtan bar kār kard*) (Hambly, *Tārīkh-i Ūljāytū*, p. 55; cf. *ibid.*, pp. 240–241). Qāshānī's vilification of Rashīd al-Dīn is unparalleled and belongs in all likelihood to the period after his master's execution (see Zaryāb Khūyī, 'Si nukta,' pp. 134–135). It seems to reflect Qāshānī's discontent and embitterment at having been deprived of material benefits, rather than with hurt authorial pride, as well as reflecting a strong anti-Jewish sentiment; see Hambly, *Tārīkh-i Ūljāytū*, pp. 54, 240–241. Qāshānī's anti-plagiarism scruples are all the more curious in view of his borrowing, in his earlier work on precious stones and aromatic compounds, *ʿArāʾis al-javāhir va nafāʾis al-aṭāyib* (compiled in 700/1300–1), a whole chunk from the *Tansūq-nāma-yi Īlkhānī* by Naṣīr al-Dīn Ṭūsī, by then also deceased (d. 672/1274), without any sort of acknowledgment; see Storey, *Persidskaja literatura*, III, p. 1395; and Zaryāb Khūyī, 'Si nukta,' p. 135.

self-awareness as an integral part of the evolution of the concept of authorship in early medieval Persian prose.

The fourth/tenth and fifth/eleventh-century medieval Persian author was far from being on guard vis-à-vis his authorial rights. While his Arab counterpart, in the person of al-Masʿūdī (d. 345/956), for example, threatened God's punishment and sent curses upon the heads of potential scoundrels if they dared alter a word or meaning or ascribed authorship to themselves of his *Murūj al-dhahab* ('The golden meadows'),[30] Persian writers did not even mention their names, leaving their works anonymous for posterity. What they did care to introduce into their texts was praise and thanks to God the Creator as well as the names of their patrons, to whom they dedicated their works. This tendency is exemplified in the most ancient extant treatise on geography, *Ḥudūd al-ʿālam min al-mashriq ilā al-maghrib* ('Borders of the world from the East to the West'), compiled not earlier than 372/982–983 and dedicated to a local prince from the Farighunid dynasty in northern Afghanistan; in the astronomical commentary *al-Mudkhal ilā ʿilm aḥkām al-nujūm* ('Introduction to the science of astronomy'), a late fourth/tenth-century translation of the Arabic work of the same name written by Abū Naṣr Ḥasan b. ʿAlī Qummī in 365/976; and in the historical composition *Tārīkh-i Sīstān* ('History of Sīstān'), whose first redaction was composed not later than 456/1063. From a theoretical viewpoint, these compositions were still produced within the conceptual framework of 'unconscious authorship,' whereby a producer perceives his work in terms of collective property, much akin to the basic principle of folk literature. He functions as a compiler, commentator or translator of materials of earlier authors, stressing by his anonymity his secondary and subsidiary role, on the one hand, and the continuity of the tradition he transmits, on the other.[31]

The simplest marker of an emerging conscious authorship appears to be the self-referential mentioning of the author's name in the body of his work. However, during the fourth/tenth – fifth/eleventh centuries one still cannot speak of any consistent pattern of authorial self-reference: Authors introduce themselves in a rather occasional,

30 See Barbier de Meynard and Pavet de Courteille, *Les Prairies d'or*, I, pp. 22–23; IX, pp. 78–80.

31 In this context, a glaring example is the omission by the Persian translator of *al-Mudkhal ilā ʿilm aḥkām al-nujūm* of his own name, while preserving intact the name of the original author. See Zanjānī, *Tarjama-yi al-Mudkhal*, p. 1.

unassuming manner. An example is Abū Saʿīd (or: Saʿd) Gardīzī, author of one of the earliest historical works, *Zayn al-akhbār* ('The Ornament of histories'), compiled between 440/1049 and 444/1053, who writes: *chunīn gūyad girdāvaranda-yi īn kitāb Abū Saʿīd ʿAbd al-Ḥayy b. al-Ḍaḥḥāk b. Maḥmūd-i Gardīzī ki* ... ('Thus says the compiler of this book, Abū Saʿīd ʿAbd al-Ḥayy b. al-Ḍaḥḥāk b. Maḥmūd Gardīzī, that ...').[32] Another random example is one of the earliest encyclopedic treatises on medicine, *Dhakhīra-yi Khᵛārazmshāhī* ('The stores [of knowledge] for the Khᵛārazmshāh'), compiled around 504/1110–1; its author, Ismāʿīl Jurjānī, introduces himself in an extremely casual and unemphatic, even low-key manner, as *banda-yi duʿāgū-yi jamʿ-kunanda-yi īn kitāb Ismāʿīl b. al-Ḥasan b. Muḥammad b. Aḥmad al-Ḥusaynī al-Jurjānī* ('a praying slave, a compiler of this book, Ismāʿīl b. al-Ḥasan b. Muḥammad b. Aḥmad al-Ḥusaynī al-Jurjānī').[33] At the same time, and in marked contrast, he is very particular and elaborate in lauding his dedicatee.[34]

That authorial self-reference in the body of the composition was still an irregular and even rare practice among prose writers of the second half of the fifth/eleventh century can be seen from the curious instance of the *Kashf al-maḥjūb* ('Revelation of the veiled'), one of the earliest extant mystical treatises, composed by *shaykh* ʿAlī Jullābī Hujvīrī in 450/1058 in Lahore. Having identified himself by his full name at the very beginning of his composition and several more times in the body of the text, Hujvīrī finds it necessary to justify his decision apologetically in a special section, termed *faṣl*:

> The reason for which I recorded my name at the beginning of the book (*ba-ibtidāʾ-i kitāb*) had to do with two things: One concerns the part of the initiated (*naṣīb-i khᵛāṣṣ*, i.e., well-versed in his field of knowledge), the other with the part of the uninitiated (*naṣīb-i ʿāmm*). As far as the ordinary persons are concerned, when those who are ignorant in this knowledge (i.e., mysticism) see a new book

32 Ḥabībī, *Zayn al-akhbār*, p. 173. For additional examples with slight variations in wording, see *ibid.*, pp. 252 and 255. Because of the lacunae at the beginning of both extant manuscripts, it is not clear whether the *Zayn al-akhbār* had a preface mentioning the author's name.

33 Dānishpazhūh and Afshār, *Dhakhīra-yi Khᵛārazmshāhī*, I, p. 2. The book is dedicated to the Khᵛārazmshāh Quṭb al-Dīn Muḥammad (r. 490–521/1097–1127), hence its title.

34 *Ibid.*, pp. 1–2.

> whose author's name is not recorded in several places, they may misappropriate [the authorship of] the book to themselves (*nisbat-i ān kitāb ba-khᵛad kunand*), and the author's purpose will not be fulfilled. For, indeed, the desire in compiling, composing and writing is none other than immortalizing the author's name by means of the book, so that its readers and students will pray favorably on his behalf (*murād az jamᶜ-u taʾlīf-u taṣnīf kardan ba-juz ān nabāshad kī nām-i muṣannif ba-d-ān kitāb zinda bāshad va khᵛānandagān-u mutaᶜllimān vay-rā duāʾ-i khayr gūyand*). [...] As for the part of the privileged ones: When they see a book and realize that its author was a learned person (*ʿālim*) in this [branch] of knowledge and science (*fann-u ᶜilm*), they will strive to perfection in keeping with the true statements [found] in the book and will be more diligent (or: serious, *ba-jiddtar*) in its reading and studying; [in this way] the desire of [both] the reader and the author will better be met.[35]

To drive his point home even more forcefully, Hujvīrī turns to his own sad experience with the literary theft and misappropriation of his works. In one case (*ḥāditha*), somebody borrowed his poetic collection (*dīvān*), which happened to be the only master-copy at his disposal. The borrower replaced the binding and deleted Hujvīrī's name from it (*nām-i man az sar-i ān biyafkand*), thus destroying all of Hujvīrī's efforts (*ranj-i man ḍāyaᶜ kard*).[36] Another unfortunate incident pertained to his treatise *Minhāj al-dīn* ('The Path of faith'), also devoted to explaining the Sufi way (*ṭarīqat-i taṣavvuf*): One of Hujvīrī's 'wicked rivals who is not even worth mentioning' (*yak-ī az muddaᶜiyān-i rakīka ki kirā-yi guftār-i ū nakunad*) erased Hujvīrī's name from the manuscript (*nām-i man az sar-i ān pāk kard*) and claimed it as his own before the uninitiated, the *ᶜavāmm*.[37] In the latter case, however, Hujvīrī did receive some consolation: The initiated and knowledgeable persons refused to believe the fraud, and the impostor eventually was punished.[38]

From the above sketch, it appears that the development of the concept of the 'author on guard,' defending his authorial rights against any kind of interference or misappropriation, was gradual. The process seems to grow more intense with the evolution and eventual fixing of

35 Zhukovskij, *Kashf al-maḥjūb*, pp. 1–2.
36 *Ibid.*, p. 2.
37 *Ibid.*
38 *Ibid.*

such paratextual units as the preface (*dībācha*) and postface (*khātima*), toward the middle of the seventh/thirteenth century.[39] However, it was by no means a diachronic, linear development. For example, the *Mujmal al-tavārīkh va-'l-qiṣaṣ* ('Collection of histories and stories'), composed in 520/1126, bears the markers of conscious authorship in its well thought-out structure and detailed exposition of the author's aims and sources, but it nevertheless obscures the author's identity. The same is true of the famous *Bakhtiyār-nāma* ('The Book of Bakhtiyār'), probably written in the early seventh/thirteenth century. Notwithstanding the work's extensive preface and postface, which elaborate the author's background, the vicissitudes of his fate and the reasons for his composing the book, the reader is never apprised of the author's identity; for some reason, he chooses not to mention his name in the preface.[40]

The 'author on guard' concept became more or less established in medieval Persian prose from the seventh/thirteenth century on, recurring with various nuances and bringing us back to Rashīd al-Dīn's notable and surprisingly self-aware authorial attitude. As an example, I shall examine the historical work *Rāḥat al-ṣudūr va āyat al-surūr* ('Ease for bosoms and marvel of happiness'), completed in 603/1206–7 by Muḥammad b. ʿAlī Rāvandī. In his extremely informative preface, occupying sixty-eight printed pages,[41] Rāvandī identifies himself as the author at key junctures, such as the chapters entitled 'Mentioning the conditions of the author of the book and praising his friends and teachers' (*Dhikr-i aḥvāl-i muṣannif-i kitāb va thanā-yi dūstān-u ustādhān-ash*) and 'The reason for composing this book and how it was composed' (*Sabab-i ta'līf-i īn kitāb va kayfiyyat-i ḥāl-i ān kichun* [sic] *būdh*).[42] He minutely describes the important events of his biography, including his education,[43] thus positioning himself and his work in space and time.

39 On defining paratexts and the significance of preface and postface as markers of authorship, see Genette, *Seuils*, pp. 150–270; on paratextual units in the context of medieval Persian literature, see Rubanovich, 'Orality,' pp. 671–672; and eadem, 'Metaphors of Authorship,' pp. 127–128.

40 The work is conventionally ascribed to a certain Daqāyiqī Marvazī, on the basis of a brief passage in the poetic anthology (*tadhkira*) *Lubāb al-albāb* by Muḥammad ʿAufī (d. ca. 630/1232). See de Bruijn, 'Daqāyeqī.'

41 Iqbāl, *Ráḥat-us-sudúr*, pp. 1–68.

42 See respectively, *ibid.*, pp. 38–39 and pp. 58, 62.

43 *Ibid.*, pp. 38–41.

He dwells on his relatives and companions[44] and explicates the aim and the merits of his composition.[45] In a section entitled *Fihrist* ('List [of contents]'), Rāvandī unfolds the range of subjects to be treated in his work.[46] He repeatedly refers to the title of his composition in the body of the preface, unapologetically and in stark contrast to Hujvīrī's stance.[47] Throughout the preface, Rāvandī refers to himself by his full name, accompanied at times with a range of his honorifics,[48] and mostly uses the first person singular. His high degree of authorial self-awareness also manifests itself in his self-designation as *mu'allif* and *muṣannif*,[49] both meaning 'author' or 'composer,' as opposed to *gird-āvaranda* or *jamʿ-kunanda* – 'compiler, assembler' – used respectively by Gardīzī and al-Jurjānī more than a century earlier.[50] Finally, Rāvandī proves himself a staunch defender of his intellectual property, a real embodiment of the 'author on guard,' in warning readers strongly – similarly to al-Masʿūdī – against any tampering with his text:

> [The author] sends one hundred thousand curses on the life, household, wife and children of the one who would remove a letter or a word from this book, or write an addition to it or delete from it, or utter [a word of] reviling [regarding it], or modify (or: misappropriate) it [in any way].

44 *Ibid.*, pp. 39–40, 47–54.
45 *Ibid.*, pp. 59–63, 67–68.
46 See *ibid.*, pp. 63–64.
47 See, e.g., *ibid.*, pp. 49, 63, 64, 68.
48 See, e.g., *ibid.*, pp. 38, 58, 64, 66. For a general remark on the usual components of the Muslim author's name, mainly in the case of late historical writing, and on the difficulties of attribution they create for modern scholars, see Sultanov, 'Authors and Authorship,' p. 23.
49 See, e.g., Iqbāl, *Ráḥat-us-sudúr*, pp. 38, 58, 62.
50 See above, at notes 32–34. One must bear in mind that self-referential terms of this kind pose a serious challenge for exact interpretation, since their meanings may vary from one author to another. To pinpoint their significations in diachronic perspective, a vast corpus of works pertaining to different genres and epochs should be examined, with a special emphasis on the correlation or lack thereof with parallel terms used in early Arabic literature. An unostentatious attempt at classifying the terms used in late Persian and Turkic historical writings (from the ninth/fifteenth century onwards) was undertaken by Sultanov, 'Authors and Authorship,' p. 24. I hope to devote a separate study to this subject.

va ṣadh hazār laʿnat ba-jān-u khānumān-u zan-u farzandān-i ān kas mīfiristadh ki az īn kitāb ḥarf-ī yā kalima-yī ḥadhf kunadh yā ziyādat-u nuqṣān-ī nivīsadh yā ṭaʿn-ī zanadh va taṣarruf-ī kunadh.[51]

The example of Rāvandī is symptomatic of the shift from unconscious to conscious authorship. Indeed, Rāvandī's authorial stance embodies all the distinctive markers of conscious authorship, including the paratextual units of preface, postface and title; a range of modes of authorial self-presentation (by name, genealogy and autobiographical details, and via the linguistic register of the first person singular and the syntactic-semantic category of the active voice); use of rhetorical means (such as curses) to establish his proprietary rights to the work as his inalienable and individual possession; and more.

The shift to conscious authorship appears to engender an awareness in the medieval Persian author of his position as an individual creator and as the sole rightful owner of his work. He undertakes to eliminate any factors that might endanger his rights to his composition and deprive him of the financial benevolence of his patron and/or the dedicatee, or, more importantly, of literary immortality (*yādgār*).[52]

In defending their rights to exert ownership of their work and control over its content, medieval Persian authors like Hujvīrī, Rāvandī and Rashīd al-Dīn participated in the textual construction of authorship towards its individualization. In focusing on the specific concept of 'the author on guard' and considering a small selection of examples from the rich reservoir of medieval Persian prose composed between the fourth/tenth and the early eighth/fourteenth centuries, I have offered a preliminary description of one of the factors that contributed to the evolution of the authorial voice in medieval Persian prose. Further investigation of this concept should include an inquiry into variations between genres in precise historical contexts, and the examination of a much larger and more differentiated corpus of works, using multiple lines of inquiry, such as the author–addressee nexus and patterns of text reception; aesthetic principles guiding the author; the range of topoi and metaphors employed by the author to describe both the

51 Iqbāl, *Ráḥat-us-sudúr*, p. 64.

52 Cf. above, note 23. An interesting example of the conscious relinquishing of authorship is found in the *Tārīkh-i Shaybānī-khān*, whose author intentionally omits his name as well as those of his father and grandfather for 'political reasons'; see Sultanov, 'Authors and Authorship,' p. 23.

process of creation and the product itself; his self-definition vis-à-vis the literary tradition, and literary canon(s) and potential critics,[53] etc. From a broader perspective, the growing influence, toward the late sixth/twelfth and early seventh/thirteenth centuries, of Arabic patterns of prose composition on Persian prose, and the increasing dependence of Persian prose on Persian poetry,[54] in which authorial self-awareness developed much earlier, should be studied carefully as the two most influential factors in accelerating the evolution of the authorial voice in medieval Persian prose.

References

Barbier de Meynard, Charles, and Abel Pavet de Courteille (ed. and transl.). Maçoudi, *Les Prairies d'or*, Paris, 1861–1877. 9 vols.

Blair, Sheila S. 'Ilkhanid Architecture and Society: An Analysis of the Endowment Deed of the Rabʿ-i Rashīdī,' *Iran*, 22 (1984), pp. 67–90.

Browne, Edward G. *A Literary History of Persia*, III, Cambridge: Cambridge University Press, 1951.

de Bruijn, J.T.P. 'Daqāyeqī,' *Encyclopædia Iranica*, Costa Mesa: Mazda Publishers, 1993, VI: pp. 660–661, s.v.

Dānishpazhūh, Muḥammad-Taqī, and Īraj Afshār (eds.). Ismāʿīl b. Ḥasan al-Ḥusaynī al-Jurjānī, *Dhakhīra-yi Khᵛārizmshāhī*, Tehran: Intishārāt-i almaʿī, 1384/2005. 2 vols. in one.

Genette, Gérard. *Seuils*, Paris: Editions du Seuil, 1987. (= Gerard Genette, *Paratexts: Thresholds of Interpretation*, English transl. by J.E. Lewin, Cambridge: Cambridge University Press, 1997.]

Ḥabībī, ʿAbd al-Ḥayy (ed.). Abū Saʿīd ʿAbd al-Ḥayy b. al-Ḍaḥḥāk b. Maḥmūd Gardīzī, *Zayn al-akhbār*, Tehran: Intishārāt-i bunyād-i farhang-i Īrān, 1347/1969.

Hambly, Mahīn (ed.). Abū al-Qāsim ʿAbd-Allāh b. Muḥammad al-Qāshānī, *Tārīkh-i Ūljāytū*, Tehran: Bungāh-i tarjuma va nashr-i kitāb, 1348/1969.

Hoffmann, Birgitt. *Waqf im mongolischen Iran: Rašīduddīns Sorge um Nachruhm und Seelenheil* (Freiburger Islamstudien, 20), Stuttgart: Franz Steiner, 2000.

53 I examine authorial safeguarding techniques in Rubanovich, 'In Anticipation of Critique and Misappropriation.'

54 On both phenomena, see, e.g., Rubanovich, 'Aspects of Medieval Intertextuality,' pp. 247–248.

Iqbāl, Muḥammad (ed.). Muḥammad ibn ʿAlī Rāvandī, *The Ráḥat-us-sudúr wa áyat-us-surúr*, Leiden–London, 1921.

Lambton, Ann K.S. 'Waḳf, iii: In Persia,' *Encyclopaedia of Islam*[2], Leiden: Brill, 2002, XI: pp. 81–87, s.v.

Melville, Charles. 'Jāmeʿ al-Tawārik̲,' *Encyclopædia Iranica*, New York: Encyclopædia Iranica Foundation, 2008, XIV: pp. 462–468, s.v.

Mīnuvī, Mujtabā, and Īraj Afshār[1] (eds.). Rashīd al-Dīn Faḍl-Allāh b. Abī al-Khayr b. ʿAlī al-Hamadānī, *Vaqf-nāma-yi Rabʿ-i Rashīdī. al-Waqfiyya al-Rashīdiyya bi-khaṭṭ al-wāqif fī bayān sharāʾiṭ umūr al-waqf wa-ʾl maṣārif*, Tehran: Anjuman-i āthār-i millī, 1350/1972 (facsimile).

Mīnuvī, Mujtabā, and Īraj Afshār[2] (eds.). Rashīd al-Dīn Faḍl-Allāh b. Abī al-Khayr b. ʿAlī al-Hamadānī, *Vaqf-nāma-yi Rabʿ-i Rashīdī. al-Waqfiyya al-Rashīdiyya bi-khaṭṭ al-wāqif fī bayān sharāʾiṭ umūr al-waqf wa-ʾl maṣārif*. Tehran: Anjuman-i āthār-i millī, 2536/1977–78.

Netzer, Amnon. 'Rashīd al-Dīn and His Jewish Background,' in Shaul Shaked and Amnon Netzer (eds.), *Irano-Judaica: Studies Relating to Jewish Contacts with Persian Culture Throughout the Ages*, III, Jerusalem: Ben-Zvi Institute, 1994, pp. 118–126.

Peters, R. 'Waḳf, i: In Classical Islamic Law,' *Encyclopaedia of Islam*[2], Leiden: Brill, 2002, XI: pp. 59–63, s.v.

Quatremère, [Étienne Marc] (ed. and transl.). *Histoire des Mongols de la Perse écrite en persan par Raschid-eldin*, I, Paris, 1836.

Rubanovich, Julia. 'Aspects of Medieval Intertextuality: Verse Insertions in Persian Prose *dāstān*s,' *Jerusalem Studies in Arabic and Islam*, 32 (2006), pp. 247–268.

—. 'Metaphors of Authorship in Medieval Persian Prose: A Preliminary Study,' *Middle Eastern Literatures Incorporating Edebiyât*, 12/2 (2009), pp. 127–135.

—. 'Orality in Medieval Persian Literature,' in Karl Reichl (ed.), *Medieval Oral Literature*, Berlin–New York: Walter de Gruyter, 2012, pp. 653–679.

—. 'The *Shāh-nāma* and Medieval Orality: Critical Remarks on the "Oral Poetics" Approach and New Perspectives,' *Middle Eastern Literatures Incorporating Edebiyât*, 16/2 (2013), pp. 217–226.

—. 'In Anticipation of Critique and Misappropriation: A Look at Safeguarding Techniques in Mediaeval Persian Prose,' Special issue of *Jerusalem Studies in Arabic and Islam* (guest editors M. Goldstein and J. Rubanovich) (2018) [forthcoming].

Storey, Ch.A. *Persidskaja literatura: Bio-bibliograficheskij obzor* (Persian Literature: A Bio-Bibliographical Survey), Russian transl. with additions and corrections by Y.E. Bregel, ed. Y.E. Borshchevsky, Moscow: Central Department of Oriental Literature, 1972. 3 vols.

Sultanov, T.I. 'Authors and Authorship in Persian and Turkic Historical Writings,' *Manuscripta Orientalia: International Journal for Oriental Manuscript Research*, 5/1 (1999), pp. 23–26.

Thackston, Wheeler M. (annotated transl.). *Classical Writings of the Medieval Islamic World: Persian Histories of the Mongol Dynasties*, III, London–New York: I.B. Tauris, 2012.

Zanjānī, Jalīl Akhavān (ed.). Anonymous, *Tarjama-yi al-Mudkhal ilā ʿilm aḥkām al-nujūm*, Tehran: Shirkat-i intishārāt-i ʿilmī va farhangī, 1375/1996.

Zaryāb Khūyī, ʿAbbās. 'Si nukta dar-bāra-yi Rashīd al-Dīn,' in *Proceedings of the Colloquium of Rashīd-al-Dīn Faḍlallāh, Tehran–Tabriz, 11–16 Aban 1348 (2–7 November 1969)* (Collected Works of Rashīd-al-Dīn Faḍlallāh, 1), Tehran: Dānishgāh-i Tihrān, 1350/1971, pp. 123–135 (Persian).

Zhukovskij, Vasilij (ed.). Abū al-Ḥasan ʿAlī b. ʿUtmān al-Jullābī al-Hujvīrī al-Ghaznavī, *Kashf al-maḥjūb*, Introduction by Qāsim Anṣārī, Tehran: Ṭahūrī, 1389/2010[11] (first edition: Leningrad 1926).

Shaul Shaked

Principal Publications

Books

As Author, Co-Author or Provider of Scholarly Comments

1. *A Tentative Bibliography of Geniza Documents* (Ecole Pratique des Hautes Etudes, Etudes Juives, 5), Paris–The Hague: Mouton & Co., 1964.
2. *Wisdom of the Sasanian Sages: An Edition, with Translation and Notes, of Denkard, Book Six* (Persian Heritage Series), Boulder, CO: Westview Press, 1979.
3. J. Naveh and S. Shaked, *Amulets and Magic Bowls: Aramaic Incantations of Late Antiquity*, Jerusalem–Leiden: Magnes Press–Brill, 1985.
4. *The History of al-Ṭabarī*, IV: *The Ancient Kingdoms*, English transl. by Moshe Perlmann; annotations of Iranian names and terms by Shaul Shaked (Bibliotheca Persica), New York: State University of New York Press, 1987.
5. J. Naveh and S. Shaked, *Magic Spells and Formulae: Aramaic Incantations of Late Antiquity*, Jerusalem: Magnes Press, 1993.
6. *Dualism in Transformation: Varieties of Religion in Sasanian Iran* (The Jordan Lectures in Comparative Religion), London: School of Oriental and African Studies, 1994.
7. Firdausi, *Shah-nama* (שאה־נאמה, ספר המלכים), I, translated into Hebrew by Eliezer Cagan, Preface and scholarly supervision by Shaul Shaked, Jerusalem: Bialik Institute, 5753/1992.
8. *Magische Texte aus der Kairoer Geniza*, I, ed. P. Schäfer and S. Shaked, in cooperation with Martin Jacobs, Claudia Rohrbacher-Sticker and Giuseppe Veltri (Texte und Studien zum antiken Judentum, 42), Tübingen: Mohr Siebeck, 1994.
9. *From Zoroastrian Iran to Islam: Studies in Religious History and Intercultural Contacts* (Collected Studies Series, CS505), Aldershot: Variorum, 1995.

10. *Magische Texte aus der Kairoer Geniza*, II, ed. Peter Schäfer and Shaul Shaked, in cooperation with Reimund Leicht, Giuseppe Veltri and Irina Wandrey (Texte und Studien zum antiken Judentum, 64), Tübingen: Mohr Siebeck, 1997.
11. *Magische Texte aus der Kairoer Geniza*, III, ed. P. Schäfer and S. Shaked, in cooperation with Reimund Leicht und Bill Rebiger (Texte und Studien zum antiken Judentum, 72), Tübingen: Mohr Siebeck, 1999.
12. Firdowsī, *Shāh-nāme* (שאה־נאמה, ספר המלכים), II, translated into Hebrew by Eliezer Cagan, edited by Shaul Shaked and Julia Rubanovich, Jerusalem: Bialik Insitute, 5763/2002.
13. *Az irān-e zardoštī tā eslām: Moṭāla'āt-i darbāre-ye tārix-e din va tamāshā-ye miyān-farhangi*, tarjome-ye Mortazi Θāqebfarr, Tehran: Entešārāt-e Qoqnus, 1381 AHS (2003) (= Persian translation of Shaked, *From Zoroastrian Iran to Islam*, 1995; above, no. 9).
14. *Le satrape de Bactriane et son gouverneur: Documents araméens du IVe s. avant notre ère provenant de Bactriane – Conférences données au Collège de France, 14 et 21 mai 2003* (Persika, 4), Paris: Editions de Bocard, 2004.
15. *Taḥavvol-e sanaviyyat: tanavvo'e ārāy-e dini dar 'aṣr-e sāsāni*, Persian transl. by Sayyed Aḥmad Reẓā Qā'emmaqāmi, Tehran: Našr-e Māhi, 1387 AHS (2009) (= Persian translation of Shaked, *Dualism in Transformation*; above, no. 6).
16. *Dīnkard-e šašom, Ḥekmat-e Farzānagān-e sāsāni*, Āðarpād Amīdān, tarjome-ye doktor Ferešte Āhangari, Tehran: Kelk-e simin, 1390 AHS (2011) (= unacknowledged Persian translation of Shaked, *Wisdom of the Sasanian Sages*; above, no. 2).
17. J. Naveh and S. Shaked, *Aramaic Documents from Ancient Bactria (Fourth Century BCE) from the Khalili Collections*, London: The Khalili Family Trust, 2012.
18. S. Shaked, J.N. Ford and S. Bhayro, *Aramaic Bowl Spells: Jewish Babylonian Aramaic Bowls*, I (Magical and Religious Literature of Late Antiquity: Manuscripts in the Schøyen Collection, 20), Leiden–Boston: Brill, 2013.
19. S. Shaked, J.N. Ford and S. Bhayro, *Aramaic Bowl Spells: Jewish Babylonian Aramaic Bowls*, II (Magical and Religious Literature of Late Antiquity: Manuscripts in the Schøyen Collection), Leiden–Boston: Brill, forthcoming.

Edited Volumes

20. *Irano-Judaica: Studies Relating to Jewish Contacts with Persian Culture Throughout the Ages*, Jerusalem: Ben-Zvi Institute, 1982.
21. S. Shaked, D. Shulman and G.G. Stroumsa, (eds.), *Gilgul: Essays on Transformation, Revelation and Permanence in the History of Religions, Dedicated to R.J. Zwi Werblowsky* (Studies in the History of Religions, Supplements to Numen, 50), Leiden: Brill, 1987.
22. S. Shaked and A. Netzer (eds.), *Irano-Judaica: Studies Relating to Jewish Contacts with Persian Culture Throughout the Ages*, II, Jerusalem: Ben-Zvi Institute, 1990.
23. I. Gruenwald, S. Shaked and G.G. Stroumsa (eds.), *Messiah and Christos: Studies in the Jewish Origins of Christianity Presented to David Flusser* (Texte und Studien zum Antiken Judentum, 32), Tübingen: J.C.B. Mohr (Paul Siebeck), 1992.
24. S. Shaked and A. Netzer (eds.), *Irano-Judaica: Studies Relating to Jewish Contacts with Persian Culture Throughout the Ages*, III, Jerusalem: Ben-Zvi Institute, 1994.
25. S. Shaked and A. Netzer (eds.), *Irano-Judaica: Studies Relating to Jewish Contacts with Persian Culture Throughout the Ages*, IV, Jerusalem: Ben-Zvi Institute, 1999.
26. S. Shaked and A. Netzer (eds.), *Irano-Judaica: Studies Relating to Jewish Contacts with Persian Culture Throughout the Ages*, V, Jerusalem: Ben-Zvi Institute, 2003.
27. *Genesis and Regeneration: Essays on Conceptions of Origins*, Jerusalem: The Israel Academy of Sciences and Humanities, 2005.
28. *Officina Magica: Essays on the Practice of Magic in Antiquity* (IJS Studies in Judaica: Conference Proceedings of the Institute of Jewish Studies, University College London, 4), Leiden–Boston: Brill, 2005.
29. S. Shaked and A. Netzer (eds.), *Irano-Judaica: Studies Relating to Jewish Contacts with Persian Culture Throughout the Ages*, VI, Jerusalem: Ben-Zvi Institute, 2008.
30. Menahem Kister, Joseph Geiger, Nadav Ne'eman and Shaul Shaked (eds.), *Ancient Gods: Polytheism in Eretz Israel and Neighboring Countries from the Second Millennium BCE to the Islamic Period* (אלי קדם: הפוליתאיזם בארץ ישראל ושכנותיה מן האלף השני לפסה"נ ועד התקופה המוסלמית), Jerusalem: Ben-Zvi Institute, 2008.

31. S. Shaked and N. Pirnazar (eds.), *Andišehā, xāṭerehā va nāmehā: Majmuʿe-i az maqālāt-e porofesōr amnon netṣer, jeld-e avval* (virāstārān: porof. šāʾul šāked, doktor nāhid pirnaẓar. Markaz-e taḥqiqāt-e yahud va irānšenāsi-ye amnon netṣer, dānešgāh-e ʿebri-ye urešlim), Los Angeles: Šarekat-e ketāb, 2009.
32. G. Bohak, Y. Harari and S. Shaked (eds.), *Continuity and Innovation in Magical Tradition* (Jerusalem Studies in Religion and Culture, 15), Leiden–Boston: Brill, 2011.
33. H. Ben-Shammai, S. Shaked and S. Stroumsa (eds.), *Exchange and Transmission across Cultural Boundaries: Philosophy, Mysticism and Science in the Mediterranean World – Proceedings of an International Workshop Held in Memory of Professor Shlomo Pines at The Institute for Advanced Studies, The Hebrew University of Jerusalem, 28 February – 2 March 2005* (Studies in the Humanities), Jerusalem: The Israel Academy of Sciences and Humanities, 2013.

Scholarly Articles

34. A.D.H. Bivar and S. Shaked, 'The Inscriptions at Shīmbār,' *Bulletin of the School of Oriental and African Studies*, 27 (1964), pp. 265–280.
35. 'Some Notes on Ahreman, the Evil Spirit, and His Creation,' in: E.E. Urbach, R.J. Zwi Werblowsky and C.H. Wirszubsky (eds.), *Studies in Mysticism and Religion Presented to G.G. Scholem*, Jerusalem: Magnes Press, 1967, pp. 227–254 (reprinted in Shaked, *From Zoroastrian Iran to Islam*, 1995; above, no. 9).
36. 'Esoteric Trends in Zoroastrianism,' *Proceedings of the Israel Academy of Sciences and Humanities*, III, no. 7 (1969), pp. 175–221 (reprinted in Shaked, *From Zoroastrian Iran to Islam*, 1995; above, no. 9).
37. 'Notes on the New Aśoka Inscription from Kandahar,' *Journal of the Royal Asiatic Society*, 101/2 (1969), pp. 118–122.
38. 'Specimens of Middle Persian Verse,' in: Mary Boyce and Ilya Gershevitch (eds.), *W.B. Henning Memorial Volume*, London: Lund Humphries, 1970, pp. 395–405.
39. Y. Kutscher, J. Naveh and S. Shaked, 'The Aramaic Inscriptions of Asoka' (הכתובות הארמיות של אשוקה), *Lešonenu*, 34 (1970), pp. 125–134.
40. 'Eschatology and the Goal of the Religious Life in Sasanian

Zoroastrianism,' in: J. Bleeker and R.J.Z. Werblowsky (eds.), *Types of Redemption* (Numen Book Series, 18), Leiden: Brill, 1970, pp. 223–230.

41. 'Judaeo-Persian Notes,' *Israel Oriental Studies*, 1 (1971), pp. 178–182.
42. 'The Notions *Mēnōg* and *Gētīg* in the Pahlavi Texts and Their Relation to Eschatology,' *Acta Orientalia*, 33 (1971), pp. 59–107 (reprinted in Shaked, *From Zoroastrian Iran to Islam*, 1995; above, no. 9).
43. J. Naveh and S. Shaked, 'A Recently Published Aramaic Papyrus,' *Journal of the American Oriental Society*, 91 (1971), pp. 379–382.
44. 'An Early Karaite Document in Judaeo-Persian' (תעודה קראית קדומה בפרסית יהודית), *Tarbiz*, 41 (5732/1972), pp. 49–58.
45. J.C. Greenfield and S. Shaked, 'Three Iranian Words in the Targum of Job from Qumran,' *Zeitschrift der Deutschen Morgenländischen Gesellschaft*, 122 (1972), pp. 37–45.
46. 'Amarkal' (Hebrew and English), in: E.Y. Kutscher (ed.), *Archive of the New Dictionary of Rabbinical Literature*, I, Ramat Gan: Bar Ilan University, 1972, pp. 112, xxxiv.
47. 'Qumran and Iran: Further Considerations,' *Israel Oriental Studies*, 2 (1972), pp. 433–446.
48. J. Naveh and S. Shaked, 'Ritual Texts or Treasury Documents?,' *Orientalia*, 42 (1973), pp. 445–457.
49. 'Ambiguous Words in Pahlavi,' *Israel Oriental Studies*, 4 (1974), pp. 227–257.
50. 'Some Terms Relating to Man in Pahlavi, I: *axw* (*ox*),' in: P. Gignoux and A. Tafazzoli (eds.), *Mémorial Jean de Menasce*, Louvain: Imprimerie Orientaliste, 1974, pp. 255–262.
51. 'Some Legal and Administrative Terms of the Sasanian Period,' in: *Monumentum H.S. Nyberg*, II (Acta Iranica, 5), Tehran–Liège–Leiden: Bibliothèque Pahlavi–Brill, 1975, pp. 213–225.
52. 'Notes on the Inscription on the Foroughi Bowl,' *Artibus Asiae*, 38 (1976), pp. 47–48 (appendix to: Guitty Azarpay, 'The Allegory of *Dēn* in Persian Art,' *ibid.*, pp. 37–47).
53. 'Observations on the Study of Oriental Jewish Communities,' *AJS Newsletter*, 18 (1976), pp. 5–6, 9.
54. 'Persia and the Origins of the Karaite Movement,' *AJS Newsletter*, 18 (1976), pp. 7–9.
55. 'Jewish and Christian Seals of the Sasanian Period,' in: M. Rosen-Ayalon (ed.), *Studies in Memory of Gaston Wiet*, Jerusalem:

Institute of Asian and African Studies, The Hebrew University of Jerusalem, 1977, pp. 17–31, pl. IV.

56. ‘Appendix in Judaeo-Persian’ (נספח ביהודית־פרסית), in: E.E. Urbach (ed.), *Pitron tora: Yalquṭ midrashim uperushim* (פתרון תורה: ילקוט מדרשים ופרושים), Jerusalem: Magnes–Jewish National and University Library, 5738/1978, pp. 347–352.
57. Review of Jürgen Hampel, *Die Kopenhagener Handschrift Cod. 27*, *Indo-Iranian Journal*, 20 (1978), pp. 102–105.
58. ‘A Persian Letter from the Time of Tamerlane from the Cairo Geniza,’ in: *Studia Orientalia Memoriae D.H. Baneth Dedicata*, Jerusalem: Magnes Press, 1979, pp. 239–244, pls I–III.
59. ‘The Heritage of Oriental Jewry and Its Research: Problems and Trends’ (מורשת יהדות המזרח ומחקרה: מגמות ובעיות), *Pe‘amim*, 1 (5739/1979), pp. 7–14.
60. ‘The Song of Songs in Judaeo-Persian’ (שיר השירים בפרסית יהודית), *Pe‘amim*, 2 (5739/1979), pp. 109–111.
61. ‘Mihr the Judge,’ *Jerusalem Studies in Arabic and Islam*, 2 (1980), pp. 1–31.
62. ‘Epigraphica Judaeo-Iranica,’ in: *Studies in Judaism and Islam presented to S.D. Goitein*, Jerusalem: Magnes Press, 1981, pp. 65–82, pl. (reprinted in Shaked, *From Zoroastrian Iran to Islam*, 1995; above, no. 9).
63. ‘Two Judaeo-Iranian Contributions,’ in: Shaked (ed.), *Irano-Judaica* (1982; above, no. 17), pp. 292–322.
64. ‘Pahlavi Notes: 1. *dahišn* “reflection”; 2. *juttar* “evil,”’ *Monumentum Georg Morgenstierne*, II (Acta Iranica, 22), Leiden: Brill, 1982, pp. 197–205.
65. ‘On Jewish Literature of Magic in Muslim Countries: Comments and Specimens’ (על ספרות הכישוף היהודית בארצות האסלאם: הערות ודוגמאות), *Pe‘amim*, 15 (5743/1983), pp. 15–28.
66. ‘The Influence of the Iranian Religion on Judaism’ (השפעת הדת האיראנית על היהדות), in: H. Tadmor and I. Eph‘al (eds.), *History of the Jewish People*, VI: *The Return to Zion – The Persian Period* (ההיסטוריה של עם ישראל: שיבת ציון, ימי שלטון פרס), Jerusalem: A. Peli, 5743/1983, pp. 236–250, 315–317.
67. ‘From Iran to Islam: Notes on Some Themes in Transmission, 1: Religion and Sovereignty Are Twins in Ibn al-Muqaffa‘’s Theory of Government; 2: The Four Sages,’ *Jerusalem Studies in Arabic and Islam*, 4 (1984), pp. 31–67 (reprinted in Shaked, *From Zoroastrian Iran to Islam*, 1995; above, no. 9).

68. 'Iranian Influences in Judaism,' *Cambridge History of Judaism*, I, Cambridge: Cambridge University Press, 1984, pp. 308–325, 441–442.
69. 'S.D. Goitein: Historian of the Jewish-Islamic Symbiosis' (ש.ד. גויטיין, חוקר השותפות ההיסטורית שבין היהדות לאסלאם), *Pe'amim*, 22 (5745/1985), pp. 4–9.
70. 'Aspects of the Early Heritage of Persian Jews' (פרקים במורשתם הקדומה של יהודי פרס), *Pe'amim*, 23 (5745/1985), pp. 22–37.
71. 'Bagdana, King of the Demons, and Other Iranian Terms in Babylonian Aramaic Magic,' in: H.W. Bailey, A.D.H. Bivar, J. Duchesne-Guillemin and J.R Hinnells (eds.), *Papers in Honour of Professor Mary Boyce*, II (Acta Iranica, 25), Leiden: Brill, 1985, pp. 511–525.
72. 'Andarz and Andarz Literature in Pre-Islamic Iran,' *Encyclopaedia Iranica*, II (1985), pp. 11–16.
73. J.C. Greenfield and Joseph Naveh (with notes on Iranian matters by S. Shaked), 'A Mandaic Lead Amulet with Four Incantations' (קמיע מנדעי בעל ארבע השבעות), *Eretz-Israel*, 18 (1985), pp. 97–107.
74. 'From Iran to Islam: On Some Symbols of Royalty,' *Jerusalem Studies in Arabic and Islam*, 7 (1986), pp. 75–91 (reprinted in Shaked, *From Zoroastrian Iran to Islam*, 1995; above, no. 9).
75. 'Iranian Loanwords in Middle Aramaic,' *Encyclopaedia Iranica*, II (1986), pp. 259–261.
76. A. Negev, with a contribution by J. Naveh and S. Shaked, 'Obodas the God,' *Israel Exploration Journal*, 36 (1986), pp. 56–60.
77. S. Shaked and J. Naveh, 'Three Aramaic Seals of the Achaemenid Period,' *Journal of the Royal Asiatic Society*, 118 (1986), pp. 21–29.
78. S. Pines and S. Shaked, 'Fragment of a Jewish-Christian Composition from the Cairo Geniza,' in: M. Sharon (ed.), *Studies in Islamic History and Civilization in Honour of David Ayalon*, Jerusalem–Leiden: Cana–Brill, 1986, pp. 307–318 (reprinted in S. Pines, *Studies in the History of Religions* [The Collected Works of Shlomo Pines, IV], Jerusalem: Magnes Press, 1996 pp. 473–486).
79. 'An Unusual Verbal Form in Early Judaeo-Persian,' in: R. Schmitt and P.O. Skjærvø (eds.), *Studia Grammatica Iranica: Festschrift für H. Humbach* (Münchener Studien zur Sprachwissenschaft), Munich: Kitzinger, 1986, pp. 393– 405.
80. M. Gil and S. Shaked, review of M.B. Morony, *Iraq after the*

Muslim Conquest (Princeton 1984), *Journal of the American Oriental Society*, 106 (1986), pp. 819–823.

81. 'Paymān: An Iranian Idea in Contact with Greek Thought and Islam,' in: *Transition Periods in Iranian History – Actes du Symposium de Fribourg-en-Brisgau (22–24 mai 1985)* (Studia Iranica, 5), Paris: Association pour l'Avancement des Etudes Iraniennes, 1987, pp. 217–240 (reprinted in Shaked, *From Zoroastrian Iran to Islam*, 1995; above, no. 9).
82. 'A Facetious Recipe and the Two Wisdoms: Iranian Themes in Muslim Garb,' *Jerusalem Studies in Arabic and Islam*, 9 (1987), pp. 24–35 (reprinted in Shaked, *From Zoroastrian Iran to Islam*, 1995; above, no. 9).
83. 'First Man, First King: Notes on Semitic-Iranian Syncretism and Iranian Mythological Transformations,' in: Stroumsa, Shaked and Shulman (eds.), *Gilgul* (1987; above, no. 21), pp. 238–256 (reprinted in Shaked, *From Zoroastrian Iran to Islam*, 1995; above, no. 9).
84. Review of J.B. Segal, *Aramaic texts from North Saqqara* (London 1983), *Orientalia*, 56 (1987), pp. 407–413.
85. 'Moreen's "Babai ibn Lutf's Chronicle,"' *Jewish Quarterly Review*, 77 (1986/7), pp. 247–250.
86. 'Ayādgār-ī Wuzurgmihr,' *Encyclopaedia Iranica*, III, fasc. 2, 1987, pp. 127–128.
87. 'Mythes d'origine comme actes de commémoration et de différenciation en Iran sasanide,' in: Ph. Gignoux (ed.), *La commémoration – Colloque du centenaire de la Section des Sciences Religieuses de l'Ecole Pratique des Hautes Etudes* (Bibliothèque de l'Ecole des Hautes Etudes, Sciences Religieuses, 91), Louvain–Paris: Peeters 1988, pp. 211–218.
88. 'An Early Magic Fragment from the Cairo Geniza,' in: R. Dan (ed.), *Occident and Orient: A Tribute to the Memory of Alexander Scheiber*, Budapest–Leiden: Akadémiai Kiadó–Brill, 1988, pp. 361–371.
89. 'An Early Geniza Fragment in an Unknown Iranian Dialect,' in: W. Sundermann, J. Duchesne-Guillemin and F. Vahman (eds.), *Barg-e sabz – A Green Leaf: Papers in Honour of Prof. J.P. Asmussen* (Acta Iranica, 28: Hommages et opera minora, 12), Leiden: Brill, 1988, pp. 219–235.
90. Review of W. Skalmowski and A. van Tongerloo (eds.), *Middle*

Iranian Studies – Proceedings of the International Symposium Organized by the Katholieke Universiteit Leuven ... May 1982 (Orientalia Lovaniensia Analecta, 16, Leuven 1984), *Bibliotheca Orientalis*, 45 (1988), pp. 155–162.

91. 'Persia as a Model for Intercultural Contact' (פרס כדגם למפגש בין תרבויות), in: *Hitbolelut uṭmi'a* (התבוללות וטמיעה: המשכיות ותמורה בתרבות העמים ובישראל), Jerusalem: Zalman Shazar Center, 1989, pp. 107–117.
92. 'Middle Persian Translations of the Bible,' *Encyclopaedia Iranica*, IV, fasc. 2 (1989), pp. 206–207.
93. 'Notes on the Preposition *be* in Judaeo-Persian,' in: C.H. de Fouchécour and Ph. Gignoux (eds.), *Etudes irano-aryennes offertes à Gilbert Lazard* (Studia Iranica, 7), Paris: Association pour l'Avancement des Études Iraniennes, 1989, pp. 315–319.
94. 'On the Interpretation of Cosmogonical Myths,' in: S. Fred Singer (ed.), *The Universe and Its Origins: From Ancient Myth to Present Reality and Fantasy*, New York: Paragon House, 1990, pp. 27–34.
95. '"Do Not Buy Anything from an Aramaean": A Fragment of Aramaic Proverbs with a Judaeo-Iranian Version,' in: *Papers in Honor of Ehsan Yarshater* (Acta Iranica, 30), Leiden: Brill, 1990, pp. 230–239.
96. '"For the Sake of the Soul": A Zoroastrian Idea in Transmission into Islam,' *Jerusalem Studies in Arabic and Islam*, 13 (1990), pp. 15–32 (reprinted in Shaked, *From Zoroastrian Iran to Islam*, 1995; above, no. 9).
97. 'Zoroastrian Polemics against Jews in the Sasanian and Early Islamic Period,' in: Shaked and Netzer (eds.), *Irano-Judaica*, II (1990; above, no. 22), pp. 85–104.
98. Review of J. Russell, *Zoroastrianism in Armenia* (Cambridge, MA, 1987), *Iranshenasi*, 2/3 (1990), pp. 65–74.
99. 'Administrative Functions of Priests in the Sasanian Period,' in: *Proceedings of the First European Conference of Iranian Studies, held in Turin, September 7th–11th, 1987 by the Societas Iranologica Europea*, Part 1, Rome: Istituto Italiano per il Medio ed Estremo Oriente 1990, pp. 261–273.
100. 'Spurious Epigraphy,' *Bulletin of the Asia Institute in Honor of R.N. Frye: Aspects of Iranian Culture*, NS 4 (1990), pp. 267–275.
101. 'Aspects of Iranian Religion in the Achaemenian Period,' in: *K.R. Cama Oriental Institute: International Congress Proceedings*, Bombay 1991, pp. 90–100.

102. 'Aspekte von Noruz, dem iranischen Neujahrsfest,' in: J. Assmann in collaboration with T. Sundermeier (eds.), *Das Fest und das Heilige: Religiöse Kontrapunkte zur Alltagswelt* (Studien zum Verstehen fremder Religionen, 1), Gütersloh: Mohn, 1991, pp. 88–102.
103. 'Irano-Aramaica: On Some Legal, Administrative and Economic Terms,' in: R.E. Emmerick and D. Weber (eds.), *Corolla Iranica – Papers in Honour of D.N. MacKenzie*, Frankfurt a.M.–Bern–New York–Paris: Peter Lang, 1991, pp. 167–175.
104. Review of Ph. Gignoux, *Noms propres sassanides en moyen-perse epigraphique* (Vienna, 1986), *Orientalia*, 60 (1991), pp. 379–387.
105. 'The Myth of Zurvan: Cosmogony and Eschatology,' in: Gruenwald, Shaked and Stroumsa (eds.), *Messiah and Christos* (1992; above, no. 23), pp. 219–240 (reprinted in Shaked, *From Zoroastrian Iran to Islam*, 1995; above, no. 9).
106. Roy Kotansky, J. Naveh and S. Shaked, 'A Greek-Aramaic Silver Amulet from Egypt in the Ashmolean Museum,' *Le Muséon*, 105 (1992), pp. 5–25.
107. 'A Palestinian Jewish Aramaic Hemerologion,' *Jerusalem Studies in Arabic and Islam*, 15: *Studies in Semitic Linguistics in Honor of Joshua Blau* (1992), pp. 28–42.
108. 'Some Iranian Themes in Islamic Literature,' in: *Recurrent Patterns in Iranian Religions: From Mazdaism to Sufism – Proceedings of the Round Table Held in Bamberg (30th September – 4th October 1991)* (Studia Iranica, 11), Paris: Association pour l'avancement des Etudes iraniennes, 1992, pp. 143–158 (reprinted in Shaked, *From Zoroastrian Iran to Islam*, 1995; above, no. 9).
109. '"Innen" und "Aussen" in der Religionsgeschichte: Einige typologische Beobachtungen,' in: J. Assmann and Theo Sundermeier (eds.), *Die Erfindung des inneren Menschen* (Studien zum Verstehen fremder Religionen, 6), Gütersloh: Mohn, 1993, pp. 15–27.
110. 'Iranian Elements in Middle Aramaic: Some Particles and Verbs,' in: W. Skalmowski and A. Van Tongerloo (eds.), *Medioiranica – Proceedings of the International Colloquium Organized by the Katholieke Universiteit Leuven from the 21st to the 23rd of May 1990*, Leuven: Uitgeverij Peeters–Departement Orientalistiek, 1993, pp. 147–156.
111. 'A Dictionary of Aramaic Ideograms in Pahlavi,' *Journal of the American Oriental Society*, 113 (1993), pp. 75–81.

112. 'Notes on the Pahlavi Amulet and Sasanian Courts of Law,' *Bulletin of the Asia Institute*, NS 7 (1993), pp. 165–172.
113. 'Two Parthian Ostraca from Nippur,' *Bulletin of the School of Oriental and African Studies*, 57 (1994), pp. 208–212.
114. 'Items of Dress and Other Objects of Common Use: Iranian Loanwords in Jewish Babylonian Aramaic,' in: Shaked and Netzer (eds.), *Irano-Judaica*, III (1994; above, no. 24), pp. 106–117.
115. 'Some Islamic Reports Concerning Zoroastrianism,' *Jerusalem Studies in Arabic and Islam*, 17 (1994), pp. 43–84.
116. 'Between Judaism and Islam: Some Aspects of Folk Religion' (בין יהדות לאסלאם: כמה עניינים בתחום הדת העממית), *Pe'amim*, 60 (5754/1994), pp. 4–19.
117. 'The Zoroastrian Demon of Wrath,' in: C. Elsas et al. (eds.), *Tradition und Translation: Zum Problem der interkulturellen Übersetzbarkeit religiöser Phänomene – Festschrift für Carsten Colpe zum 65. Geburtstag*, Berlin–New York: De Gruyter, 1994, pp. 285–291.
118. 'Jewish Sasanian Sigillography,' in: R. Gyselen (ed.), *Au carrefour des religions:* Mélanges offerts à Philippe Gignoux (Res Orientales, 7), Bures-sur-Yvette, 1995, pp. 239–256.
119. 'Qumran: Some Iranian Connections,' in: Z. Zevit, M. Sokoloff and S. Gitin (eds.), *Solving Riddles and Untying Knots: Biblical, Epigraphic, and Semitic Studies in Honor of Jonas C. Greenfield*, Winona Lake, IN: Eisenbrauns, 1995, pp. 265–269.
120. '"Peace Be upon You, Exalted Angels" on Hekhalot, Liturgy and Incantation Bowls,' *Jewish Studies Quarterly*, 2 (1995), pp. 197–219.
121. Review of Mary Boyce, *Zoroastrianism: Its Antiquity and Constant Vigour* (1992), *Bulletin of the School of Oriental and African Studies*, 58 (1995), pp. 375–379.
122. 'A Persian House of Study, A King's Secretary: Irano-Aramaic Notes,' *Acta Orientalia Academiae Scientiarum Hungaricae* (Zsigmond Telegdi Memorial Volume), 48 (1995), pp. 171–186.
123. 'Jewish and Iranian Visions of the Talmudic Period' (חזונות יהודיים ואיראניים בתקופת התלמוד), in: A. Oppenheimer, I. Gafni, and D. Schwartz (eds.), *The Jews in the Hellenistic and Roman World – Studies in Memory of Menahem Stern* (היהודים בעולם ההלניסטי והרומי – מחקרים לזכרו של מנחם שטרן), Jerusalem: Zalman Shazar Center–Historical Society of Israel, 5756/1996, pp. 467–486.
124. 'The Traditional Commentary on the Avesta (Zand): Translation,

Interpretation, Distortion?,' in: *La Persia e l'Asia Centrale da Alessandro al X secolo* (Atti dei convegni Lincei, 127), Rome: Accademia nazionale dei Lincei, 1996, pp. 641–656.

125. Review of Rika Gyselen, *Sceaux magiques en Iran sassanide* (Paris, 1995), *Journal of the American Oriental Society*, 117 (1997), pp. 612–615.
126. Review of Haskell D. Isaacs, with the assistance of Colin F. Baker, *Medical and Para-Medical Manuscripts in the Cambridge Genizah Collections* (Cambridge, 1994), *Journal of the American Oriental Society*, 117 (1997), pp. 615–616.
127. 'Two Types of Esotericism,' in: Aleida Assmann and Jan Assmann (eds.), *Schleier und Schwelle: Geheimnis und Öffentlichkeit* (Archäologie der literarischen Kommunikation, V/1), Munich: Wilhelm Fink, 1997, pp. 221–233.
128. 'Popular Religion in Sasanian Babylonia,' *Jerusalem Studies in Arabic and Islam*, 21 (1997), pp. 103–117.
129. 'Gerāyeshā-ye nehāni [rāzvarāne] dar āyin-e zartošt,' in: Shiva Kaviani (research and translation), *Rāzvari dar āyin-e zartošt (ʿerfān-e zartošti)* (Zoroastrian mysticism), Tehran: Qoqnoos, 1377 AHS (1998) (= Persian translation of 'Esoteric Trends in Zoroastrianism,' above, no. 36).
130. 'New Data on the Jews of Afghanistan in the Middle Ages' (ידיעות חדשות על יהודי אפגאנסתאן בימי הביניים), *Pe'amim*, 79 (5759/1999), pp. 5–14.
131. 'Jews, Christians and Pagans in the Aramaic Incantation Bowls of the Sasanian Period,' *Mediterraneum*, Atlanta, GA: Scholars Press, 1999.
132. 'Quests and Visionary Journeys in Sasanian Iran,' in: J. Assmann and Guy G. Stroumsa (eds.), *Transformations of the Inner Self in Ancient Religions* (Studies in the History of Religions, Numen Book Series, 83), Leiden–Boston–Köln: Brill, 1999, pp. 65–86.
133. 'The Poetics of Spells: Language and Structure in Aramaic Incantations of Late Antiquity, 1: The Divorce Formula and Its Ramifications,' in: Tzvi Abusch and Karel van der Toorn (eds.), *Mesopotamian Magic: Textual, Historical, and Interpretative Perspectives* (Ancient Magic and Divination, 1), Groningen: Styx Publications, 1999, pp. 173–195.
134. 'Parole des dieux, parole des anges: À propos des coupes magiques de la Babylonie sassanide,' in: *Union Académique Internationale:*

Soixante-treizième session annuelle du Comité, Cracovie, du 20 au 26 juin 1999 – Compte rendu, Brussels: Secrétariat administratif de l'UAI, 1999, pp. 17–33.

135. 'Jesus in the Magic Bowls: Apropos Dan Levene's "... and by the Name of Jesus ...,"' *Jewish Studies Quarterly*, 6 (1999), pp. 309–319.
136. 'M.J. Kister and the Study of Early Islam' (מ"י קיסטר וחקר האסלאם הקדום), in: M.J. Kister, *Studies in the Formation of Islam* (מחקרים בהתהוות האסלאם), Hebrew transl. by Aharon Amir, ed. M. Lecker, Jerusalem: Magnes, 1999, pp. 11–17.
137. 'List of Judaeo-Persian Bible Translations' (רשימת תרגומי המקרא לפרסית־יהודית) *Pe'amim*, 84 (5760/2000), pp. 12–20.
138. 'Medieval Jewish Magic in Relation to Islam: Theoretical Attitudes and Genres,' in: B.H. Hary, J.L. Hayes and F. Astren (eds.), *Judaism and Islam: Boundaries, Communications and Interactions – Essays in Honor of W.M. Brinner*, Leiden–Boston–Köln: Brill, 2000, pp. 97–109.
139. 'Manichaean Incantation Bowls in Syriac,' *Jerusalem Studies in Arabic and Islam*, 24 (2000), pp. 58–92.
140. 'The Moral Responsibility of Animals: Some Zoroastrian and Jewish Views on the Relations of Humans and Animals,' in: M. Stausberg (ed.), *Kontinuität und Brüche in der Religionsgeschichte: Festschrift für Anders Hultgård zu seinem 65. Geburtstag am 23.12.2001* (Ergänzungsband zum Reallexikon der Germanischen Altertumskunde, 31), Berlin: De Gruyter, 2001, pp. 578–595.
141. 'Iran, 2: Judentum,' in: *Religion in Geschichte und Gegenwart*[4], IV (2001), pp. 224–225.
142. 'Healing as an Act of Transformation,' in: D. Shulman and G.G. Stroumsa (eds.), *Self and Self-Transformation in the History of Religions*, Oxford: Oxford University Press, 2002, pp. 121–130.
143. 'Jews, Christians and Pagans in the Aramaic Incantation Bowls of the Sasanian Period,' in: Adriana Destro and Mauro Pesce (eds.), *Religions and Cultures: First International Conference of Mediterraneum* (Academic Studies in Religion and the Social Order), Binghamton: Global Publications–Binghamton University, 2002, pp. 61–89.
144. 'Towards a Middle Persian Dictionary,' in: Philip Huyse (ed.), *Iran: Questions et connaissances – Actes du IVe Congrès européen des études iraniennes organisé par la Societas Iranologica Europaea, Paris, 6–10 septembre 1999* (Studia Iranica, 25), I, Paris:

Association pour l'Avancement des Études Iraniennes, 2002, pp. 121–134.

145. 'The Science of Religion in Israel, with Notes on Interlocking Circles of Tradition,' in: G. Wiegers in association with J. Platvoet (eds.), *Modern Societies & the Science of Religion – Studies in Honour of Lammert Leertouwer* (Studies in the History of Religions, Numen Book Series, 115), Leiden: Brill, 2002, pp. 258–271.
146. 'Sarah (Sorour) Soroudi, a Scholar of Iranian Jewry and Folk Literature' (שרה [סורור] סורודי, חוקרת יהודי איראן וספרותם העממית), *Pe'amim*, 91 (5762/2002), pp. 188–190.
147. 'On the Study of Jewish Communities in the East' (על חקר קהילות ישראל במזרח) *Pe'amim*, 92 (5762/2002), pp. 8–10.
148. 'Zoroastrianism and Judaism,' in: Pheroza J. Godrej and Firoza Panthakey Mistree (eds.), *A Zoroastrian Tapestry: Art, Religion and Culture*, Mumbai: Mapin Publishing, 2002, pp. 199–209.
149. 'Eliezer Cagan, Translator of the *Shah-nama*' (אליעזר כגן, מתרגם השאהנאמה), in: Firdowsī, *Shāh-nāme*, II (2002; above, no. 12), pp. vii–ix.
150. 'Hadith as Influenced by Iranian Ideas and Practices,' *Enyclopaedia Iranica*, XI, fasc. 5 (2002), pp. 453–457.
151. 'Scripture and Exegesis in Zoroastrianism,' in: M. Finkelberg and G.G. Stroumsa (eds.), *Homer, the Bible and Beyond: Literary and Religious Canons in the Ancient World* (Jerusalem Studies in Religion and Culture, 2), Leiden–Boston: Brill, 2003, pp. 63–74.
152. 'Haman,' *Encyclopaedia Iranica*, XI, fasc. 6 (2003), p. 629.
153. J. Naveh and S. Shaked, 'A "Knot" and a "Break": Terms for a Receipt in Antiquity,' *Israel Exploration Journal*, 53 (2003), pp. 111–118.
154. 'Between Iranian and Aramaic: Iranian Words Concerning Food in Jewish Babylonian Aramaic, with Some Notes on the Aramaic Heterograms in Iranian,' in: Shaked and Netzer (eds.), *Irano-Judaica*, V (2003; above, no. 26), pp. 120–137.
155. 'Early Judaeo-Persian Texts, with Notes on a Commentary to Genesis,' in: Ludwig Paul (ed.), *Persian Origins: Early Judaeo-Persian and the Emergence of New Persian – Collected Papers of the Symposium, Göttingen 1999* (Iranica, 6), Wiesbaden: Harrassowitz, 2003, pp. 195–219.
156. '"Mind" and "Power" in the Gāthās: Ritual Notions or Cosmic Entities?,' in: Carlo G. Cereti, Mauro Maggi and Elio Provasi (eds.),

Religious Themes and Texts of Pre-Islamic Iran and Central Asia – Studies in Honour of Professor Gherardo Gnoli on the Occasion of His 65th Birthday on 6th December 2002 (Beiträge zur Iranistik, 24), Wiesbaden: Ludwig Reichert, 2003, pp. 391–398.

157. 'De Khulmi à Nikhšapaya: Les données des nouveaux documents araméens de Bactres sur la toponymie de la région (IVe siècle av. n. è.),' *Comptes rendus de l'Académie des Inscriptions et Belles-Lettres* (2003), pp. 1517–1535.

158. 'The Yasna Ritual in Pahlavi,' in: Michael Stausberg (ed.), *Zoroastrian Rituals in Context* (Studies in the History of Religions, Numen Book Series, 102), Leiden–Boston: Brill, 2004, pp. 333–344.

159. 'David Asheri, Scholar of Greek–Persian Contacts' (דוד אשרי, חוקר המגעים בין יוונים לפרסים), in: *David Asheri – In Memoriam* (לזכרו של דוד אשרי), Jerusalem: The Israel Academy of Sciences and Humanities, 5764/2004, pp. 24–27.

160. 'Judaeo-Persian Letter from Dandan-Uiliq,' in: S. Whitfield (ed.), *The Silk Road: Trade, Travel, War and Faith*, London: The British Library, 2004, pp. 221–222.

161. 'Zoroastrian Origins: Indian and Iranian Connections,' in: J.P. Arnason, S.N. Eisenstadt and B. Wittrock (eds.), *Axial Civilizations and World History* (Jerusalem Studies in Religion and Culture, 4), Leiden–Boston: Brill 2005, pp. 181–200.

162. 'Cosmic Origins and Human Origins in the Iranian Cultural Milieu,' in: Shaked, *Genesis and Regeneration* (2005; above, no. 27), pp. 210–222.

163. S. Shaked and R. Jacoby, 'An Early Torah Pointer from Afghanistan,' *Ars Judaica*, 1 (2005), pp. 147–152.

164. S. Shaked, and C.G. Cereti, 'A Middle Persian Dictionary: Project Proposal,' in: C.G. Cereti and M. Maggi (eds.), *Middle Iranian Lexicography – Proceedings of the Conference Held in Rome, 9–11 April 2001* (Orientalia Romana, 8; Serie Orientale Roma, 98), Rome: Istituto Italiano per l'Africa et l'Oriente, 2005, pp. 181–190.

165. 'Incantation Bowls and Amulet Tablets: How Does One Get Rid of Demons and Harmful Beings?' (קערות השבעה ולוחות קמיע: כיצד נפטרים משדים ומזיקים?), *Qadmoniot*, 38/129 (2005), pp. 2–13.

166. 'Form and Purpose in Aramaic Spells: Some Jewish Themes (The Poetics of Magic Texts),' in: Shaked, *Officina magica* (2005; above, no. 28), pp. 1–30.

167. 'Iranian Words Retrieved from Aramaic,' in: D. Weber (ed.), *Languages of Iran: Past and Present – Iranian Studies in Memoriam David Neil MacKenzie*, Wiesbaden: Harrassowitz, 2005, pp. 167–176.
168. 'Isaiah, Book of,' *Encyclopaedia Iranica*, 13 (2006), pp. 611–612.
169. '*Dramatis Personae* in the Jewish Magic Texts: Some Differences between Incantation Bowls and Geniza Magic,' *Jewish Studies Quarterly*, 13 (2006), pp. 363–387.
170. 'Professor Franz Rosenthal,' *Jerusalem Studies in Arabic and Islam*, 31 (2006), pp. i–vi.
171. 'Notes on Some Jewish Aramaic Inscriptions from Georgia,' *Jerusalem Studies in Arabic and Islam*, 32 (2006), 503–510.
172. 'The Iranian Canon of Scriptures and Writings,' in: F. Vahman and C.V. Pedersen (eds.), *Religious Texts in Iranian Languages – Symposium Held in Copenhagen, May 2002*, Copenhagen: Det Kongelige Danske Videnskabernes Selskab, 2007, pp. 11–26.
173. 'New Early Judeo-Persian Finds,' in: Shaked and Netzer (eds.), *Irano-Judaica*, VI (2008; above, no. 29), pp. 222–252.
174. 'Classification of Linguistic Features in Early Judeo-Persian Texts,' in: W. Sundermann, A. Hintze and F. De Blois (eds.), *Exigisti Monumenta – Festschrift in Honour of Nicholas Sims-Williams* (Iranica, 17), Wiesbaden: Harrassowitz, 2009, pp. 449–461.
175. 'A Jewish Aramaic Amulet from Afghanistan,' in: K.D. Dobos and M. Köszeghy (eds.), *With Wisdom as a Robe – Qumran and Jewish Studies in Honour of Ida Fröhlich*, Sheffield: Phoenix Press, 2009, pp. 485–494.
176. 'Spells and Incantations between Iranian and Aramaic,' in: D. Durkin-Meisterernst, Chr. Reck und D. Weber (eds.), *Literarische Stoffe und ihre Gestaltung in mitteliranischer Zeit – Kolloquium anlässlich des 70. Geburtstages von Werner Sundermann* (Beiträge zur Iranistik, 31), Wiesbaden: Dr. Ludwig Reichert Verlag, 2009, pp. 233–244.
177. 'Who Gives Lordship to Ohrmazd? A Zoroastrian Debate,' in: C. Allison, A. Joisten-Pruschke and A. Wendtland (eds.), *From Daēnā to Dîn: Religion, Kultur und Sprache in der iranischen Welt – Festschrift für Philip Kreyenbroek*, Wiesbaden: Harrassowitz, 2009, pp. 209–212.
178. 'Aramaic Loan-Words in Middle Persian,' *Bulletin of the Asia Institute*, 19 (2009), pp. 159–168.
179. '"No Talking during a Meal": Zoroastrian Themes in the Babylo-

nian Talmud,' in: C. Bakhos and M. R. Shayegan (eds.), *The Talmud in Its Iranian Context* (Texts and Studies in Ancient Judaism, 135), Tübingen: Mohr Siebeck, 2010, pp. 161–177.

180. 'La vision humaine selon les livres pehlevis: Quelques observations,' *Studia Asiatica*, 11 (2010) pp. 105–166.
181. 'Time Designations and Other Recurrent Themes in Aramaic Incantation Bowls,' in: J. Stackert et al. (eds.), *Gazing on the Deep – Ancient Near Eastern and Other Studies in Honor of Tzvi Abusch*, Bethesda, MD: CDL Press, 2010, pp. 221–234.
182. 'Human Identity and Classes of People in the Pahlavi Books,' in: C.G. Cereti (ed.), *Iranian Identity in the Course of History – Proceedings of the Conference Held in Rome, 21–24 September 2005* (Serie Orientale Roma, CV; Orientalia Romana, 9), Rome: IsIAO, 2010, pp. 331–345.
183. 'A Note on Hebrew-Script Tombstones from Jam, Afghanistan,' *Journal of Jewish Studies*, 61 (2010), pp. 305–307.
184. 'On Hebrew Words Derived from Persian' (על המלים העבריות שמקורן בפרסית), in: David Yeroushalmi (ed.), *Light and Shadows: The Story of Iran and the Jews* (אורות וצללים: סיפור איראן והיהודים), Tel Aviv: Bet Hatfutsot, 2010, pp. 101–102.
185. 'Persian-Arabic Bilingualism in the Cairo Genizah Documents,' in: B. Outhwaite and S. Bhayro (eds.), *'From a Sacred Source': Genizah Studies in Honour of Professor Sefan C. Reif* (Cambridge Genizah Studies Series, 1; Etudes sur le Judaïsme medieval, 42), Leiden: Brill, 2011, pp. 319–330.
186. 'The Transmission and Transformation of Magical Formulae: The Case of the Jewish Babylonian Bowls,' in: G. Bohak, Y. Harari and S. Shaked (eds.), *Continuity and Innovation in the Magical Tradition* (Jerusalem Studies in Religion and Culture, 15), Leiden: Brill, 2011, pp. 187–217.
187. 'Shlomo Dov Goitein – In Memoriam' (זכרון לראשונים: שלמה דב גויטיין), *Katharsis*, 15 (Spring 5771/2011), pp. 86–123.
188. 'Questions of Identity and Difference' (שאלות של זהות ושוני), *Pe'amim*, 125–127 (5771/2010–2011), pp. 17–36.
189. 'New Jewish Writings Discovered in a Cave in Afghanistan' (כתבים יהודיים חדשים שנתגלו במערה באפגניסטאן), *Masu'ah*, 13 (Year 7, April 2012), p. 9.
190. 'Master of West-Semitic Palaeography and Epigraphy – On the Death of Joseph Naveh, Scholar of Semitic Script' (אמן הפענוח של כתובות ארץ־ישראל: עם מותו של יוסף נוה, חוקר של הכתב השמי), *Haaretz*,

Seventh Day of Pesaḥ supplement, Thursday, 20 Nisan 5772/2012, p. 1.

191. Obituary: Joseph Naveh, *Israel Exploration Journal*, 62/1 (2012), pp. 113–116.

192. Gideon Bohak, 'From Qumran to Cairo: The Lives and Times of a Jewish Exorcistic Formula' (with an appendix by Shaul Shaked), in: Ildikó Csepregi and Charles Burnett (eds.), *Ritual Healing: Magic, Ritual and Medical Therapy from Antiquity until the Early Modern Period*, Florence: Sismel–Edizioni del Galluzzo, 2012, pp. 31–52.

193. 'Joseph Naveh (1928–2011)' (יוסף נוה [1928-2011]), *Qadmoniot*, 143 (2012), pp. 46–47.

194. 'Religious Actions Evaluated by Intention: Zoroastrian Concepts Shared with Judaism,' in: S. Secunda and S. Fine (eds.), *Shoshanat Yaakov: Jewish and Iranian Studies in Honor of Yaakov Elman*, Leiden–Boston: Brill, 2012, pp. 403–413.

195. 'Early Persian Documents from Khorasan,' *Journal of Persianate Studies*, 6 (2013), pp. 153–162.

196. 'The Sayings of Wuzurgmihr the Sage: A Piece of Sasanian Wisdom Transmitted into Arabic,' in: Ben-Shammai, Shaked and Stroumsa, *Exchange and Transmission across Cultural Boundaries* (2013; above, no. 33), pp. 216–275.

197. 'The Zoroastrian Calendar in Another Document from Ancient Bactria,' in: S. Tokhtasev and P. Lurje (eds.), *Commentationes Iranicae Vladimiro f. Aaron Livschits Nonagenario Donum Natalicium*, St. Petersburg, 2013, pp. 249–252.

198. 'Magic in Zoroastrianism,' *Fezana Journal*, 28/4 (2014), pp. 59–63.

199. 'Islam,' in: M. Stausberg and Y. Sohrab-Dinshaw Vevaina, with the assistance of Anna Tessmann (eds.), *The Wiley Blackwell Companion to Zoroastrianism*, Chichester: Wiley Blackwell, 2015, Chap. 31, pp. 491–498.

200. 'Rabbis in Incantation Bowls,' in: Markham J. Geller (ed.), *The Archaeology and Material Culture of the Babylonian Talmud*, Leiden–Boston: Brill, 2015, pp. 97–120.

201. 'Orality and Esotericism: Reflections on Modes of Transmission in Late Antiquity,' in: Julia Rubanovich (ed.), *Orality and Textuality in the Iranian World: Patterns of Interaction across the Centuries* (Jerusalem Studies in Religion and Culture, 19), Leiden–Boston: Brill, 2015, pp. 43–62.

202. ‘Jews in Khorasan before the Mongol Invasion,’ *Iran Namag*, 1/1 (2016), pp. iv–xvi.
203. ‘Assimilation or Survival: The Kai Feng Jews According to Their Own Documents’ (טמיעה או השתמרות: יהודי קאיפנג על פי תעודות העדה), in Avi Elqayam and Yosef Kaplan (eds.), *Conceal the Outcasts: Jews with Hidden Identities* (סתרי נידחים: יהודים עם זהויות חבויות), Jerusalem: Ben-Zvi Institute, 2016, pp. 345–351.
204. ‘A New Aramaic Inscription from the Hatra region’ (כתובת ארמית חדשה מאזור חטרה), in: J. Aviram, S. Ahituv, I. Eph‘al, A. Yardeni and A. Mendel-Gavrovitz (eds.), *Eretz-Israel: Studies in the Geography and Antiquities of Israel* (ארץ ישראל: מחקרים בידיעת הארץ ועתיקותיה), 32 (Joseph Naveh Volume), Jerusalem 2016, pp. 191–197.
205. ‘Joseph Naveh, Master of West-Semitic Palaeography and Epigraphy’ (יוסף נוה, חוקר הכתב השמי, אמן הפענוח של כתובות ארץ ישראל), *ibid.*, pp. יא-יב (English version: *ibid.*, pp. xi–xiii).
206. ‘Zoroastrian Views on Suffering,’ in: Enrico Morano, Elio Provasi and Adriano V. Rossi (eds.), *Studia Philologica Iranica – Gherardo Gnoli Memorial Volume* (Università degli Studi di Napoli ‘L’Orientale,’ Dipartimento Asia, Africa e Mediterraneo; ISMEO – Associazione Internazionale di Studi sul Mediterraneo e l’Oriente), Rome: Scienze e Lettere, 2017, pp. 435–448.
207. ‘Yima in a Newly Discovered Manuscript,’ in: جشن نامه استاد جلال خالقی مطلق (Festschrift Jalāl Khāleqi-Motlaq), Tehran, 2018.
208. Domenico Agostini and Shaul Shaked, ‘Two Sasanian Seals of Priests,’ *Bulletin of the Asia Institute*, NS 27 (2013, publ. 2018), pp. 99–106.
209. Shaul Shaked and Rivka Elitzur-Leiman, ‘An Aramaic Amulet for Winning a Case in a Court of Law,’ *Jewish Studies Quarterly* (2018), forthcoming.
210. ‘Some Lexical Items in Pahlavi,’ in: *Adriano Rossi Festschrift*, forthcoming.
211. ‘A Fragment of the Book of Jeremiah in Early Judaeo-Persian,’ in: J. Rubanovich (ed.), *Irano-Judaica*, VII, Jerusalem: Ben-Zvi Institute, 2018, forthcoming.
212. ‘Dualists against Monotheists,’ in: Ch. Markschies and Y. Friedmann (eds.), *Rationalization in Religions*, Berlin: Walter de Gruyter, 2018, forthcoming.

Contributors to This Volume

Gideon Bohak
Professor, Department of Jewish Philosophy and Talmud, Tel Aviv University

Yohanan Friedmann
Professor Emeritus, Department of Arabic Language and Literature, The Hebrew University of Jerusalem, and Department of Islamic and Middle Eastern Studies, Shalem College, Jerusalem
Member, The Israel Academy of Sciences and Humanities

Ofir Haim
The Mandel School for Advanced Studies in the Humanities, The Hebrew University of Jerusalem

Yuval Harari
Professor, Department of Jewish Thought, Ben-Gurion University of the Negev

Geoffrey Herman
Directeur d'études, Judaïsmes antiques et littérature rabbinique classique, Section des sciences religieuses, École Pratique des Hautes Études, PSL, Paris

Moshe Idel
Professor Emeritus, Department of Jewish Thought, The Hebrew University of Jerusalem
Member, The Israel Academy of Sciences and Humanities

Etan Kohlberg
Professor Emeritus, Department of Arabic Language and Literature, The Hebrew University of Jerusalem
Member, The Israel Academy of Sciences and Humanities

Julia Rubanovich
Senior Lecturer in Persian Language and Literature, Department of Islamic and Middle Eastern Studies, The Hebrew University of Jerusalem

Michael Shenkar
Senior Lecturer in Pre-Islamic Iranian Studies, Department of Islamic and Middle Eastern Studies, The Hebrew University of Jerusalem

Sara Sviri
Professor Emerita, Department of Arabic Language and Literature and Department of Religious Studies, The Hebrew University of Jerusalem

תוכן העניינים

מסת"ב 978-965-208-232-9

עריכת לשון: גילה ברנד
התקנה והבאה לדפוס: דבורה גריינימן
הפקה: יהודה גרינבאום
סדר: אירית נחום
נדפס בישראל בדפוס איילון, ירושלים

מחקרים לכבוד שאול שקד

בעריכת

יוחנן פרידמן ואיתן קולברג

ירושלים תשע"ט

האקדמיה הלאומית הישראלית למדעים

עיונים במדעי הרוח

כתבי האקדמיה הלאומית הישראלית למדעים
החטיבה למדעי הרוח

מחקרים לכבוד שאול שקד